Lecture Notes in Computer Science 9821

Commenced Publication in 1973
Founding and Former Series Editors:
Gerhard Goos, Juris Hartmanis, and Jan van Leeuwen

More information about this series at http://www.springer.com/series/7409

Efthimios Tambouris · Panos Panagiotopoulos
Øystein Sæbø · Maria A. Wimmer
Theresa A. Pardo · Yannis Charalabidis
Delfina Sá Soares · Tomasz Janowski (Eds.)

Electronic Participation

8th IFIP WG 8.5 International Conference, ePart 2016
Guimarães, Portugal, September 5–8, 2016
Proceedings

 Springer

Editors
Efthimios Tambouris
Applied Informatics
University of Macedonia
Thessaloniki
Greece

Panos Panagiotopoulos
School of Business and Management
Queen Mary University
London
UK

Øystein Sæbø
University of Agder
Kristiansand
Norway

Maria A. Wimmer
Universität Koblenz-Landau
Koblenz, Rheinland-Pfalz
Germany

Theresa A. Pardo
Center for Technology in Government
University at Albany
Albany, NY
USA

Yannis Charalabidis
University of Aegean
Karlovassi, Samos
Greece

Delfina Sá Soares
United Nations University Operating Unit on
    Policy-Driven Electronic Governance
Guimarães
Portugal

Tomasz Janowski
Policy-Driven Electronic Governance
United Nations University Operating Unit
Guimarães
Portugal

ISSN 0302-9743   ISSN 1611-3349   (electronic)
Lecture Notes in Computer Science
ISBN 978-3-319-45073-5   ISBN 978-3-319-45074-2   (eBook)
DOI 10.1007/978-3-319-45074-2

Library of Congress Control Number: 2016948293

LNCS Sublibrary: SL3 – Information Systems and Applications, incl. Internet/Web, and HCI

Printed on acid-free paper

This Springer imprint is published by Springer Nature
The registered company is Springer International Publishing AG Switzerland

Preface

Under the auspices of the International Federation for Information Processing (IFIP) Working Group 8.5 (Information Systems in Public Administration), or IFIP WG 8.5 for short, the dual IFIP EGOV-ePart conference 2016 presented itself as a high-caliber five-track conference and a doctoral colloquium dedicated to research and practice on electronic government and electronic participation.

Scholars from around the world have used this premier academic forum for over 15 years, which has given it a worldwide reputation as one of the top two conferences in the research domains of electronic, open, and smart government, and electronic participation.

This conference of five partially intersecting tracks presents advances in the socio-technological domain of the public sphere demonstrating cutting-edge concepts, methods, and styles of investigation by multiple disciplines.

The Call for Papers attracted over 135 submissions of completed research papers, work-in-progress papers on ongoing research (including doctoral papers), project and case descriptions, as well as four workshop and panel proposals. Among the full research paper submissions, 14 papers (empirical and conceptual) from the General ePart Track and the Policy Modeling and Policy Informatics Track were accepted for Springer's LNCS EGOV proceedings, whereas another 24 papers of completed research papers from the General EGOV Track, the Open Government and Open/Big Data Track, and the Smart Governance/Government/Cities Track went into the LNCS EGOV proceedings (vol. 9820).

The ePart Track aims to bring together researchers of distinct disciplines in order to present and discuss advances in eParticipation research. As the field of eParticipation is multidisciplinary in nature, this track provides an excellent opportunity for researchers with backgrounds in different academic disciplines to share and discuss current research on foundations, theories, methods, tools, and innovative applications of eParticipation. In addition, ePart provides a fruitful ground to nurture and plan future cooperation.

The Policy Modeling and Policy Informatics Track focuses on supporting public policy making with innovative ICT therewith involving relevant stakeholders. It heavily involves multidisciplinary research. The scope ranges from policy analysis and conceptual modeling to programming and visualization of simulation models, to help policy makers and stakeholders deliberate and evaluate policy decisions and explore new models of governance.

This volume includes completed research organized in four topical threads as follows:

- Theoretical Foundations
- Critical Reflections
- Implementations
- Policy Formulation and Modeling

As in previous years, IOS Press published accepted work-in-progress papers and workshop and panel abstracts in a complementary open-access proceedings volume. In 2016, this volume covers over 60 paper contributions, workshop abstracts, and panel summaries from all tracks, workshops, posters, and the PhD colloquium.

All submissions were blind peer reviewed by at least three reviewers (and in most cases by four reviewers) from the Program Committee. The quality of the conference tracks is directly related to the quality of the peer reviews and we would like to once again acknowledge the work done by the members of the Program Committee.

As in the previous years and per recommendation of the Paper Awards Committee under the lead of the honorable Prof. Olivier Glassey of the University of Lausanne, Switzerland, the dual IFIP EGOV-ePart 2016 Conference Organizing Committee again granted outstanding paper awards in three distinct categories:

- The most interdisciplinary and innovative research contribution
- The most compelling critical research reflection
- The most promising practical concept

The winners in each category were announced in the award ceremony at the conference dinner, which has always been a highlight of each dual IFIP EGOV-ePart conference.

The dual IFIP EGOV-ePart 2016 conference was jointly hosted in Guimarães, Portugal, by UMinho and UNU-EGOV. Established in 1973, UMinho operates on three campuses, one in Braga, and two in Guimarães, educating approximately 19,500 students by an academic staff of 1,300 located in eight schools, three institutes, and several cultural and specialized units. It is one of the largest public universities in Portugal and a significant actor in the development of the Minho region in the north of Portugal. UNU-EGOV is a newly established UN organization focused on research, policy, and leadership education in the area of digital government, located in Guimarães and hosted by UMinho. The organization of the dual conference was partly supported by the project "SmartEGOV: Harnessing EGOV for Smart Governance", NORTE-01-0145-FEDER-000037, funded by FEDER in the context of Programa Operacional Regional do Norte.

Although ample traces of Celtic and Roman presence and settlements were found in the area, Guimarães became notable as the center of early nation building for Portugal in the late eleventh century, when it became the seat of the Count of Portugal. In 1128, the Battle of São Mamede was fought near the town, which resulted in the independence of the Northern Portuguese territories around Coimbra and Guimarães, which later extended further south to form the independent nation of Portugal. Today, Guimarães has a population of about 160,000. While it has developed into an important center of textile and shoe industries along with metal mechanics, the city has maintained its charming historical center and romantic medieval aura. It was a great pleasure to hold the dual IFIP EGOV-ePart 2016 conference at this special place.

Many people make large events like this conference happen. We thank the over 100 members of the dual IFIP EGOV-ePart 2016 Program Committee and dozens of additional reviewers for their great efforts in reviewing the submitted papers. Delfina Sá Soares of the Department of Information Systems at the University of Minho (UMinho) and Tomasz Janowski of the United Nations University Operating Unit on Policy-Driven Electronic Governance (UNU-EGOV) and their respective teams in Guimarães, Portugal, were major contributors who helped organize the dual conference and manage zillions of details locally. We would also like to thank the University of Washington organizing team members Kelle M. Rose and Daniel R. Wilson for their great support and administrative management of the review process and the compilation of the proceedings.

September 2016

Hans Jochen Scholl
Olivier Glassey
Marijn Janssen
Bram Klievink
Ida Lindgren
Peter Parycek
Efthimios Tambouris
Maria A. Wimmer
Tomasz Janowski
Delfina Sá Soares
Yannis Charalabidis
Mila Gascó
Ramon Gil-Garcia
Panos Panagiotopoulos
Theresa A. Pardo
Øystein Sæbø
Anneke Zuiderwijk

Organization

Conference Chairs

Hans Jochen Scholl	University of Washington, USA
Marijn Janssen	Delft University of Technology, The Netherlands
Maria A. Wimmer	University of Koblenz-Landau, Germany
Efthimios Tambouris	University of Macedonia, Greece
Tomasz Janowski	United Nations University Operating Unit on Policy-Driven Electronic Governance, Portugal
Delfina Sá Soares	University of Minho, Portugal

General Electronic Participation Track Chairs

Efthimios Tambouris	University of Macedonia, Greece (Lead Chair)
Øystein Sæbø	Agder University, Norway
Panos Panagiotopoulos	Queen Mary University of London, UK

The Policy Modeling and Policy Informatics Track Chairs

Maria A. Wimmer	University of Koblenz-Landau, Germany (Lead Chair)
Theresa A. Pardo	Center for Technology in Government, University at Albany, SUNY, USA
Yannis Charalabidis	University of Aegean, Greece

Program Committee and Reviewers

Ayman Alarabiat	University of Minho, Portugal
Renata Araujo	UNIRIO, Brazil
Yannis Charalabidis	University of Aegean, Greece
Peter Cruickshank	Edinburgh Napier University, UK
Ahmed Darwish	Ministry of State of Administrative Development, Egypt
Todd R. Davies	Stanford University, USA
Fiorella De Cindio	Università di Milano, Italy
Annelie Ekelin	Linneaus University/BTH, Sweden
Elsa Estevez	United Nations University, Portugal
Sabrina Franceschini	Regione Emilia-Romagna, Italy
Andras Gabor	Corvinno technology Transfer Center Nonprofit Public Ltd., Hungary
Katarina Gidlund	Midsweden University, Sweden
Dimitris Gouscos	University of Athens, Greece

Contents

Theoretical Foundations

A Metamodel for the E-Participation Reference Framework

Sabrina Scherer(✉) and Maria A. Wimmer(✉)

Institute for IS Research, University of Koblenz-Landau, Universitätsstr. 1,
56070 Koblenz, Germany
{scherer,wimmer}@uni-koblenz.de

Abstract. E-participation projects are complex socio-technical constructs integrating different concepts such as participation techniques, stakeholders, objectives, information artefacts, and technical facilities. To conceptualise comprehensive solutions of e-participation projects in a holistic way – i.e. comprehensively integrating the different concepts forming an e-participation project–, enterprise architecture frameworks are increasingly studied. Effective use of enterprise architecture frameworks demands a comprehensive conceptualisation of e-participation projects, which should embark on a common metamodel. In this paper, we study existing conceptual models structuring the e-participation domain and metamodels of enterprise architecture frameworks. From the insights of the comparative analysis, the e-participation metamodel is developed using design science research. The metamodel provides the conceptualisation and taxonomy for an e-participation reference framework to develop comprehensive architectures in e-participation projects. It is presented in a UML 2.0 diagram and involves six viewpoints: Participation Scope, Participant Viewpoint, Participation Viewpoint, Data & Information Viewpoint, E-participation Viewpoint, and Implementation & Governance Viewpoint.

Keywords: Metamodel · E-participation · Architecture framework · Domain model · E-participation project

1 Introduction

Over the past decade, several attempts have been made to conceptualise the e-participation domain [9, 12, 19, 22, 29, 31, 32, 36, 37]. The concepts brought forward vary in their intended purposes and results. What they have in common is that they systemise the interdisciplinary research field and identify relevant concepts forming e-participation initiatives. Each of them can be seen as a kind of e-participation metamodel, understood as a conceptual definition and description of an e-participation project. The purpose of such a conceptual description can be

- To define a vocabulary of e-participation usable in design and implementation [26],
- To model the e-participation domain [9],
- To structure the e-participation research [36], or
- To contribute to the proper understanding of the domain [9].

Published by Springer International Publishing Switzerland 2016. All Rights Reserved
E. Tambouris et al. (Eds.): ePart 2016, LNCS 9821, pp. 3–16, 2016.
DOI: 10.1007/978-3-319-45074-2_1

An e-participation metamodel conceptualising an architecture of an e-participation project was identified as part of a reference framework for e-participation in our earlier research [25, 26]. To derive such a metamodel, this paper analyses e-participation models and enterprise architecture frameworks. Enterprise architecture frameworks are instruments consisting of conventions, principles, and practices that guide the development of an enterprise architecture [30]. An enterprise architecture is a conceptualisation of an enterprise (such as an e-participation project) with a common set of goals [33]. As such they can be a means to support the development and implementation of an e-participation project [26]. In this paper, we perform a comparative analysis of existing conceptual models of e-participation and develop an e-participation metamodel that systematically combines the results of existing research into one comprehensive model. As the objective of this work is to construct a metamodel as an artefact that guides the design of e-participation initiatives along an enterprise architecture framework, this research applies Design Science Research. Design science research aims to design artefacts that define ideas, practices, models, frameworks, and products to support the analysis, design, implementation and use of information systems [7, 17].

The remainder of the paper is as follows: Sect. 2 presents the comparative analysis of related work in e-participation. Subsequently, these results are further combined with a comparative analysis of metamodels of enterprise architecture frameworks in Sect. 3. Both sections provide the foundations for the metamodel for e-participation, which is introduced in Sect. 4. Finally, Sect. 5 provides concluding remarks.

2   Comparative Analysis of Related Work in E-Participation

Conceptual models present entities and their relationships, which characterise the e-participation domain. As such, they can be a means to structure e-participation projects and to identify relevant entities, their attributes and relationships. This section studies conceptual models and analyses them concerning viewpoints and entities identified.

To start with, e-participation literature often refers to the evaluation framework proposed by Macintosh and Whyte [13] (referred to e.g. in [10, 19]), which distinguishes three viewpoints described as overlapping (pp. 20–21): *Democratic* considering criteria to understand how e-participation affects democracy, *Project* considering the aims, objectives, and methods of public engagement, and *Socio-technical* considering to what extent ICT design affects the outcomes. Kubicek and Aichholzer state that this framework "*covers almost any aspect that has been mentioned in the literature as relevant or interesting in order to assess and evaluate (e-)participation*" ([10] p. 30), while at the same time admitting that these viewpoints are overlapping (ibid. p. 31) – i.e. Macintosh and Whyte's framework does not consider interrelations between these viewpoints. Furthermore, Kubicek and Aichholzer criticise the Project viewpoint as particularly heterogeneous, because it considers too many different aspects [10]. As an example, they mention that this viewpoint includes the participation process as well as managerial objectives.

In an earlier work, Macintosh presents an analytical framework for e-participation, which emerged from work for the OECD e-government group. This framework proposes to study the characteristics of e-participation projects based on the following ten key dimensions: level of participation, stages in the policy making lifecycle, actors, technology used, rules of engagement, duration and sustainability, accessibility, resources and promotion, evaluation and outcomes, and critical success factors [12]. This work is the basis for several further models emerging in literature over time, such as:

- In 2007, Wimmer presents an ontology for an e-participation virtual resource centre with the aim to structure information available in e-participation research [36]. It bases on Macintosh's work [12], yet reduces the core dimensions of the ontology to: stages in policy making, level of engagement, stakeholders and participation areas.
- In 2008, Kalampokis et al. introduce a domain model for e-participation, which aims to represent important aspects and relationships to characterise e-participation. The authors suggest three sub-domains: ICT tool, participation process, and stakeholder [9]. Finally, they combine the sub-domains into one model to visualise the key relationships between them.
- In 2008, Phang and Kankanhalli put forward a framework of ICT exploitation for e-participation initiatives [18]. The framework examines how suitable various ICT tools are to achieve e-participation objectives. The work is based on Glass' work [6], who analyses offline participation techniques with regards to achieving different objectives of citizen participation programs.
- In 2011, Sæbø et al. present an exploration of actors, activities, contextual factors, effects, and evaluation approaches addressed in the e-participation literature [22]. Medaglia visualises this exploration and adopts it as a guideline to analyse how the e-participation research field develops [15].
- Also in 2011, Smith et al. present a framework of e-participation analysis levels [29] based on the generic impact analysis and measurement reference system by Millard [16]. This framework differentiates results by their focus on operational objectives = outputs, on specific objectives = outcomes, and on general objectives = impacts.
- In 2014, Yusuf et al. introduce a model as the result of evaluating other frameworks [37]. The approach categorises entities of other models such as [9], and [12] in a new way and includes barriers and drivers of e-participation.
- In 2016, Porwol et al. propose an ontology for next generation initiatives [19], which aims at facilitating operations of e-participation initiatives and improving knowledge exchange between similar initiatives. The ontology covers the views Platform, Project, and Democratic Process[1].

A comparative analysis of entities included in the models studied above shows that each of these conceptual models focusses on and considers slightly different e-participation characteristics. The models in [9] and [36] are comprehensive but neglect objectives and a further differentiation of participation results as [29] provides. Porwol et al. focus on the comparison of different e-participation projects and do not consider specifics of participation processes and involvement of actors [19]. None of

---

[1] Based on the perspectives proposed in Macintosh and Whyte [13].

the models considered can provide a comprehensive picture of an e-participation project and, thus, cannot serve alone as an e-participation metamodel to be used to describe e-participation architectures in a reference framework.

The analysis and synthesis of above conceptual models leads us to a comprehensive list of structural elements of an e-participation project, which contains: stakeholder/ actor, role, stage in policy-making, level of participation, participation area, participation activity, participation technique, participation process, ICT (application/ICT, tool, tool category, and technology), channel, objective, driver, barrier, input, output, outcome, impact. Each of the elements can further be analysed. For this paper, we investigate the stakeholders and actors proposed in the conceptual models. The following stakeholder/actor types list shows the union set of entities described in the literature: academia; advisory board, industry/business (in particular consultancies); elected representative; government executive; policy maker; political party/politician; citizen/citizen group; NGO/CSO; the media. Relevant roles that stakeholders can take over in an e-participation project are put forward e.g. in Kalampokis et al. [9], Macintosh (describing some activities that can be interpreted as roles) [12], Sæbø et al. [21]. Furthermore, Rozanski and Woods put forward relevant roles in software engineering [20]. The roles, which the authors describe, can be both, internal (part of the project team) and external. The analysis of the actor/stakeholder roles results in the following list: input provider and lurker as participant; decision maker; administrator, consultant, evaluator, expert of the particular policy, facilitator, initiator, ICT developer, ICT maintainer; ICT provider, moderator, marketing/promotion, owner, project manager, and support staff.

Based on above analysis of conceptualisations of e-participation, and in particular on the works of Karalampokis et al. [9] and Macintosh and Whyte [13], we select the following four viewpoints as an initial structure of the metamodel, which separates participation from management processes and methods – therewith also clustering above number of elements in a systematic way:

- *Participation Viewpoint* (participation process, democratic objectives),
- *Implementation & Governance Viewpoint* (managerial objectives),
- *E-participation Viewpoint* (socio-technical), and
- *Participant Viewpoint* (stakeholder, target groups).

However, our experience from past e-participation projects [see e.g. 23, 24] shows that the list of identified elements is not sufficiently complete to design the architecture of an e-participation project. In particular, elements to design managerial aspects (e.g. risks, which may hamper the achievement of objectives) or a data architecture are missing. As EA frameworks are used in the information systems domain to design complex socio-technical systems, we therefore analyse a selection of metamodels of EA frameworks to complement e-participation conceptual models (see next section).

3   Comparative Analysis of Enterprise Architecture Frameworks

Multiple (enterprise) architecture frameworks exist on the market [14] provided from commercial consultancies, industry consortia, governments or the military. The following frameworks are analysed in this research:

- The *Zachman Framework for Information System Architecture* [38] is a reference point for many EA frameworks published later on [28]. It presents an architecture-based systematisation of what needs to be defined and implemented in information systems development and enterprise engineering.
- *The Open Group Architecture Framework (TOGAF)* [33] is an industry standard for developing enterprise architectures (EAs). It represents an international approach, commonly agreed upon by many industry players, and it complements the Zachman Framework by e.g. providing a detailed architecture development method. TOGAF is the EA framework most often used in industry [3].
- The *Federal Enterprise Architecture Framework (FEAF)* [5] provides a framework for developing processes and information structures between U.S. agencies.
- The *Department of Defence Architecture Framework (DoDAF)* [35] serves as standard for military information system development, but is used also for enterprise architecture development outside the military domain.
- The *ArchiMate* Specification 2.1 [34] is an integrated architectural approach and language for enterprise modelling [11]. The Open Group qualifies ArchiMate as "fully aligned with TOGAF"[2] [4], even if some differences to TOGAF exist.

DoDAF states the purposes of a metamodel as (1) to define a vocabulary, (2) to specify data exchange semantics and formats, (3) to improve comprehensibility of EA data, and (4) to provide a basis for semantic precision. It proposes a conceptual data model, a logical data model and a physical exchange schema. The FEAF metamodel is called the Consolidated Reference Model [5] and aims to provide such a reference model. The TOGAF metamodel aims to formally structure the terms for ensuring consistency and guiding organisations [33]. It proposes a core model ("a basic model with the minimum feature set" [33]) and several extensions, e.g. for process or motivation. ArchiMate [34] defines the entities used in the modelling language.

In our comparative analysis (see Table 1), we map the architecture framework metamodel entities with the elements identified in e-participation frameworks in the previous section, leading to two additional viewpoints (informed by the EA frameworks studied): Since the e-participation metamodels (cf. previous section) do not cover data, which the project will produce, store, or edit in different activities, we add the *Data & Information Viewpoint*. In addition, the motivation aspect (vision, objectives, etc. driving the e-participation) is not covered in e-participation metamodels, hence we add the *Participation Scope Viewpoint*. This way, objectives can be defined at a higher level, and can be broken down subsequently into participation objectives, socio-technical objectives and operational objectives along with relevant measures.

---

[2] See http://www.opengroup.org/subjectareas/enterprise/archimate [accessed 29 May 2016].

Table 1. Mapping entities identified in e-participation conceptual models with entities in architecture framework metamodels

Framework	Viewpoint					
	Participation scope	Participant	Participation	E-participation	Data & Information	Implementation & Governance
Initial Set of E-participation Entities (Sect. 2)	Input, Output, Outcome, Impact, Objective, Driver, Barrier, Guideline	Actor, Organisation Unit, Role	Policy-making Stage, Participation Level/Area, Participation Activity, Technique, Decision-making/Participation Process	Tool, Tool Category, Technology		Resource, Promotion, Funding
TOGAF [33]	Requirement	Actor, Organisation Unit, Role	Process, Business Service, Function, Event	Application/Technology Component, Platform Service, Service Interface	Data Entity	Location, Event
DoDAF [35]	Guidance	Actor, Organisation, Person/Organisation Type	Activity	System, Service, Service Channel	Resource	Condition, Measure, Capability, Location, Event
FEAF [5]	Goals, Assets (Investments, Programes), Purpose	Person	Functions, Services, Assets (Processes)	IT Assets, Application (System, Component, Interface), Infrastructure (Platform, Facility, Network), Interface	Data Assets (Domain, Subject, Topic),	Business Capabilities, Measurement Areas/Categories, Risk, Control
ArchiMate [34]	Requirement, Assessment	Business actor, Stakeholder, Business role	Product	Application Component, Interface, Application Function, System Software	Data Object	Location, Event

The comparison of elements of existing metamodels (Table 1) shows that it is not necessary to develop a new metamodel from scratch. However, there are two reasons for arguing the need for a customised metamodel for the e-participation domain:

1. The existing e-participation metamodels do not include some entities needed to design e-participation in a comprehensive way,
2. Existing Enterprise Architecture metamodels are too business-oriented or are not customised towards e-participation contexts.

As the e-participation metamodel should consider specific entities relevant to e-participation projects (e.g. particular stakeholder groups and roles to ease its application for e-participation experts) to effectively support the EA framework for e-participation [25, 26], we put forward a comprehensive e-participation metamodel. This metamodel is derived from above investigations by (a) selecting common entities in existing metamodels, and (b) adapting them to the needs and specifications of e-participation.

4 The E-Participation Metamodel

Six viewpoints structure the e-participation metamodel, which are derived from the above analysis of existing metamodels and which are described in more detail below:

1. *Participation Scope Viewpoint*: motivation and objectives of the project.
2. *Participant Viewpoint*: stakeholder engagement and management.
3. *Participation Viewpoint*: participation services and processes.
4. *Data & Information Viewpoint*: production and use of data.
5. *E-participation Viewpoint*: e-participation tools and support of techniques.
6. *Implementation & Governance Viewpoint:* operations, administration and management of the e-participation project.

Relationships exist between these viewpoints as visualised in Fig. 1.

4.1 Participation Scope Viewpoint

The purpose of the *Participation Scope Viewpoint* is to capture the objectives, and to link them with measures to achieve them. Furthermore, it provides information needed by the owners to decide if they will carry out the project or not and the basis for further developments after a positive decision. Using this viewpoint makes it possible to determine the purpose of e-participation. It is also foreseen to estimate the potential impacts of e-participation throughout its lifecycle through a high-level view on how the objectives can be achieved by participation techniques. Stakeholders may be the owner and management as well as participants wishing to understand the purposes of participation. The Participation Scope Viewpoint employs scenario building to describe the participation vision. The analysis begins by determining which objectives support the vision. A solution for achieving these objectives is defined on a high level. Therefore, any entities of other viewpoints can be associated with entities from the Participation Scope, e.g. to determine actors' requirements or objectives.

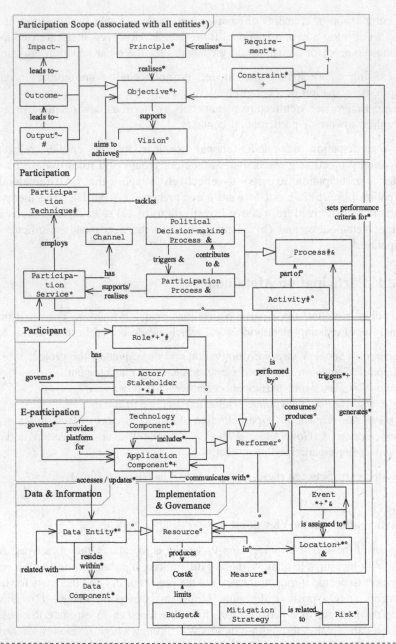

Legend: UML class diagram. Symbols represent the sources of the entities: * TOGAF, + ArchiMate, ° DoDAF, ~ Smith et al., # Kalampokis et al., § Phang and Kankanhalli, & Porwol et al.

Fig. 1. Overview of the e-participation metamodel

A *Vision* is a mental image of the intended future [cp. inputs in 35] with regards to what the project aims to achieve and the context. A vision tackles participation levels, a policy cycle stage and participation areas. An *Objective* is the goal of e-participation. Objectives can be defined on different levels: general objectives (impacts), specific objectives (outcomes) and operational objectives (outputs) [16]. A *Principle is* "a qualitative statement of intent that should be met by" [33, p. 22] the e-participation architecture. Principles are "general rules and guidelines [...] that inform and support the way in which an organisation sets about fulfilling its mission" [33, p. 235]. A *Requirement* is "a statement of need that must be realised" [34, p. 120]. An *Output* is an operational objective that the project generates through its construction [29]. An *Outcome* is a specific objective that describes a benefit for stakeholders [29]. An *Impact* is a general objective, i.e. a societal objective or public value that describes an overall goal [29]. A *Constraint* is an external factor or restriction influencing the way in which the project can be realised [33, 34].

4.2 Participant Viewpoint

The purpose of the *Participant Viewpoint* is to identify and manage the stakeholders, who are actively and passively engaged in the project or affected by the policy under consideration. It provides information needed to allocate roles to participants. Stakeholders of this viewpoint may be the owner and management, as well as participation analyst. Nevertheless, it is also for ICT engineers to derive access rights. The Participant Viewpoint employs stakeholder analysis. It needs to model Actor/Stakeholder, Role, Organisation type, Organisation. The enumeration Actor Type specifies the kind of stakeholder/actor, while the enumeration Organisation Type defines the kind of organisations. A *Performer* is any entity or complex of entities responsible to perform an activity and provide a capability [35]. A *Stakeholder* is "an individual, team, or organization (or classes thereof) with interests in, or concerns relative to, the outcome of the architecture" [33]. Stakeholder can be seen as "a motivational role [...] that an actor may fulfil" [34]. An *Actor* is an organisational entity that is capable of performing behaviour [34]. An *Actor Type* is a particular kind of actor: citizen, elected representative, government executive, employee, policy maker, decision maker, politician, lobbyist, other. An *Organisation* is a self-contained unit of people and other resources with objectives [33, 35]. An *Organisation Type* is a particular kind of organisation: academia, government, industry, political party, non-governmental organisation, media, and advisory board. A *Role* is the part and the contribution an actor plays in the e-participation project [33], as e.g. administrator, decision-maker, policy expert, facilitator, moderator, input provider, lurker.

4.3 Participation Viewpoint

The purpose of the *Participation Viewpoint* is the design of participation services, processes and activities necessary to carry out the e-participation project. It considers the political decision-making processes and plans how to integrate participation processes in a meaningful way. Participation analysts who are interested in planning the participation procedures are obvious stakeholders. In addition, the owners, managers, and participants who want to see how participation is carried out are stakeholders.

This viewpoint employs process analysis and management. The analysis is performed in two steps [27]: First, the decision-making processes are analysed. Afterwards the participation processes are planned. The planning needs to consider the participation techniques and the roles that perform activities in the processes as well as inputs and outputs. There is a need to model Event, Process, Activity, Participation Service, Channel, and Participation Technique. Furthermore, it is necessary to link Performer of related viewpoints and Objective of the Participation Scope Viewpoint. An *Activity* transforms input resources into output resources or changes the states of resources [35]. A *Participation Technique* is a method or instrument applied to involve or engage individuals or groups in the participation process [9]. A *Participation Service* is a specific service to involve or engage target groups based on participation techniques employed. A *Process* is an entity that groups behaviour based on an ordering of activities [34]. Processes are differentiated in policy-making and participation processes. A *Decision-making Process* is a set of coordinated activities with certain start and end points that are performed by a government with the aim to set a policy on the political agenda, formulate a policy, decide a policy, implement a policy and/or evaluate a policy [1, 2, 8]. A *Participation Process* presents the activities to engage stakeholders in policy-making processes. An *Event* is a state change, inside or outside the e-participation initiative, which triggers activities or processes [33].

4.4   Data & Information Viewpoint

The *Data & Information Viewpoint* describes the data, which performers produce or consume within e-participation. The purpose of the viewpoint is the development of a data and information architecture. It aims to ensure that the information relevant in e-participation project operations is managed [according to the Data and Information Viewpoint in 35]. Using this viewpoint makes it possible to conceptualise the data and information. Editorial team, marketing, ICT engineer are interested in these views: The editorial team and marketing to identify participation data and information, which are to be provided. ICT architects and engineers to design appropriate applications. The Data & Information Viewpoint describes the Resources, which performers produce or consume within e-participation. The entities are *Data Entity* representing data and information, *Data Component* to store data entities, and *Data Type*. A *Data Entity* is a specific encapsulation [33] or information that is materialised in any medium or form and communicated or received [35]. It is represented in a formalised manner suitable for communication, interpretation, or processing by humans or by automatic means [35].

4.5   E-Participation Viewpoint

The purpose of the *E-participation Viewpoint* is the technical representation of the applications required to implement the participation architecture, its deployment and operation. It therefore describes the general architecture of the applications: their structure, distributions and how they are interconnected, and a technical description of the applications. Stakeholders are the ICT engineers, suppliers, developers and administrators, i.e. those who are responsible for implementing the ICT facilities supporting the participation. When employing the viewpoint, the requirements manager analyses the Requirements considering input by all stakeholders. The ICT engineers/architects and participation analysts in charge decide on the Application Components supporting the Participation Services and Requirements. Next, the ICT engineers select appropriate *Technology Components*, which provide the platform for the *Application Components*. Afterwards, they develop the software architecture. An Application Component is a group of interacting or interdependent ICT elements, which can be functional, physical or behaviour related [35]. A group of integrated application components form an e-participation tool or e-participation platform. A Technology Component is an "encapsulation of technology infrastructure" [33, p. 631].

4.6 Implementation & Governance Viewpoint

The purpose of the *Implementation & Governance Viewpoint* is the operational management of the e-participation project and governance of architecture implementation. It addresses the concern of determining the constraints of carrying out e-participation (e.g. of managerial or environmental nature) and evaluating the outcomes. Some likely stakeholders for the viewpoint are the project managers. The managers need to model the Budget by estimating the Costs of Resources. A Resource is something that is consumed or produced by an activity [35]. Resources include the underlying infrastructure necessary to construct the e-participation [29]. Project managers define a project plan and need to work out important Events. Furthermore, Measures are defined for Objectives consolidated. The viewpoint employs risk management [a risk management framework is e.g. described in [33], pp. 313–317]. Mitigation Strategies are developed for Risks identified. A *Risk* describes a danger, which might influence if objectives are achievable.

5   Conclusion

This paper studied e-participation and enterprise architecture metamodels and derived from this research a e-participation metamodel, which serves as a structure in the design and implementation of e-participation projects. The research combined a comparative analysis of literature on conceptual models structuring the e-participation domain and metamodels of architecture frameworks. Comparative analysis showed that the different attempts complement each other, but a comprehensive approach is still missing. This paper combined the elements from the different models to develop a comprehensive metamodel for e-participation, and it is structured by the following six viewpoints: participation scope, participant, participation, data & information, e-participation, and implementation & governance. The metamodel formalises the architecture of an e-participation project, the relationships between the entities, and enables an EA tool mapping. The latter is a particular additional value that the proposed metamodel provides in comparison with the existing e-participation metamodels resulting from the comparison with EA framework metamodels. Another benefit is that this metamodel integrates managerial as well as data and information aspects necessary to design the architecture of an e-participation project. Furthermore, the breaking down into viewpoints supports the stakeholders in managing the complexity, as particular stakeholders are able to focus on their concerns.

The research on the metamodel is part of research work putting forward an e-participation reference framework [25, 26]. This framework is designed to guide the design and implementation of e-participation so that the architecture enables project success with optimised processes and ICT, and a lower total cost of ownership. Its target group is the group of stakeholders responsible for designing and implementing an e-participation project. The strategic, top-down perspective on the project enables project management, initiators, owners, executives and decision makers to plan, organise, and combine their activities in a comprehensive way. The metamodel provides the base vocabulary and structural concept.

References

1. Anderson, J.E.: Public Policymaking, 7th edn. Cengage Learning, Wadsworth (2010)
2. Birkland, T.A.: An Introduction to the Policy Process: Theories, Concept and Models of Public Policy Making. M. E. Sharpe, Armonk/London (2004)
3. Cameron, B.H., McMillan, E.: Analyzing the current trends in enterprise architecture frameworks. J. Enterp. Archit. **9**(1), 60–71 (2013)
4. Estrem, W.A., Gonzalez, S.: TOGAF® framework and ArchiMate® modeling language harmonization. Content metamodel harmonization. Entities and relationships. The Open Group White Paper (2014)
5. Federal Enterprise Architecture Program Management Office: Federal enterprise architecture framework, version 2 (2013)
6. Glass, J.J.: Citizen participation in planning: the relationship between objectives and techniques. J. Am. Plan. Assoc. **45**(2), 180–189 (1979). doi:10.1080/01944367908976956
7. Hevner, A., Chatterjee, S.: Design science research in information systems. In: Hevner, A., Chatterjee, S. (eds.) Design Research in Information Systems. Theory and Practice, vol. 22, pp. 9–22. Springer, Boston (2010)
8. Howlett, M., Ramesh, M., Perl, A., et al.: Studying Public Policy. Policy Cycles and Policy Subsystems, vol. 163, 3rd edn. Cambridge University Press, Don Mills (1995)
9. Kalampokis, E., Tambouris, E., Tarabanis, K.A.: A domain model for eParticipation. In: Mellouk, A., Bi, J., Ortiz, G., et al. (eds) Proceedings of the Third International Conference on Internet and Web Applications and Services, pp. 25–30. IEEE Computer Society, Los Alamitos (2008)
10. Kubicek, H., Aichholzer, G.: Closing the evaluation gap in e-Participation research and practice. In: Aichholzer, G., Kubicek, H., Torres, L. (eds.) Evaluating e-Participation, pp. 11–45. Springer International Publishing, Switzerland (2016)
11. Lankhorst, M.: Enterprise Architecture at Work: Modelling, Communication and Analysis. The Enterprise Engineering Series. Springer, New York (2009)

12. Macintosh, A.: Characterizing e-participation in policy-making. In: Proceedings of the 37th HICSS. IEEE Computer Society, Los Alamitos (2004)
13. Macintosh, A., Whyte, A.: Towards an evaluation framework for eParticipation. Transform. Gov. People Process Policy 2(1), 16–30 (2008). doi:10.1108/17506160810862928
14. Matthes, D.: Enterprise Architecture Frameworks Kompendium. Xpert.press. Springer, Heidelberg (2011)
15. Medaglia, R.: eParticipation research: moving characterization forward (2006–2011). Gov. Inf. Q. (GIQ) 29(3), 346–360 (2012). doi:10.1016/j.giq.2012.02.010
16. Millard, J.: eGovernment measurement for policy makers. Eur. J. ePractice 4, 1–14 (2008)
17. Peffers, K., Tuunanen, T., Rothenberger, M.A., et al.: A design science research methodology for information systems research. J. Manag. Inf. Syst. 24(3), 45–77 (2007). doi:10.2753/MIS0742-1222240302
18. Phang, C.W., Kankanhalli, A.: A framework of ICT exploitation for e-participation initiatives. Commun. ACM 51(12), 128–132 (2008). doi:10.1145/1409360.1409385
19. Porwol, L., Ojo, A., Breslin, J.G.: An ontology for next generation c-participation initiatives. Gov. Inf. Q. (2016). doi:10.1016/j.giq.2016.01.007
20. Rozanski, N., Woods, E.: Software Systems Architecture. Working with Stakeholders Using Viewpoints and Perspectives, 2nd edn. Addison-Wesley, Upper Saddle River (2012)
21. Sæbø, Ø., Flak, L.S., Sein, M.K.: Understanding the dynamics in e-Participation initiatives. Looking through the genre and stakeholder lenses. Gov. Inf. Q. 28(3), 416–425 (2011). doi:10.1016/j.giq.2010.10.005
22. Sæbø, Ø., Rose, J., Flak, L.S.: The shape of eParticipation. Characterizing an emerging research area. Gov. Inf. Q. 25(3), 400–428 (2008). doi:10.1016/j.giq.2007.04.007
23. Scherer, S., Neuroth, C., Schefbeck, G., Wimmer, M.A.: Enabling eParticipation of the youth in the public debate on legislation in Austria: a critical reflection. In: Macintosh, A., Tambouris, E. (eds.) ePart 2009. LNCS, vol. 5694, pp. 151–162. Springer, Heidelberg (2009)
24. Scherer, S., Wimmer, M.A.: A regional model for e-participation in the EU: evaluation and lessons learned from VoicE. In: Tambouris, E., Macintosh, A., Glassey, O. (eds.) ePart 2010. LNCS, vol. 6229, pp. 162–173. Springer, Heidelberg (2010)
25. Scherer, S., Wimmer, M.A.: Reference framework for e-participation projects. In: Tambouris, E., Macintosh, A., Bruijn, H. (eds.) ePart 2011. LNCS, vol. 6847, pp. 145–156. Springer, Heidelberg (2011)
26. Scherer, S., Wimmer, M.A.: E-participation and enterprise architecture frameworks: an analysis. Inf. Polity 17(2), 147–161 (2012). doi:10.3233/IP-2012-0270
27. Scherer, S., Wimmer, M.A., Ventzke, S.: Hands-on guideline for e-participation initiatives. In: Rosemann, M., Janssen, M., Lamersdorf, W., Pries-Heje, J. (eds.) EGES 2010 and GISP 2010. IFIP AICT, vol. 334, pp. 49–61. Springer, Heidelberg (2010)
28. Schönherr, M.: Enterprise architecture frameworks. In: Aier, S. (ed.) Enterprise Application Integration. Serviceorientierung und nachhaltige Architekturen, vol. 2, pp. 3–48. Gito-Verlag (2004)
29. Smith, S., Macintosh, A., Millard, J.: A three-layered framework for evaluating e-participation. Int. J. Electron. Gov. 4(4), 304–321 (2011). doi:10.1504/IJEG.2011.046013
30. Software and Systems Engineering Standards Committee of the IEEE Computer Society: Systems and software engineering - architecture description (ISO/IEC/IEEE 42010:2011) (2011)
31. Tambouris, E., Kalampokis, E., Tarabanis, K.: A survey of e-participation research projects in the European Union. Int. J. Electron. Bus. (IJEB) 6(6), 554–571 (2008)

32. Tambouris, E., Liotas, N., Tarabanis, K.: A framework for assessing eParticipation projects and tools. In: Proceedings of the 40th Annual Hawaii International Conference on System Sciences. IEEE Computer Society Press, US (2007)

33. The Open Group: The Open Group Standard TOGAF Version 9.1, Document Number: G116. TOGAF Series. The Open Group (2011)

34. The Open Group: ArchiMate® 2.1 Specification. Open Group Standard, C13L. The Open Group, United Kingdom (2013)

35. U.S. Department of Defense: The DoDAF Architecture Framework Version 2.02 (2011)

36. Wimmer, M.A.: Ontology for an e-participation virtual resource centre. In: Janowski, T., Pardo, T.A. (eds.) Proceedings of the 1st International Conference on Theory and Practice of Electronic Governance, pp. 89–98. ACM, New York (2007)

37. Yusuf, M., Adams, C., Dingley, K.: A novel framework of e-participation. In: Ionas, A. (ed.) Proceedings of the 14th European Conference on eGovernment, p. 363. Academic Conferences Limited (2014)

38. Zachman, J.A.: A framework for information systems architecture. IBM Syst. J. **26**(3), 277–293 (1987). doi:10.1147/sj.263.0276

Towards a Research Framework of Computer-Supported Organizational Participation

Thomas Wagenknecht[1(✉)], René Filpe[1], and Christof Weinhardt[2]

[1] FZI Research Centre for Information Technology, Berlin, Germany
{wagenknecht,filpe}@fzi.de
[2] Karlsruhe Institute of Technology, Karlsruhe, Germany
weinhardt@kit.edu

Abstract. Employees demand high responsibility and empowerment, while keeping their work communal and flexible. Initiatives that foster organizational participation can contribute to the fulfilment of such work conditions. Research in sociology and psychology demonstrated positive effects on job satisfaction as well as productivity. However, although adoption of social software is widely spread in firms, research on the determinants of computer-supported organizational participation is scarce. We conduct 20 guided expert interviews to propose a research framework for computer-supported organizational participation. We describe the elements to consider when designing processes that aim to be beneficial for both the employer as well as the employees. Building on the expert interviews, our process model includes a topic horizon and a collaboration phase, which creates proposals that have to be decided on in order to produce results. We show how employee competence and leadership commitment are as important as the workload and supporting features as well as an option for anonymous communication. We propose a set of features and discuss implications for researchers and practitioners.

Keywords: Organizational participation · eParticipation · Group decision support systems · Expert interviews

1 Introduction

Many companies offer their staff social software such as employee portals and Enterprise Social Networks (ESNs) to support information exchange and collaboration [2]. Yet, in a network society, more and more areas of our lives become democratized [3]. This democratization has reached the workplace as today's employees demand high responsibility and empowerment as well as communal and flexible work environments [4]. Initiatives that foster employee participation can nurture these demands. Organizational participation (OP) and its positive effects on job satisfaction and productivity have been well studied [5, 6]. However, little attention has been paid to the exploration of how these processes can be incorporated by and designed with social software. Yet, considering the eParticipation practices in eGovernment on one hand [8, 27], and the progressively strong grip that social software holds over current work

© IFIP International Federation for Information Processing 2016
Published by Springer International Publishing Switzerland 2016. All Rights Reserved
E. Tambouris et al. (Eds.): ePart 2016, LNCS 9821, pp. 17–28, 2016.
DOI: 10.1007/978-3-319-45074-2_2

practices on the other, computer-supported organizational participation (CSOP) becomes increasingly relevant [7].

Nonetheless, research on CSOP is scarce. This is especially problematic as it is not clear which parts of existing social software for participation – e.g. from the political sphere [8] – can be applied in the corporate contexts. Hence, the main purpose of this paper is to further our understanding of the design of eParticipation in firms. We conduct 20 guided interviews with experts from a variety of industries, including services as well as manufacturing, in order to derive a model that describes the relevant determinants of CSOP. The results provide a basis for a framework that informs future research on the main areas where studies are needed. We derive a set of CSOP use cases and draw implications for practitioners.

The remainder of this article is organized as follows. In Sect. 2, we illustrate the theoretical background on organizational participation, eParticipation and group decision support systems. Section 3 presents our study design, including our data set and the structure of the expert interviews. We report the results in Sect. 4 and propose a framework of CSOP in Sect. 5. Section 6 draws a conclusion.

2 Theoretical Background and Related Work

We begin by introducing the fundamental theories behind OP from sociology and psychology, and highlight some of its positive as well as negative effects. Thereafter, we introduce information systems literature to establish the connection to eParticipation and group decision support systems (GDSS).

2.1 Fundamentals of Participation

Typically, there are four basic theoretical lines of thinking that shape OP: democratic, socialist, human growth and development as well as those focusing on productivity and efficiency [9, 10]. The democratic view emphasizes participation in a form that includes as many employees and stakeholders as possible. The socialist assumption departs from the notion of participation as increasing workers' control of the production process, while simultaneously educating them to the point that they can replace their managers [11]. Furthermore, human growth and development theories extend the latter aspect by highlighting self-development and self-fulfillment. Finally, theories on productivity regard participation as having the goal of increasing employee satisfaction and commitment as well as a generally increasing productivity and efficiency by means of better decision quality [10]. Empowerment is a management style that incorporates many of these aspects. Kanter [12] suggests that empowerment is a form of ability to mobilize resources. She argues that individuals gain power by having access to information, support and resources as well as space to foster their soft and hard skills. Empowerment is understood as a process that allows employees to gain and retain power to act autonomously [13].

Typically, research in organizational and work psychology categorizes OP along eight steps, which moves from a low to a high degree of employee decision-making authority. The steps include employee information, consultation (employees can have their say), co-determination (employees have to be involved in the discussion) and control [5, 6, 10]. The latter can range from voting on selected issues, to having a veto right, shared leadership or even final decision-making authority. Dachler and Wilpert [10] also stress the complexity, topic and the point in time that participative elements are used in the decision-making process as important factors for OP.

2.2   Effects of Participation

Participation is often implemented with regards to its positive effects in terms of employee motivation, satisfaction and performance [5, 13, 14]. For instance, in a meta-analysis, Miller and Monge [14] find that participative leadership contributes to more sustainable and effective learning and personal development. Moreover, employees increase intrinsic motivation, job satisfaction, organizational commitment and feelings of self-efficacy [15, 16]. This in turn can help companies to increase effectiveness [12, 13, 17].

However, OP is not without risks. For instance, decision quality could actually be decreased if lower-level employees are not knowledgeable enough to take appropriate decisions [17]. Moreover, participative processes could prolong decision-making as they take more time than usual top-down decisions. Besides time, employers could also fear that they lose power and authority. Among the common explanations for the reluctance of senior managers to implement employee empowerment practices are two psychological factors established by Pfeffer et al. [18]. First, the researchers demonstrated that people have a tendency to believe in the supervision effect. Controlling for the quality, they suggest that observers assume a work product to be better the greater the degree of supervision. Moreover, Pfeffer et al. [18] were able to show in an experiment that the more participants were involved in the supervision of the creation of a product, the more favorably participants evaluated it. This self-enhancement effect is well documented as people regularly evaluate their work to be above that of their peers [19].

Interestingly, there is no need for managers to fear losing control completely when introducing OP. Markey et al. [20] found that workers who felt appreciated by their senior management did not desire more influence. However, those who were under the impression that they did not learn new things and did not receive sufficient information on important decisions, changes and future plans indicated that they want to have more influence.

2.3   eParticipation and Group Decision Support Systems

If there is limited ground for reluctance against OP, why has OP not spread further despite the benefits? One reason might be that many firms face difficulties with its realization [21]. For instance, Arnold et al. [22] point out that it is crucial for employers to constantly support and inform employees during participative processes to demonstrate that their input is taken seriously. GDSS offer support in the computer-mediated generation, presentation and synthesis of proposals [23]. They are also popular tools to lower dysfunctional effects in the decision-making of groups, like boards, units or teams [24, 25]. Such dysfunctions include social effects that usually occur in group decision-making such as conformity pressure, groupthink or limited information apprehension [13, 26].

Political parties, government agencies and non-governmental groups alike are already using GDSS to enable eParticipation processes for citizens [8, 27]. These software tools often facilitate information sharing, collaboration and collective action (such as voting) [1]. We understand CSOP as social software that technologically enables participative elements specifically in firms. Extant research already proposed success factors for eParticipation in eGoverment intiatives [8]. However, factors from the political sphere might not yield the same results in the corporate field [28]. For instance, as enterprises are slowly beginning to implement OP through means of GDSS, one approach is to use ESNs [29]. However, ESNs can be understood as "social media used for communication and interaction within the workplace" [2]. Thus, these information systems are by no means automatically fully equipped to serve as facilitators for CSOP, suggesting that further research is needed.

All in all, current research proposes that OP offers many benefits to both employees as well as employers. However, they need to be considered against their risks, which can be partially mitigated through the use of GDSS. Although ESNs are fairly widespread, research on eParticipation tools for the specific context of OP is very scarce. Thus, we seek to close this gap by proposing a research framework that incorporates the components and requirements for GDSS to enable participation in firms. We choose to interview experts in diverse organizations in order to elicit possible challenges and opportunities in implementing CSOP. This will yield a framework with testable propositions that is able to guide future research as well as practical implementations.

3   Study Design

We aim to capture tacit knowledge from experts in organizations based on guided expert interviews [30]. We consider this as the most promising and insightful method to develop a framework with verifiable propositions and hypotheses for future research. For instance, a general survey might be too broad and a field study in a single firm too case-specific. Therefore, we focus on expert interviews with executives with more than five years of work experience in the HR and/or IT department. These experts can be considered decision makers when it comes to implementing CSOP.

We interviewed a total of 20 participants that all had extensive experience with organizational participation in practice. Two thirds of the experts were working in the services and information and communication technologies industry. Production industry was home to five experts. Only one of the companies had less than 100 employees. In two thirds of the companies, there was a more or less active workers council.

Based on the theoretical background presented in Sect. 2, we developed an interview guide. Our interviews began by introducing the concepts of OP. We then asked for the level of workers' representation (i.e. trade unions, workers council) and examined the corporate culture by asking about the corporate hierarchy and formal decision-making processes. Thereafter, we explored the usage of collaborative software tools such as ESNs. Following this part, we interviewed the experts on their experience with OP processes and asked for challenges and opportunities of a possible computer-supported implementation.

Interviews lasted, on average, 45 min. We recorded them both in writing and audio. Three research assistants transcribed the interviews following the approach of Weston et al. [30]. Inter-coder reliability was ensured by repeated crosschecks. Three research assistants resolved discrepancies with the help of an independent third party. Transcriptions were then processed using MAXQDA 12.1.3 [31]. We created a codebook with 98 codes. Codebooks were crosschecked to increase validity. We took an iterative and dynamic approach, developing the codebook further as we went on to derive codes in vivo during the analysis of the interviews. We coded snippets, phrases and paragraphs and cross-checked the final coding.

Based on the theoretical background and the expert interviews, we develop a nascent framework, which will be described in detail as follows.

4 Results

Table 1 shows the use cases for which experts carried out OP. Most commonly, employees were simply informed about firm developments. Furthermore, we observed a form of what we call "coffee kitchen participation", which includes employee voting on decisions that are not business-relevant such as the color of the canteen walls, where to go for a Christmas party or the type of coffee to be bought. Moreover, the interviewees stated that participative processes in their companies asked for the staff's well-being and for idea generation (i.e. suggestions for improvements of products, procedures and work conditions). In addition, experts said that employees were invited to set the agenda of board meetings and corporate events, propose mission statements and work on strategy plans or corporate policies. All of the use cases happened both with and without the support of IT tools. Also, most use cases were located at a corporate-wide level, but one that was exclusive to the unit level. In most cases our interviewees told us about, employees were only able to decide on "light-weight" issues. The creation of mission statements or strategies was rare. More often, OP was

Table 1. Use cases for organizational participation

Use case	Using IT-tools	Unit level	Corporate level
Information	X	X	X
Coffee kitchen participation	X	X	–
Employee well-being	X	X	X
Idea generation	X	X	X
Agenda setting	X	–	X
Mission statements	X	–	X
Strategy & corporate policy	X	–	X

happening in form of suggestion schemes, surveys on well-being and by means of coffee kitchen participation.

The vast majority of the experts made positive experiences with OP. They reported affirmative reactions from their employees, who appreciated the effort as promoting equal opportunities. As expected, the interviewees said that participation lead to increased job satisfaction. Some experts also told us that they experienced a change in the corporate culture with more feedback and trust as a sign for a willingness for organizational transformation. Moreover, OP reportedly led to an increase in decision quality and more (product and process-optimizing) ideas. Many interviewees also said that OP was positively received by the companies' leadership. Some were frankly surprised by the high quality of the results and the overall effects.

However, in the past experience with OP many experts reported critical problems too. A major issue was the low rate of response among employees, which the interviewees traced back to four reasons. First, some employees were unable to identify themselves and their job with the chosen topics. Thus, they had no interest in participating and did not feel involved. Second, many companies simply were not ready for OP as their corporate culture lacked the formal and informal framework (e.g. employees did not dare to express their opinion or were unable to do so because of hierarchical structures). Third, the experts acknowledged that an OP process needs some marketing to attract users. An interviewee explained it the following way: "*When you put up something for discussion, you can be happy if there is some degree of participation at all. We call it the empty dancefloor: There always needs to be someone who starts dancing first, so that other people follow*". Fourth, companies used software tools to organize the participative process, which were often perceived as insufficient because of their high complexity in terms of both the time it took to learn the functions as well as the resources employees had to put into the process besides their normal job tasks. An expert stated: "*There are usually employees who say, they feel simply overloaded with the tasks they already have. They perceive the introduction of new software tools as an additional burden*". Moreover, interviewees reported that some employees did not trust the (technical) systems due to a lack of anonymity. Some experts also reported that reticent employees were discriminated by the process as they did not get equal opportunities to have their say. Furthermore, employees that were less tech-savvy were disadvantaged too. Due to these four main reasons described above, low employee participation diminished a processes' representative status in the eyes of the experts.

In general, our experts recognized that OP in their companies was often structured inefficiently. For instance, discussions were sometimes perceived as off-topic and not constructive. This happened when there was a lack of priority and when responsibilities were unclear. Experts regularly reported of a lack of commitment by the leadership because it was not clear how the senior management would deal with results or simply did not show much interest. Many experts also think that the leadership could effectively block decisions or derail the participative process, so that employees lose interest and trust in the whole process. Another problem occurred especially in the field of idea generation. In a few cases, results were so disappointing that the experts assumed that employees did not have sufficient expertise to propose and discuss certain ideas. Instead the experts stressed that they faced a high workload in evaluating and eventually dismissing ideas.

A small number of experts reported that their firms used dedicated software tools for OP. Yet, most experts said that they were relying on offline measures, their Intranet or ESNs. Thus, when introduced to an online GDSS specifically designed for CSOP, most experts had to depend on hypothetical knowledge. In general, most suggested that such a system is especially appropriate for firms with more than one location and a larger number of (spatially dispersed) employees. They expect employees to have positive reactions for CSOP. In particular, experts expect more constructive discussions as a result of mutual rating of proposals and filtering of bad ideas. This in turn would lead to higher acceptance and approval from the leadership. Many interviewees also think that such software tools can support employees regardless of their position and social status. Some experts also predict increased transparency of the decision-making process. They envision dedicated software to make the whole process clearer, which could increase the efficiency of CSOP. Moreover, some experts recognized that GDSS might be more motivating through means of rankings and gamified elements. Experts were divided over the questions of anonymity and moderation. For instance, some assume that employees would only use it to write complaints or might even use the forum as a way to compromise and attack their superiors. As one expert stated: *"With anonymity we made the experience that a very small part of the participants who dislike everyone and everything can have a big negative impact on the discussion overall"*. Contrarily, other experts emphasized the need for anonymity as it would be the only way to comply with legal requirements and, more importantly, enable open discussions on sensitive issues. In their view, anonymous comments would protect employees from repressions of their superiors. Notably, we found the same controversy among experts in terms of the need for moderators.

In conclusion, we captured tacit knowledge on CSOP from a variety of experts. We found that firms rarely use dedicated software for OP, although the experts envision that CSOP could diminish negative effects of offline processes while emphasizing the positive sides. GDSS seemed promising especially because of their ability to make the structure of the overall process more transparent and accessible, as well as more engaging. However, the interviewees also stressed that GDSS might be misused by some employees. Thus, based on these results we can derive the determinants for a CSOP framework.

5   Framework

The expert interviews offer a critical analysis of existing practices in OP. Based on these results, we describe a framework that describes the determinants of CSOP in a way so that it will improve both the efficiency and equality of employers and employees; leading to a win-win situation for both. We aim to describe valid constructs for firms with spatially and timely dispersed teams and more than 50 employees. Figure 1 shows our framework of CSOP. We describe it in more detail as follows.

Topic Horizon. In order to fulfil its purpose, CSOP needs a process that allows employees and employers to discuss a range of ideas and topics. We call this the topic horizon, which defines the issues that can be discussed in detail throughout the

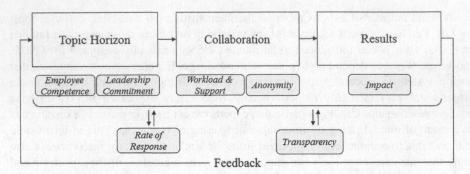

Fig. 1. Framework of computer-supported organizational participation

participation process. These issues can range along all use cases discovered in Table 1 – from seemingly trivial topics, such as the color of the cafeteria, to mission statements and strategic decisions. The topic horizon also sets the boundaries of who can propose what type of issue. The topic horizon is defined by both the employees' competence as well as the leadership's commitment. The first means both competence as a function of the expertise of the employees (Do they have enough knowledge and skills to work on a certain topic?) as well as what rights and obligations are granted to them (What can employees decide on?). Topics should be chosen in such a way, so that they are relevant to employees in order to ensure identification. On the other hand, commitment asks for how much the leadership is actually involved in the whole participation process (How much do they engage?) and what they plan to do with the results (Are results binding or just a form of consultation?). Both characteristics set the boundaries of the topic horizon. These characteristics significantly impact the topics that can then be proposed in the collaboration phase.

Collaboration. After agreeing on a topic horizon, members of the participation process can propose issues they want to discuss in more detail. At the moment of the inception of the first proposals, the participation process enters into a phase of collaboration that develops these proposals further. Depending on the goals of a certain process, this can include commenting, editing and rating – either by regular users or (internal as well as external) moderators. The means of collaboration dictate the workload that is imposed on both employees (How much effort is asked for to propose and work on an idea?) and employers (What degree of oversight is needed?). In addition, collaboration also includes support for the members of a participation process. For instance, in cases where the topic horizon exceeds the employees' expertise (but not the relevance), firms could implement supporting collaboration tools or structures that ensure the required level of information apprehension. Anonymity is another important characteristic of the collaboration phase. In some countries, anonymous discussion might be legally advised. Moreover, anonymous communication seems generally useful when employees discuss sensitive issues, because users can express their opinion more honestly and do not have to fear repression from their superiors [24]. We propose a few features and remarks on implementation below. Finally, the collaboration phase ends by presenting the final proposals.

Results. These proposals are subject to decision-making (i.e. voting) and, hence, become results. The results have a (more or less disruptive) impact on the employees, the employers and the firm's market. While the results and their form are heavily dependent on the form of the topic horizon and the collaboration phase, they also define future participation processes. For instance, if the results produce disruptive product ideas, both employees and employers will be more inclined to start another participation process. They might even widen the topic horizon by committing more strongly and granting more competencies. However, if the feedback is negative, another round of participation might have a narrower topic horizon. In the end, the members of the CSOP process decide on the proposals in the form that they have been developed into during the collaboration phase. Thereafter, the outcomes enter a feed-back loop, which determines the conditions of whether another round of the participation process will be initiated.

Feedback. Furthermore, the process as a whole is dependent on the rate of response and level of participation. Naturally, if more members take part in the discussion, the leadership will be inclined to commit more strongly to the results. However, if a certain threshold cannot be reached, there is less of an incentive because the process has a limited representative status. Likewise, if many members enter a discussion, it becomes more engaging. Yet, these effects are interdependent and a type of chicken-and-egg problem. Additionally, the way the process is designed en bloc determines its degree of transparency for every construct. Transparency is a basis for trust in the whole process. If the leadership communicates clearly how the CSOP process is set out, employees know what to do and what to expect. This makes decision-making more easy to understand and will spark participation. A transparent process will also ensure that employees feel appreciated [20].

The success of CSOP is highly dependent on the goals and the appropriate selection of the tools and features necessary to fulfil these goals. First, a successful CSOP procedure is dependent on the corporate culture. Some companies might be able to adapt CSOP more easily due to their flat hierarchies and open discussion culture, while others might take longer because of a more formalized way of communication. Second, the experts interviewed stressed several times that some employees will be easily engaged in a participative process. However, others might feel overwhelmed. Thus, participation should be voluntary and competition between employees should be kept at compatible levels. Nonetheless, if employees spent much time on participation, they could also ask for some rewards. Third, participation is by no means a sure-fire success. One expert said: "*Marketing is essential to ensure acceptance of the tool.*" Hence, we advise to implement (on- and offline) marketing measures before, during and after the participation process. These might include trainings and workshops. Furthermore, the implementation should consider how a participation process can be integrated in the existing enterprise IT infrastructure.

A myriad of features can be used to pronounce the positive and mitigate the negative effects of CSOP postulated by the experts. These include idea filtering techniques [32], delegated voting [33], gamified approaches [34] or could make use of text mining tools, such as term extraction and topic modeling [35].

6   Discussion, Limitations and Conclusion

We proposed a nascent framework of CSOP. Based on 20 guided expert interviews, we derived a set of use cases for CSOP. Thereafter, we propose a model that incorporates a topic horizon, a collaboration phase and results as its basic constructs. These are highly dependent on their respective characteristics. First, the topic horizon is determined by the employee's competence – both in terms of expertise as well as the relevance of the topics to them. Additionally, the commitment by the leadership is crucial as it defines which stakeholders are involved and in what way results will be dealt with. According to these boundaries set for the topic horizon, CSOP enters into a collaboration phase. Depending on how the workload is shared among employees and employers and what measures for support are chosen, as well as whether anonymous communication is enabled, collaboration entails certain forms of proposal editing, commenting and developing. In result, these proposals are decided on and will reveal a more or less disruptive impact for the employees, the leadership and the firm's market. CSOP is heavily reliant on the features that are chosen for the design of the process. We also suggest that the whole process is profoundly depending on the rate of response by the employees, which determines the representative status of the whole CSOP initiative. Moreover, the transparency of the process defines how well the decision-making process can be understood and accessed by employees and employers. However, these two latter constructs are interdependent with the aforementioned constructs. The design of CSOP is very context-specific. Hence, practitioners should also consider a thorough assessment of a firm's corporate culture and the diversity of their employees as well as marketing measures.

In line with extant research, our framework incorporates the three forms of online communities – information sharing, collaboration and collective action [1]. It mirrors some of the common success factors identified for public eParticipation [8], while we emphasize workload and support as well as anonymity more strongly. Future research could compare our model to other public eParticipation frameworks in more detail, which was beyond the scope of this study. Despite our best efforts to diversify our set of experts, future research could consider surveying a broader (and more international) set of employers and employees. All in all, our framework can only be the first step of research in progress, where the model needs to be tested in practice.

Acknowledgement. This study is part of the research project "Participation as a Service" (PaaS), funded by the German Federal Ministry of Education and Research. We are grateful for the support of our interviewed experts, our research partners at HRpepper GmbH & Co. KGaA, partou eG and Liquid Democracy e.V., as well as three anonymous reviewers.

References

1. Spagnoletti, P., Resca, A., Lee, G.: A design theory for digital platforms supporting online communities: a multiple case study. J. Inf. Technol. **30**(4), 364–380 (2015)
2. Leonardi, P.M., Huysman, M., Steinfield, C.: Enterprise social media. Definition, history, and prospects for the study of social technologies in organizations. J. Comput.-Mediat. Commun. **19**(1), 1–19 (2013)
3. Castells, M.: The Rise of the Network Society. The Information Age: Economy, Society, and Culture, 2nd edn. Wiley, Hoboken (2011)
4. Tumasjan, A., Strobel, M., Welpe, I.M.: Employer brand building for start-ups. Which job attributes do employees value most. J. Bus. Econ. **81**(6), 111–136 (2011)
5. Wegge, J., et al.: Promoting work motivation in organizations. J. Pers. Psychol. **9**(4), 154–171 (2010)
6. Wilkinson, A., et al. (eds.): The Oxford Handbook of Participation in Organizations. Oxford University Press, Oxford (2010)
7. Majumdar, A., Krishna, S., Bjorn, P.: Managers' perceptions of social software use in the workplace. Identifying the benefits of social software and emerging patterns of its use. In: Proceedings of the 19th Americas Conference on Information Systems (AISeL) (2013)
8. Panopoulou, E., Tambouris, E., Tarabanis, K.: Success factors in designing eParticipation initiatives. Inf. Organ. **24**(4), 195–213 (2014)
9. Greenberg, E.S.: The consequences of worker participation: a clarification of the theoretical literature. Soc. Sci. Q. **56**(2), 191–209 (1975)
10. Dachler, H.P., Wilpert, B.: Conceptual dimensions and boundaries of participation in organizations. A critical evaluation. Adm. Sci. Q. **23**(1), 1–39 (1978)
11. Vranicki, P.: Socialism and the problem of alienation. Praxis **1**, 307–317 (1965)
12. Kanter, R.M.: Men and Women of the Corporation. Basic Books, New York (1977)
13. Wilkinson, A.: Empowerment: theory and practice. Pers. Rev. **27**(1), 40–56 (1998)
14. Miller, K.I., Monge, P.R.: Participation, satisfaction, and productivity. A meta-analytic review. Acad. Manag. J. **29**(4), 727–753 (1986)
15. Spreitzer, G.M.: Psychological empowerment in the workplace. Dimensions, measurement, and validation. Acad. Manag. J. **38**(5), 1442–1465 (1995)
16. Humborstad, S.I.W.: When industrial democracy and empowerment go hand-in-hand. A co-power approach. Econ. Indus. Democr. **35**(3), 391–411 (2014)
17. Harrison, J.S., Freeman, R.E.: Special topic. Democracy in and around organizations. Is organizational democracy worth the effort. Acad. Manag. Exec. **18**(3), 49–53 (2004)
18. Pfeffer, J., Cialdini, R.B., Hanna, B., Knopoff, K.: Faith in supervision and the self-enhancement bias. Two psychological reasons why managers don't empower workers. Basic Appl. Soc. Psychol. **20**(4), 313–321 (1998)
19. Brown, J.D.: Evaluations of self and others. Self-enhancement biases in social judgments. Soc. Cogn. **4**(4), 353–376 (1986)
20. Markey, R., Ravenswood, K., Webber, D.J., Knudsen, H.: Influence at work and the desire for more influence. J. Ind. Relat. **55**(4), 507–526 (2013)
21. Scholl, W., Schermuly, C., Klocke, U.: Wissensgewinnung durch Führung. Die Vermeidung von Informationspathologien durch Kompetenzen für Mitarbeiter (Empowerment). In: Grote, S. (ed.) Die Zukunft der Führung, pp. 391–413. Springer, Berlin Heidelberg (2012)
22. Arnold, J.A., Arad, S., Rhoades, J.A., Drasgow, F.: The empowering leadership questionnaire: the construction and validation of a new scale for measuring leader behaviors. J. Organ. Behav. **21**(3), 249–269 (2000)

23. Desanctis, G., Gallupe, R.B.: A foundation for the study of group decision support systems. Manag. Sci. **33**(5), 589–609 (1987)
24. Postmes, T., Lea, M.: Social processes and group decision making. Anonymity in group decision support systems. Ergonomics **43**(8), 1252–1274 (2000)
25. Briggs, R.O., Nunamaker, J.F., Sprague, R.H.: 1001 unanswered research questions in GSS. J. Manag. Inf. Syst. **14**(3), 3–21 (1998)
26. Stroebe, W., Diehl, M.: Why groups are less effective than their members. On productivity losses in idea-generating groups. Eur. Rev. Soc. Psychol. **5**(1), 271–303 (1994)
27. Tambouris, E., Macintosh, A., Smith, S., Panopoulou, E., Tarabanis, K., Millard, J.: Understanding eParticipation state of play in Europe. Inf. Syst. Manag. **29**(4), 321–330 (2012)
28. Bayley, C., French, S.: Designing a participatory process for stakeholder involvement in a societal decision. Group Decis. Negot. **17**(3), 195–210 (2008)
29. Richter, A., Heidemann, J., Klier, M., Behrendt, S.: Success measurement of enterprise social networks. In: 11th International Conference on Wirtschaftsinformatik (2013)
30. Weston, C.: Analyzing interview data the development and evolution of a coding system. Qual. Sociol. **24**(3), 381–400 (2001)
31. Corbin, J., Strauss, A.: Basics of Qualitative Research. Techniques and Procedures for Developing Grounded Theory, 3rd edn. Sage Publications, Los Angeles (2008)
32. Klein, M., Garcia, A.C.B.: High-speed idea filtering with the bag of lemons. Decis. Support Syst. **78**, 39–50 (2015)
33. Behrens, J., Kistner, A., Nitsche, A., Swierczek, B.: The Principles of LiquidFeedback. Interaktive Demokratie eV, Berlin (2014)
34. Hamari, J., Koivisto, J., Sarsa, H.: Does gamification work. A literature review of empirical studies on gamification. In: Proceedings of the 47th Hawaii International Conference on System Sciences, pp. 3025–3034 (2014)
35. Blei, D.M., Lafferty, J.D.: Topic models. In: Text Mining. Classification, Clustering, and Applications, p. 71. CRC Press (2009)

A New Path for the Public Sector: How to Design a Co-created Strategy in Higher Education

Maximilian Rapp[1(✉)], Markus Rhomberg[2], Giordano Koch[3], and Ken White[1]

[1] College of William & Mary, Williamsburg, USA
maximilian.rapp@hyve.net, Ken.white@mason.wm.edu
[2] Zeppelin University, Friedrichshafen, Germany
markus.rhomberg@zu.de
[3] HYVE AG, Munich, Germany
giordano.koch@hyve.net

Abstract. The use of collaborative platforms and eParticipation has turned out to be a promising channel to integrate citizens and external experts in various scenarios. While initiatives from institutions like political parties, governments or municipalities have been the target of influential research, another public service, namely higher education, seem to run below radar level. In this paper we analyze the project "Tomorrow's MBA" of the College of William & Mary, Virginia, and show through hands-on insights key success factors on how co-creation initiatives have to be designed in the field of higher education. The bottom-up strategy to create a new MBA program together with external stakeholders, students and the faculty delivers substantial results, which can be transferred to other fields within the public sector.

Keywords: Open government · eGovernment · eParticipation · Co-creation · Open education

1 Introduction and Theoretical Background

Ever since the philosophy of Open Innovation emerged, firms dwelled upon the question which tasks in value creation would be suited for the active integration of consumers (*Co-Creation*) [1]. In contrast, the strategic use of co-creation -in times of web 2.0- within the public sector needed more time to flourish, even though the active participation of citizens –in an offline format- has a way longer tradition [2]. The research often refers to the Obama administration with its White Gov-initiative [3], when similar to a snowball effect, eParticipation spread overseas to Europe and led to pilot, and later on long-term citizen sourcing projects, like participatory budgets, online consultations, city dialogues or collaborative strategy discussions. Best practices like in Ontario to use an online discussion platform to re-structure their voting system, or in Bavaria, where the Christian Social Union searched collaboratively for concepts for its new party program [4] nearly blossomed out of thin air in the years after.

© IFIP International Federation for Information Processing 2016
Published by Springer International Publishing Switzerland 2016. All Rights Reserved
E. Tambouris et al. (Eds.): ePart 2016, LNCS 9821, pp. 29–40, 2016.
DOI: 10.1007/978-3-319-45074-2_3

These paths lead the way for various researchers to explore potentials and challenges public organizations are facing when using innovative co-creation methods to actively engage citizens [5]. Nam for instance, focused on the differentiation and definition of Open Government and Open Government 2.0 as well as citizens' attitudes toward their integration [3]. He found out that the use of existing e-Government services does not significantly influence citizens' attitudes toward Open Government, while those who value the use of e-Government have a more positive attitude regarding Open Government and Government 2.0. Interesting findings have been identified by Schlozman et al., who state that the use of the new medium to foster citizens' engagement has mainly turned out to be a weapon of the strong [6]. Hereby they refer to the use of Open Government possibilities majorly by those, who are already interested and engaged in socio-political processes. According to Walters et al. there are five purposes to integrate public opinions: (1) the search for definitions, alternatives or criteria; (2) educating the public about an issue or alternatives; (3) measuring public opinion; (4) persuading the public; and (5) legitimize government decisions [7]. In contrast, King et al. identified three barriers to the effective participation: (1) the nature of life in contemporary society, (2) administrative processes and (3) techniques for participation [2]. In 1981 Kweit & Kweit analyzed the reasons for participation success and structured those in three characteristics: (1) the structures of participation mechanism and organizations; (2) the target organization, its resource base and member attitude and (3) the environment such as stability, form of government or community size. These research insights show us in other words that especially following guidelines are important regarding the integration of the public: (1) Why integrating the public, (2) how and, (3) with what expectations? [8].

The basis for a more open political approach, as mentioned above, was not laid through modern technologies and ICTs, but has already been addressed by democratic thinkers since the Antique. Back then people were defined as "idiots" [9], when not participating in everyday politics. While Aristoteles '*zôon politikón* can be seen as the individuals' obligation to interact and participate with the society to be fulfilled and create a strong and vital *polis*, Barber points out that representative democracy through politicians without participatory elements, where citizens can engage actively, are strongly dangerous for innovative societies and should thus be pursued actively [9]. In the same vein Corrado and Fireston concluded that online discussions will create a "conversational democracy" in which both the citizen as well as the political leaders will meet in a new (online) and existing (offline) way [10]. As Wright and Street summarized in their article on Democracy, deliberation and design "will promote the development of more democratic forms of government where citizens will be able to develop a more meaningful voice in their government" [11]. When looking further into the argumentation of a public administration perspective, the most obvious shift within the general development lays in the object of analysis. Whereas traditional research has mainly focused on the administration itself, many recent perspectives on public service provision focused on the relationship between citizen and government referring to the basic idea that government officials need to provide public services support [12].

Even though the literature on the use of co-creation and open innovation in the public sector is growing rapidly, it covers mainly the primary institutions like political parties, governments, politicians, administrations or unions and their need or approach to execute co-creation initiatives. In this paper we aim to broaden this approach on another field of the public service, namely higher education. We are interested, if openness and the method of co-creation can also be applied on this sector. Interestingly, the discussion about co-creation within higher education (open education) in general has led to major findings about the question if higher education should be free of tuition, but just a few insights about using those methods at universities have been delivered [13, 14]. Hereby we want to identify critical success factors and answer the research question on how to concept, design and execute a bottom-up co-creation project within higher education. Within the field of higher education we seek to focus on universities. However, universities have no hands-on products to co-create, so, the integration of public opinions and ideas for strategies or programs seem to be most likely. However, the lack of literature surprises, as you might think the step from opening up companies to consumers or governments to citizens, is logically followed by universities, which are opening up to students or external experts.

2 Empirical Approach

To answer our research question and to bridge the gap between the rich and already existing body of literature and cases from the open innovation research community and the upcoming paradigm in the educational sector, we introduce a five objective framework, which was originally developed by Li and Bernoff to analyze the outcome of co-creation and crowdsourcing projects [15]. We will now use this framework to better understand and analyze a co-creation project in the public sector, specifically for strategies within higher education. Due to the fact that many open strategies are struggling in the implementation phases, we will introduce a sixth dimension labeled "living", which will focus on the actual implementation and realization success of a co-creation campaign (Fig. 1).

- *Energizing:* The first dimension focuses on the recruitment, activation and motivation of the relevant target group to participate in the open call for ideas. Within this approach for universities, not just students and faculty staff should have the possibility to contribute, but also academics, experts or innovators around the globe to gather as much insights and knowhow as possible. Energizing and addressing these target groups is especially important as they have to be seen as a diverse and locally disperse crowd. An activation and motivation strategy will help to identify the most relevant target groups, which will be more engaged due to their knowledge and experience, but also their topic or task related responsibility.
- *Listening:* Generally, this dimension describes the use of an open innovation platform to involve the outside of the organization or administration to "listen" to a larger peer group of users/consumers (external academics, students) or own employees (teaching staff). As students and the teaching staff are dealing with the processes and content of a university on an everyday basis, they should have an influence on what they are learning or teaching at least have a possible feedback channel for proposing improvements or changes. Therefore, "listening" can be described as a key dimension as it aims and describes the steps how to open up the

Dimension	Open Innovation objectives within higher education
Energizing	Energizing aims to actively embrace students, academics, alumni and experts to engage in the given setup and to motivate sustainably in order to share their experience and knowledge.
Listening	Listening can be described as a key dimension as it aims to opening up the internal administrative barriers to integrate the voices from external experts and target groups sustainably.
Talking	Talking can be described as an external communication channel, which aims to promote the public initiative in order to generate more awareness for the respective project.
Supporting	Supporting seems to be the hard ground work of open public collaboration initiatives as its objective is to actively give feedback to shared ideas and to motivate the target group throughout the live phase of the co-creation initiative.
˙ Embracing	The goal of embracing is to guarantee that an open public initiative is backed up by the majority of stakeholders and responsible persons within the institution.
Living	Living can be described as a term that stands for the strong will to implement the results of the initiative, which were discussed and evaluated together with the crowd.

Fig. 1. Objectives for open innovation formats within higher education

internal administrative barriers to sustainably integrate the voices from internal as well as external.

- *Talking:* Although the main objective should focus on the generation of qualitative output, the communication and marketing dimension of such an initiative has to be seen as key factor. This dimension can be subdivided in communication efforts aiming on community growth, on output development, or on more general, not directly related communication efforts. So, "talking" might in other words be described as an external communication channel, which aims to promote the public initiative in order to generate more awareness and traffic on the platform as well as addressing the defined target group.
- *Supporting:* Open Innovation processes are based on the idea of peer-to-peer feedback. This implicates the participative and collaborative aspect since platform participants may support each other. Within the public sector setting such an approach within higher education can be a viable means to get in touch with other academics, students or likeminded users, connect with experts or the faculty staff and get feedback from them. Especially during the planning, implementation, and realization phases of an open innovation campaign relevant peer-to-peer feedback is considered very helpful. Moreover, a continuous and professional management and guidance of the initiative helps to identify relevant multipliers and motivate contributors to give them a positive feedback. Therefore, "supporting" seems to be the

hard ground work as its objective is to actively give feedback to shared ideas and to motivate the target group throughout the initiative.

- *Embracing:* The final dimension introduced by Li and Bernoff focuses on embracing relevant stakeholders. We know that the successful implementation of ideas and concepts, submitted within such a campaign, often fail due to the lack of motivated and engaged people within the organization. However, this implicates that the systematic integration of relevant experts and especially multipliers may be a success factor. By using a more open process these people can be identified, invited, motivated, and specially treated (embraced) to profit from their central and influencing role. Consequently, through the dimension of "embracing" the project owner tries to guarantee that an open public initiative is backed up by the majority of stakeholders and responsible persons within the institution.
- *Living:* Since public driven strategies usually in general, but especially with a more open approach, can be evaluated and reviewed by the public itself, a new dimension of transparency is achieved. However, the chance to be integrated leads inevitable to certain expectations of those, who contributed and spend time to help. If nothing happens with ideas and concepts or if there is no certain feedback to the engagement, negative rebound effects can arise. So, open approaches may also serve as a valuable mechanism to report, discuss and evaluate the consequences of the actual purpose. Even through an open strategy mechanisms no ground breaking input has been generated, the transparent communication of what is going to happen with the concepts and the initiative itself, is strikingly important.

Based on the foundation provided by literature on open innovation, crowdsourcing and co-creation and especially on the introduced framework of open innovation objectives for higher education, we executed a crowdsourcing project for the Mason A. School of Business at the College of William and Mary in Williamsburg, Virginia, USA. The initiative targeted the reorganization and development of the MBA. In this scope stakeholders of the program, e.g. students, managers, alumni were addressed to co-create a more consumer-focused and improved Master in Business Administration.

Since we were not able to draw on already existing research from other open strategy projects within the public sector, we applied a rather explanatory and thus qualitative research approach focusing on one single case. To get a better understanding of the effects between more open participatory approaches and the functions of governmental organizations, we chose a methodology that combined participatory and qualitative research approaches. "Participatory Action Research Approach" (PAR) refers to a research process that makes scientists become active participants and participants become scientists in the project that needs to be analyzed [16]. By creating a clear structure for planning, implementation, execution as well as systematic learning loops, it can be ensured that a new phenomenon in all its complexity is analyzed in a concrete use case. Therefore PAR is an approach primarily used for research questions that have only been analyzed very little, where scientists actually have to actively immerse themselves in the project. Consequently, the participatory project was conducted in close arrangement with the leaders of the College of William & Mary, the implementing consultancy and the research team. The research team was part of the entire project, as an observing and actively supporting instance.

3 Empirical Case: Creating Tomorrow's MBA

In 2015, the Raymond A. Mason School of Business at the College of William and Mary decided to collaboratively design the future of their MBA. The nucleus of this decision has been the international experience of influential enterprises and organizations, which use co-creation in order to find new trends, innovate their products or improve their services. While different researches have shown that the use of crowdsourcing and methods like innovation contests can be successfully applied in industry and the governmental sector, not many higher education institutions have tested this approach in field and especially for their own use. The major difference was the focus on a strategy, as companies usually co-create new services or products. Therefore, the target group differed tremendously from classical co-creation approaches. In order to integrate different stakeholders, but not necessarily from the covered home turf USA, a community as a virtual table for discussion was initiated. This community was approved by the William & Mary CI and enabled interested experts to register (with e-mail, professional background, username) and afterwards submit ideas, comment on others or evaluate contributions. The user-friendly ideation platform www.tomorrowsmba.mason.wm.edu was equipped with various social media shares to spread the word of mouth. Up in front the project team existing of the faculty and a professional innovation consultancy decided to frame the community within an eight-week idea contest to trigger gamification on the community. After the submission phase (end date December 23rd 2015) an independent jury of influential business professionals decided upon the winning ideas. The whole process was transparently displayed on the community as well as further information about the current MBA program. During the community activation phase MBA students, the teaching staff, business professionals, academics, alumni and experts around the globe were able to share their ideas on how the future of the MBA and business administration could like on the open access platform. During the ideation phase 200 ideas from over 5.000 unique visitors from more than 80 different countries worldwide were submitted. 307 of them registered actively and shared various information about their professional background as well as their contact details. Moreover, 265 comments on shared ideas and 537 evaluations have been made by the community (Fig. 2).

4 Discussion and Findings

As described, the research team observed the co-creation process during the live-phase in order to understand how faculty staff, experts and students might cope with the platform and especially what key success factors could be identified. The conclusions help to improve the set up and design of co-creation initiatives in higher education. In order to provide a structured project analysis we will use the initially introduced framework to present as well as reflect our insights.

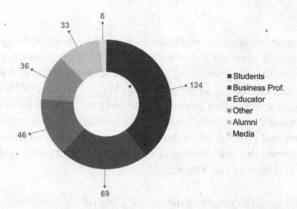

Fig. 2. Background of the registered community members

4.1 Energizing

Energizing the target group to participate and to help a public institution to generate ideas is crucial. To do so the right set-up and framework has to be found:

- Activation Strategies: Typically citizens and experts can be motivated intrinsically or extrinsically. However, we have learned that unlike to open innovation initiatives in the industry, public sector eParticipation should mainly offer intrinsic motivation, because citizens want to influence politics sustainably. We therefore used a gamification approach by framing the project as an idea contest, where participants compete to other members of the platform community. Furthermore, we focused by the prizes for the winning ideas on non-cash incentives. The reason for this is the demand of participants to have an influence on an important strategy, but also the chance to show their experience and push profiling. The winner was eternalized in the university with a visible badge as well as an invitation as an interviewee in the successful business podcast of the school (Leadership & Business). Moreover, due to an active community management, we aimed on establishing a strong social grid between all community members, motivating feedback, additional materials, constructive comments, and evaluation. Technical functionalities like e-mail notifications etc. supported re-activation of rather passive platform participants. Social networking functionalities, like the usage of personal profiles with a picture and message boards enriched the communication between the target groups.
- Community Management: In line with research on open innovation projects, we identified a pro-active community management as a further crucial factor to really energize the growing community. The research team participated as community managers on the platform performing the following tasks: monitoring (e.g. content screening & reporting), technical support activities, conflict management, activation (e.g. welcome messages, feedback, sharing and evaluating ideas) and triggering active participation. Thereby, we were immediately able to find solutions to task-related or technical problems and, even more important, establish a well guided and interrelated network structure. The latter addresses especially the fact that different community roles must be addressed and differently motivated to be "energized".

4.2 Listening

One of the strongest arguments for conducting public sector strategy development processes more openly aims on the potential to profit from external knowledge but obviously also from the experiences of all related students. Hence, finding the most appropriate ways of establishing an efficient and effective process of "listening" seems crucial. Generally, this dimension focuses on the abilities to profit from external inputs of the project initiator or the strategy owner. Traditionally, public administrations are used to consult internal experts, when developing new political strategies. During this project we have learned that this dimension subsumes different potential starting points, which should be reflected in the following:

– Capacity Building: Before starting the online phase of the community the faculty of the university came together in order to discuss the crucial topics of the MBA program and to reflect already failed ideas. This guidance was then mirrored to the community in the scope of different categories on the platform. Here, the target group was able to contribute ideas to the provided guidelines, namely (1) Courses, Focus & Skills, (2) Formats, (3) Scholarship & Financing, (4) Lifelong Learning & Community and (5) Marketing & Branding (overall concepts with all dimensions were possible as well as submitting ideas affecting multiple categories). In each category the faculty came up with initial ideas within a workshop to give the community a certain orientation point. However, listening starts already during the planning and conception phase of a public sector open strategy project. Integrating the faculty and the member of the university board has to be seen as a key success factor as important stakeholders within the organization might issue a "not invented here problem". So, to trigger an early enough capacity building process, we conducted lectures and workshops aiming on approach related (open innovation, open strategy, citizen participation) as well as project related (recruiting, tasks, roles etc.) topics (Fig. 3).

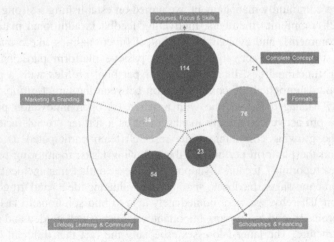

Fig. 3. Submitted ideas per category

– Engagement on the Platform: the second aspect focuses on the actual engagement on the open strategy platform. We observed that those experts from the public administration who participated actively on the platform, where more likely to positively participate und constructively use the platform output within the following strategy formulation phase.

4.3 Talking

The dimension of "talking" in public sector might seem to be tremendously interesting, as "getting the word out" is one of the big challenges when initiating a co-creation project. Finding the right target group, communicating the content and actually "market" the own purposes can be highlighted as key success factor.

– Recruiting Activities: In order to identify and activate relevant target groups, we learned that an online focused activation and recruiting strategy, accompanied by project related offline events, like workshops and conferences seems totally sufficient. Due to budget restrictions, we did not use traditional media like newspaper ads to promote the co-creation strategy project. Besides the very successful approach of identifying topic related bloggers, forums, and online journalists as virtual multipliers, we also shared the content in influential social media groups as well as in existing channels like linkedIn, Facebook or Twitter. Interestingly, one of the most influential blogs on MBAs (Poets & Quants) wrote an article about the initiative and selected it in the aftermath as one of the most innovative campaign in higher education in 2015. Furthermore, the College of William & Mary used existing alumni newsletter, institutional social media channels and networks. On the other hand we initiated various events and information campaign to gather ideas in the offline world. As most promising approaches the execution of personal interviews with leading experts in this field (here professors and top managers) as well as Meet-Ups with students can be identified. The latter was based on round-table discussions in universities like the LMU or TU in Munich or the College of William and Mary in Williamsburg. However, the acceptance among external stakeholders and students lead to a broad interest also in classical media like newspaper, which reported about the campaign and automatically shared the word of mouth (f.e. Virginia Gazette). Even the info stands on different universities and selected guest lectures (f.e. University of Lübeck) led to a broad engagement all over the world, seeing that 78 different nations were registered as users on the platform.

4.4 Supporting

The dimension of "supporting" focuses less on a citizen/administration relationship, but rather on a horizontal interconnection of different platform participants. The open strategy process showed how relevant and important qualitative feedback is in order to improve concepts, rework ideas and connect input from different participants with each other.

- Focusing on the dimension "supporting" we found out that the welcoming and motivation of participants, by leaving messages on their personal pin-walls established a trustable and transparent setting, which leads to a constructive, creative, and feedback orientated community.
- Expert Engagement: The integration of internal experts is not just inevitable for capacity building, but also for the feedback management. Ideas from various stakeholders on the community should be feed backed to activate the discussion and to share the insights from the institutions. A collaborative dialogue is the intentioned consequence. Consequently, without the permanent feedback of other platform participants and the support of the experts, many ideas would not have been qualitative enough to influence the strategy (in average every idea has been feed backed four times -either evaluated or commented; 200 ideas/848 interactions on the platform in general).

4.5   Embracing

As stated before, a co-creation process by integrating the opinion and ideas from external -but also from extended internal- target groups, needs an open mind set within the institution. By conducting capacity workshops in the first place, you create a decent working atmosphere with a common goal. In the long run, this process has to be intensified, especially with the faculty in the university, as their task is to bring the final strategy to life. Even though the whole co-creation format is a bottom-up approach due to the participation of a broad basis, the institution itself should integrate the head of the university/program to have to reputation to push the process through the internal stage-gate.

- Systematic Further Capacity Building: To integrate the internal stakeholders from ideation to implementation, it helps to have responsible and constant project owners throughout the process. This team needs to focus on pushing the underlying idea of an open strategy format, integrating topic related experts from the faculty and ensure a sustainable project progress.

4.6   Living

The dimension "living" addresses the needs of an open strategy approach with respect to the sustainable development and implementation of a co-creation strategy for the higher education. From projects in the public sector we know that a lack of implementation might lead to further distrust and disappointment within the target groups [17].

- Transparent Communication: Right from the start of the online platform, the project owners have to clarify the rules and terms & conditions on when input from the co-creation process might be implemented in the strategy. Here it is inevitable to not raise false hopes and to explain the essential credo of the institution. Hence, the participants knew from the start what will happen to their ideas and what goals the initiator address in the process. As a consequence, no negative rebound effects have been measured or frustrated posts on the co-creation platform were registered.

- Output Formulation and Implementation: the final aspect emphasizes the importance of finding an appropriate mode of summarizing the content from the platform and analyzing as well as condensing the most important insights. One key take away from this study is to integrate the above mentioned experts from the faculty also as "consultants" in the post-platform realization and implementation phase. Furthermore, for the evaluation and further elaboration of the ideas, an independent jury of influential professionals (f.e. CEO of Canadian Tire) was consolidated to select the best ideas for the idea contest. So, the selection of best ideas (selected from the faculty and then the jury) is currently (2016) in progress to be implemented in the strategy, which will be communicated in 2016/2017.

5 Conclusion and Further Research

The "Tomorrow's MBA" co-creation strategy development process was a unique approach, systematically accompanied by research and practical partners in the public sector. The initiative aimed at integrating external stakeholders like business professionals or students as well as the internal organization (faculty). Consequently, the insights generated in this study are not generalizable. Further research might exactly jump in here and try to compare our results to the experience in other public sectors to find key differences. Furthermore, a detailed analysis of the implementation strategy, compared to other sectors, might be interesting to address.

However, while linking our research to already existing open strategy research in the public sector, we conclude that the approach was a powerful tool to co-create an important strategy in higher education. Summarizing the insights gained from open government literature, we were able to further elaborate and extent the five dimension framework, originally introduced by Li and Bernoff. Overall, the study was able to show that an open co-creation strategy approach is also applicable within a public sector setting, specifically in higher education. Hence, our discussions and insights contribute more or less a manual on how to design and execute a co-creation initiative within the public sector, more precise within the public sector and open education research community.

References

1. Füller, J., Mühlbacher, H., Matzler, K., Jawecki, G.: Consumer empowerment through internet-based co-creation. J. Manag. Inf. Syst. **26**(3), 71–102 (2009)
2. King, S., Feltey, K.M., Susel, B.: The question of participation: toward authentic public participation in public administration. Public Adm. Rev. **58**(4), 317–326 (1998)
3. Nam, T.: Citizens' attitudes toward open government and government 2.0. Int. Rev. Admin. Sci. **78**(2), 346–368 (2012)
4. Rapp, M., Hoffmann, C.P., Kröger, N.: Beteiligung an open government fördern. HMD Praxis der Wirtschaftsinformatik **301**(52), 161–171 (2015)

5. Lee, S.M., Hwang, T., Choi, D.: Open innovation in the public sector of leading countries. Manag. Decis. **50**(1), 9 (2011)
6. Schlozman, K.L., Verba, S., Brady, H.E.: Weapon of the strong? Participatory inequality and the internet. Perspect. Polit. **8**(2), 487–509 (2010)
7. Walters, L., Miller, A.: Putting more public in policy analysis. Public Adm. Rev. **50**(4), 435–445 (2000)
8. Kweit, M., Kweit, W.: Implementing Citizen Participation in a Bureaucratic Society: A Contingency Approach. Praeger, New York (1981)
9. Massing, P., Breit, G., Buchstein, H.: Demokratietheorien: von der Antike bis zur Gegenwart. Wochenschauverlag, Schwalbach (2000)
10. Corrado, A., Firestone, C.M.: Elections in Cyberspace: Towards a New Era in American Politics. Brookings Institutions, Washington D.C. (1997)
11. Wright, S., Street, J.: Democracy, deliberation and design: the case of online discussion forums. New Media Soc. **9**(5), 849–869 (2007)
12. Boivard, T.: Developing new forms of partnership with the 'market' in the procurement of public services. Public Adm. **84**(1), 81–102 (2006)
13. Padilla-Meléndez, A., Garrido-Moreno, A.: Open innovation in universities: what motivates researchers to engage in knowledge transfer exchanges. Int. J. Entrepreneurial Behav. Res. **18**(4), 417–439 (2012)
14. Kux, B.: Universities and open innovation: a new research paradigm. In: Dual, J., Schwyzer, N. (eds.) Essays 2030: Visionen für die Zukunft der ETH Zürich. Neue Zürcher Zeitung NZZ libro (2005)
15. Li, C., Bernoff, J.: Groundswell: Winning in a World Transformed by Social Technologies. Harvard Business School Press, Harvard (2011)
16. Checkland, P., Holwell, S.: Action research: its nature and validity. In: Kock, N. (ed.) Information Systems Action Research: An Applied View of Emerging Concepts and Methods, pp. 3–17. Springer, Boston (2007)
17. Fishkin, J.S.: When the People Speak: Deliberative Democracy and Public Consultation. Oxford University Press, London (2009)

Electronic Participation with a Special Reference to Social Media - A Literature Review

Ayman Alarabiat[1](✉), Delfina Sá Soares[1,2], and Elsa Estevez[2,3]

[1] Department of Information Systems, University of Minho,
Guimarães, Portugal
aymanalarabiyat@gmail.com, dss@dsi.uminho.pt
[2] Operating Unit on Policy-Driven Electronic Governance,
United Nations University, Guimarães, Portugal
ecestevez@gmail.com
[3] Department of Computer Science and Engineering,
Universidad Nacional del Sur, Bahia Blanca, Argentina

Abstract. As a consequence of the interdisciplinary nature of Electronic Participation (e-Participation), current research on the field is fragmented and scattered. The exciting blurry boundaries and the immature identity of the field are making difficult the understanding of the main domain themes being investigated, in particular for "neophytes" researchers. In practice, several e-Participation initiatives often attract a wide audience but face serious limitations regarding involvement of those who attract. Recently, the potential of using social media to address citizens' involvement deficit has been subject of academic debate. By consulting 44 e-Participation papers, considered highly relevant to the aforementioned challenges, this paper produces a general overview of e-Participation research, particularly through social media. The findings show that the e-Participation field still faces the challenge of identity and strive for gaining wider recognition as an independent research area. Concerning e-Participation through social media which seems to be partly overlooked in the field research, the politicians-citizen's interaction has dominated scholars' attention and the adoption of such initiatives sponsored and driven by governments are rarely examine. Based on the findings, several research suggestions, which could play a significant contribution to advance future e-Participation research, are proposed.

Keywords: Electronic Participation · Social media · Literature review · Electronic government · Electronic democracy

1 Introduction

Research on the use of digital technologies for the purpose of facilitating greater citizen participation in policy decision-making process (e-Participation) has witnessed explosive growth over the last few years. However, it has been widely acknowledged that the research area of e-Participation has been fragmented, immature, and

E. Tambouris et al. (Eds.): ePart 2016, LNCS 9821, pp. 41–52, 2016.
DOI: 10.1007/978-3-319-45074-2_4

under-theorized [1–4]. While prior reviews have been made [2–5], the field of e-Participation is yet to own cohesive "identity" and clearly defined boundaries, which are significantly preventing the field to be recognized as a distinct research area [3, 6].

In practice, while there are some successful e-Participation initiatives showing positive results, a low level of citizens' engagement is often recognized in the majority of them, and few have attained tangible citizens' influences into policy making process [1, 7–10]. For enhancing citizens engagement, policy makers – politicians and governments – have been encouraged to go where citizens are, rather than expecting them to move from their actual online location, namely social media space [11–13]. Nevertheless, despite such attempts for using social media, the challenges of e-Participation initiatives to attract and engage more citizens still remains [14–16].

The aim of this paper is twofold. First, to provide an overall view of the state of the art on e-Participation. Second, to review the emerging research on e-Participation through social media. In doing so, we first address how e-Participation is understood (Sect. 3.1), implemented (Sect. 3.2), and later we review emerging research on e-Participation through social media (Sect. 4).

Motivated by numerous calls for developing the field maturity [1, 3–5], an effective review significantly advances such ambition [17]. For that, we argue that after more than a decade of introducing the concept of e-Participation in 2004 [18], the time is right for it to be treated as distinct field. The current review contributes towards clear understanding of e-Participation, either in its own right or within "neighboring" fields such as e-Democracy and e-Government, and to support current efforts for reaching a "self-identity" of the field [1, 4, 6]. It also addresses recent calls to encourage further research on e-Participation and social media [2, 4].

The rest of this paper is structured as follows. Section 2 explains the methodology adopted to carry out the research. Sections 3 presents the state of the art on e-Participation, while specific findings of e-Participation through social media are introduced in Sect. 4. Section 5 offers some topical propositions and implications for further research. Finally, Sect. 6 concludes the paper.

2 Research Methodology

The research methodology used to carry out the current review comprises four phases: (1) defining the assessment framework; (2) collecting relevant papers; (3) selecting papers; and (4) classifying the selected papers. The phases are briefly explained below.

2.1 Assessment Framework

In the recent years, high priority has been given towards systematizing and scoping the e-Participation field, addressing research gaps, and driving future research directions [1–5]. Based on the major findings of such studies, considering the multi-disciplinary nature of e-Participation, and addressing the current review objectives, this phase aims at defining the assessment framework for the research work. The adopted assessment framework is based on three main categories: (1) e-Participation "self-identity" (includes e-Participation concept and e-Participation boundaries); (2) e-Participation Initiatives and Projects; and (3) e-Participation through Social Media.

2.2 Collecting Relevant Papers

Given the lack of a specific set of key publication venues on e-Participation, it is difficult to select a limited number of major journals as the primary source for identification of literature [3]. Therefore, we decided to base our search on Scopus, ISI-Web of Science, and EBSCO Host database indexes. The search was conducted for the years (2004–2015) using two keywords "e-Participation" and "Electronic Participation", and returned 507 papers - 311 in Scopus, 69 ISI-Web of Science, and 127 in EBSCO Host. We followed two-stage filtering process for selecting most relevant papers as we explained in the next section. We highlight that this study does not duplicate findings of previous e-Participation literature reviews presented in 2007 [5], 2008 [3], and 2012 [2, 4]. However, we built on them, enriching their findings with latest results.

2.3 Selecting Papers

The selection process applied two filtering stages consistent with the aim of this review. The first aim is to present a general view and the identity of e-Participation research. In this stage, titles, abstracts, and keywords of the retrieved papers were scanned. All candidate papers had to meet one major criteria to be further used: the paper should address e-Participation as a central subject or as essential theme of discussion. In other words, any paper that did not focus on e-Participation but barely mentioned the term as just a concept, or merely mentioned e-Participation along with other political and government/governance topics for a general coverage was excluded. This decision relies on devoting more efforts towards considering e-Participation as a distinct research field, which in results is expected to contribute to the realization of the "self-identity" of the field [4]. The process selected 44 papers. The second aim is to investigate e-Participation through social media initiatives. Thus, the previous 44 identified papers were scanned once again to find those focused on e-Participation through social media. During this stage, 19 papers were selected.

2.4 Classifying Selected Papers

Table 1 shows a breakdown of the selected papers for each of the three categories of the research assessment framework: 12 papers concern e-Participation "self-identity",

Table 1. Distribution of papers per category

Category	Papers	# Papers
E-Participation "self-identity"	[1–6, 8, 18–22]	12
E-Participation initiatives and projects	[9–11, 13, 23–31]	13
E-Participation through social media	[7, 12, 14–16, 32–45]	19

13 papers focus on e-Participation initiatives and projects (the analysis of these 25 former papers is presented in Sect. 3), and 19 papers refer to e-Participation through social media (the analysis of these latter papers is explained in Sect. 4).

3   E-Participation State of the Art

This section fulfills the first aim of this review – generating an overview of the state of the art in e-Participation field. The findings are presented in two subsections: e-Participation "self-identity" and e-Participation initiatives and projects.

3.1   E-Participation "Self-identity"

We analyze the identity of e-Participation by studying: (a) the concept and (b) the boundaries of the domain, as presented in the following sections.

E-Participation Concept. To date, there is no established or widely adopted consensus among scholars concerning the definition of e-Participation [3–5, 10, 34], and this fact may be influencing the development and the maturity of the research domain [4]. The cross-disciplinary research field of e-Participation is mainly related to political science and public administration disciplines [1, 3, 5]. Subsequently, this brings a number of different understandings, philosophies and research traditions inside the e-Participation field [3, 4, 24]. Thus, it is not surprising to find many definitions and perceptions for e-Participation. Generally, the term of e-Participation is used within a number of near synonyms such as engagement, involvement and empowerment [13], and sometimes interchangeably used with "Political Participation".

An early study [18] introduces e-Participation as one of two sub areas of e-Democracy. According to the author, e-Voting and e-Participation are two technological means and mechanisms to support representative democratic decision making. However, the term became closely associated only with e-Voting, which created some problems for those who believe that e-Participation is more than just voting [3, 5, 19]. A broader definition was provided later by [46:85]. These authors defined e-Participation as "the use of information and communication technologies (ICT) to broaden and deepen political participation by enabling citizens to connect with one another and with their elected representatives". This definition has gained scholars' attention, especially for those interested in political activities. As evidenced by the previous definitions, researchers have primarily associated e-Participation with political participation and e-Democracy field [4, 5]. However, the definitions excludes other types of political engagements as well as interactions between citizens and government officials who are not directly elected [24].

A new definition provides more details of e-Participation, "the use of ICT to support information provisioning and "top-down" engagement i.e. government-initiated citizen participation, or "ground-up" efforts to empower citizens, civil society organizations and other democratically constituted groups to gain the support of their elected representatives" [24:17]. In such view, citizens are seen as more integrated in administrative and policy processes either with their elected politicians or assigned officials.

A broader perspective also sees e-Participation as an act intrinsically concerned with shaping government policy decision making by citizen's involvement in government and governance processes through digital technologies [3, 5]. According to these authors, e-Participation aims to increase citizens participation in digital governance, which includes citizens participation in political process likewise in transformation of digital government information and services [3, 5]. Such view considered e-Participation as contributing to discussions or activities related not only to political issues such as voting, but also to public issues that shape day-to-day relationships between citizens and their governments [19]. In this respect, citizen participation can occur through actions that aimed at selecting citizens' representatives and at influencing decisions taken either by those who were elected or by government officials. Then, the main principle of e-Participation could also be implemented through citizens' participation in public affairs, i.e. citizen participation in a decision making process for the development a "COVE" of five acres, located near of a Norwegian city center [45].

In conclusion, we believe that e-Participation is a budding field that leverages on available digital technologies to enable and strengthen more opportunities for citizen's involvement in political and public affairs tailored for influencing policy making. Such approach is a useful mechanism for governments to fulfill the 2030 Sustainable Development Agenda.

E-Participation Boundaries. Overall, e-Participation research is mainly placed into e-Democracy and e-Government fields. In fact, much of the discussions of e-Participation are conducted in these two literature fields. Accordingly, the boundaries between e-Participation and the two other fields are not clear yet [3, 4]. The intersection of e-Participation with e-Democracy is understood since e-Participation by its origin and definition is largely related to e-Democracy and political context [18, 46]. Likewise, it is closely related to e-Government and Open Government [3, 4]. Hence, e-Participation has to be placed on a well-established field [3]. This section may not be able to clearly delineate such boundaries; however, it paves the way for a better understanding of the intersections between them.

There is no deny that e-Participation was born as a response to a perceived decline in political engagement (decline in election turnout), and a disconnection between citizens and their elected representatives [18]. Thus, the crossing between e-Participation and e-Democracy started early, when Macintosh (2004) claimed that e-Participation seek to achieve the principles of e-Democracy [18]. Since then, to a certain degree, e-Participation has been applied widely strictly in a political context [4, 5, 19, 20], that seeks to increase citizens' political participation in order to overcome the growing democratic deficit [22, 28, 47]. Consequently, e-Participation is widely considered as an integral part of e-Democracy [10, 18] – in other cases, both concepts are misconceived as synonymous [4, 20]. Recently, some researchers studied the common perception that e-Participation is equal to e-Democracy [4]. The authors came to the conclusion that e-Participation scope is much broader and encompasses citizens' participation in various processes that are not necessarily political, e.g. in patient participation [4].

In government context, there were several advancements towards restoration of government role in addressing "democratic deficit" through participation initiatives [20, 48]. Nowadays, the development of enhanced e-Participation initiatives is at the heart of worldwide e-Government strategies [49]. In such context, it is common to find that e-Participation is considered an integral part of e-Government [10, 50]. However, government-led e-Participation initiatives is mainly informational and do not promote interactivity since they usually focus on information dissemination, enhancing e-service delivery, and fostering transparency [9, 51]. Accordingly, e-Government overall impact on enhancing citizen participation and strengthening democratic processes has been quite modest [48].

In summary, e-Participation research is pervaded with syntactically similar notions, such as e-Democracy and e-Government. These notions related to e-Participation have often lack any accurate differentiation or boundaries, in result the research of e-Participation is still "fragmented and disjointed". In fact, the field is still torn between them. In addition, e-Participation has various stakeholders including citizens, politicians and government officials, who posse a wide variety of needs, aims, activities, and purposes [2, 3, 10]. Consequently, e-Participation is asked to seek different tasks and address different objectives according to the context in which the initiatives occur (e.g. in e-Democracy, or in e-Government) [3, 4, 10].

3.2   E-Participation Initiatives and Projects

The notion of e-Participation has attracted considerable attention from governments worldwide especially in Europe. It is being seen as a way to increase government transparency, to legitimize their decisions, and, consequently, enhance citizens political participation and address the growing democratic deficit [10, 13, 18, 22, 28].

Recent studies identified the existence of around 255 e-Participation initiatives from 23 European countries [27, 28], 53 of which have been funded with over 120 million Euros by the European Union between 1990 and 2010 [31]. Despite the high costs and great interest, findings show that the majority of them generated low citizens participation [29], and that they were mainly focused on information provision [13, 27].

Overall, European e-Participation initiatives apparently failed to meet expectations [8, 29, 30] particularly in reaching and sustaining wider audiences, as well as in increasing their participation [8]. While the success of e-Participation may depend on understanding citizens' needs [9], European e-Participation projects are giving more attention towards delivering technical digital solutions than to the understanding the needs of citizens [30]. Furthermore, the highly sophisticated e-Participation tools and the weak communication means that were used to reach and to interact with citizens in such projects appear as other reasons for the low level of engagement achieved [11, 29]. An evaluation study of various e-Participation project has found a positive impact between providing citizens with attractive and easy-to-use e-Participation tools and their participation rate [41]. Other study demonstrates that limited amount of administrative support available (i.e. few staff) might affect the success of such projects in sustaining citizen's participation [23].

4   E-Participation Through Social Media

This section addresses the second aim of this review – investigating e-Participation through social media initiatives. While social media enables a new dimension to the e-Participation field, and has the potential role of enhancing citizen participation at different stages of policy making processes [1, 2, 4, 12], there is a further lack of research on social media and participation [2, 4, 52]. Recently, new attempts aim at summarizing and organizing the literature on e-Participation through social media [53, 54].

While the first documented attempt of introducing social media for e-Participation was in 2009 [12], the topic of e-Participation through social media has been developed at a slow pace, since many of retrieved studies have been published after 2012. Furthermore, the majority of discussions around social media for e-Participation are more placed in e-Government and e-Democracy research rather than in the e-Participation field [53, 54]. Another relevant aspect is that e-Participation through social media initiatives are more informative than interactive [14, 40, 44], and few initiatives have been found that aim at considerably enhancing citizen participation in policy decision making processes [33, 53, 54].

There are two major criticisms of the existing literature on e-Participation through social media. On the one hand, typical e-Participation through social media research is more driven towards political system processes activities [15, 42, 44] - e.g. e-Voting, e-Campaign [14, 34–36, 38, 39], which might nearly discuss similar ideas as in the e-Democracy field. The majority of e-Participation initiatives in such "political setting" have been mainly addressed by politicians and the pursued aim was to enable them to disseminate information, to promote themselves, and to seek potential vote-gaining during election time [44, 53]. The focus has often been on making the interactions easier and more beneficial for the politicians, not the citizens. Hence, this view of e-Participation can be seen as communication, rather than truly participation [55].

On the other hand, except few cases [16, 37, 43, 45], e-Participation through social media studies rarely capture, and examine citizens' involvement in e-Participation projects that are sponsored and driven by governments, which seems that the e-Participation field community is reluctant to move towards the e-Government context. Such findings confirm that the e-Participation field focuses mostly around political process. As general observation, e-Participation concept in e-Government research context has been superficially examined along with other government principles or public policy objectives, such as openness, transparency, and accountability. For sure, e-Participation has direct relation with and impact on those principles and objectives [10]. Nevertheless, e-Participation for openness, accountability, and transparency does not inevitably mean a truly participation [8, 9, 33, 51].

5   Propositions and Implications

Based on the analysis of major e-Participation challenges identified in the review, we derive a number of propositions that may assist future research. Such propositions were discussed and agreed among researchers of the project team.

Proposition 1: E-Participation Concept and Boundaries. The lack of cohesive definitions and clear boundaries within the field of e-Participation shape the consequential difficulties in research, application, and indeed for the identification of the field identity [4, 6]. Further work for both conceptual clarification and boundaries is still needed [1, 3–6]. Many lessons can be drawn from specific insights generated by other disciplines that have experienced similar challenges and suffered from similar symptoms, e.g. e-Government [56]. Those challenges refer to how such disciplines shaped their identities, and cleared what are their core subjects matter [57, 58]. For example, Information Systems (IS) academic discipline had been earlier exposed and encountered a great difficulty in establishing itself among other related disciplines, i.e. Information Science and Computer Science, [58, 59]. Thus, e-Participation discipline can get inspiration and learn from IS accumulative experience in the matter. Around two decades ago, some authors set forward a theoretical framework of the main areas of the IS by undertaken "Delphi" method survey [57]. Since the Delphi method has been successfully employed to systemize new concepts and to propose frameworks within IS research [60], that gives a good reason that the emergent research field of e-Participation is demanding for such studies.

Proposition 2: Remedy E-Participation Internal Disciplinary Boundaries [4]. While e-Participation knowledge puts forward arguments on why separating the technological or social perspectives appear inadequate to explain and investigate e-Participation [1, 21, 22, 50], few studies overcome the internal disciplinary boundaries that exist at the moment among e-Participation research [4]. The internal disciplinary boundaries appear in the lack of researches that link and interlace several e-Participation themes together, such as connecting stakeholders, tools and environment when they are studying e-Participation topics [4].

Indeed, neither the technological nor the social perspectives alone can be successful when implementing and investigating e-Participation [22], but in the possibility for their interweaving by taking multi-approaches and perspectives. In this sense, integrated a balanced sociology and psychology perspectives with technological one could be more convenient to understand e-Participation [21]. The current review reaffirms these arguments and further suggests that there is a great opportunity for harnessing and transforming knowledge from one area to another [61], in order to get a more comprehensive overview of e-Participation. The IS discipline for instance, significantly contributes to advance the maturity of e-Government field [56, 62]. In thus, IS can offer similar contributions for maturing e-Participation.

Proposition 3: E-Participation Diversity. It is interesting to find some recent applications of e-Participation related to the governance field but in specific contexts [4], such as in students' online participation in higher education processes [63], in environmental protection initiatives [64], and global climate change [65]. Such efforts highlight more evidence that today's e-Participation research does not necessarily need to be centered on political activities. Our argument is similar to the one used in IS, - i.e. the use of Information Technologies (IT) artifacts it does not necessarily imply that IT is the core subject matter of IS studies [58]; likewise, e-Voting and e-Campaign activities are not required to be the core subjects matter of e-Participation studies.

E-Participation-related research may start under the e-Democracy discipline or following a political interest. However, our conclusion is that strictly following a banner of research that is only interested in political activities will result in a micro focus for e-Participation research and, in turn, puts e-Participation as subdivision of e-Democracy field. Similarly, more researches are also demanding to differentiate "typical" e-Government projects from other government projects related to e-Participation [8]. The field needs theoretical comparative studies contributing to this debate and researchers should be aware of such differences when advancing e-Participation studies.

Accepting a smaller role and viewing political activities as the core subject matter of the e-Participation field will limit the potential contributions and significance of the e-Participation field in other areas. Moreover, it may further make more difficult for e-Participation to be recognized as independent research area.

6 Conclusions

The current findings challenge the optimistic argument that e-Participation may soon emerge as an independent research area. Perhaps, it may take longer time than what was expected, not because the concept may lose its usefulness, but, on the contrary, because it may be fully integrated in "more matured fields" such as e-Government.

While political activities are the focal point of e-Participation through social media studies, few contributions focus specifically on studying such initiatives to involve citizens in government policy decision making process. The e-Participation community has a great story to tell and thus this paper questions that the political activities should not be viewed as the only core matters of the e-Participation field. In practice, the majority of e-Participation initiatives, particularly through social media, have been heavily performed as one-way communication method, rather than as tools enabling citizens to be actually involved in the decision-making process.

A limitation of this study is the number of analyzed papers. Although the sample is small, it could be argued that this is due to the restricted approach that has been followed to fulfill the specific aims of this research work. Future work includes expanding the literature review to propose a more detailed outline of the field.

References

1. Macintosh, A., Coleman, S., Schneeberger, A.: eParticipation: the research gaps. In: Macintosh, A., Tambouris, E. (eds.) ePart 2009. LNCS, vol. 5694, pp. 1–11. Springer, Heidelberg (2009)
2. Medaglia, R.: eParticipation research: Moving characterization forward (2006–2011). Gov. Inf. Q. 29, 346–360 (2012)
3. Sæbø, Ø., Rose, J., Flak, L.S.: The shape of eParticipation: characterizing an emerging research area. Gov. Inf. Q. 25, 400–428 (2008)
4. Susha, I., Grönlund, Å.: eParticipation research: systematizing the field. Gov. Inf. Q. 29, 373–382 (2012)

5. Sanford, C., Rose, J.: Characterizing eParticipation. Int. J. Inf. Manag. **27**, 406–421 (2007)
6. Medaglia, R.: The challenged identity of a field: the state of the art of eParticipation research. Inf. Polity **12**, 169–181 (2007)
7. Charalabidis, Y., Loukis, E.N., Androutsopoulou, A., Karkaletsis, V., Triantafillou, A.: Passive crowdsourcing in government using social media. Transform. Gov.: People Process Policy **8**, 283–308 (2014)
8. Sæbø, Ø., Flak, L.S., Sein, M.K.: Understanding the dynamics in e-Participation initiatives: looking through the genre and stakeholder lenses. Gov. Inf. Q. **28**, 416–425 (2011)
9. Sanchez-Nielsen, E., Lee, D.: eParticipation in practice in Europe: the case of "puzzled by policy: helping you be part of EU." Presented at the 2013 46th Hawaii International Conference on System Sciences (HICSS) (2013)
10. Tambouris, E., Macintosh, A., Dalakiouridou, E., Smith, S., Panopoulou, E., Tarabanis, K., Millard, J.: eParticipation in Europe: current state and practical. E-Gov. Success Around the World: Cases Empir. Stud. Pract. Recomm. 341 (2013)
11. Karantzeni, D., Gouscos, D.G.: eParticipation in the EU: re-focusing on social media and young citizens for reinforcing European identity. Transform. Gov.: People Process Policy **7**, 477–500 (2013)
12. Sæbø, Ø., Rose, J., Nyvang, T.: The role of social networking services in eParticipation. In: Macintosh, A., Tambouris, E. (eds.) ePart 2009. LNCS, vol. 5694, pp. 46–55. Springer, Heidelberg (2009)
13. Smith, S., Dalakiouridou, E.: Contextualising public (e)Participation in the governance of the European Union. Eur. J. ePract. **7**, 4–14 (2009)
14. Rustad, E., Sæbø, Ø.: How, why and with whom do local politicians engage on Facebook? In: Wimmer, M.A., Tambouris, E., Macintosh, A. (eds.) ePart 2013. LNCS, vol. 8075, pp. 69–79. Springer, Heidelberg (2013)
15. Wakabi, W., Grönlund, Å.: When SNS use doesn't trigger e-Participation: case study of an African Authoritarian Regime. Int. J. E-Polit. (IJEP) **6**, 14–29 (2015)
16. Wahid, F., Sæbø, Ø.: Affordances and effects of promoting eParticipation through social media. In: Tambouris, E., Panagiotopoulos, P., Sæbø, Ø., Tarabanis, K., Wimmer, M.A., Milano, M., Pardo, T. (eds.) ePart 2015. LNCS, vol. 9249, pp. 3–14. Springer, Heidelberg (2015)
17. Webster, J., Watson, R.T.: Analyzing the past to prepare for the future: writing a literature review. Manag. Inf. Syst. Q. **26**, 3 (2002)
18. Macintosh, A.: Characterizing e-participation in policy-making. Presented at the 37th Annual Hawaii International Conference on System Sciences (HICSS 2004) (2004)
19. Avdic, A., Hedström, K., Rose, J., Grönlund, Å.: Understanding eParticipation: contemporary Ph.D. eParticipation research in Europe (2007)
20. Grönlund, Å.: ICT is not participation is not democracy – eParticipation development models revisited. In: Macintosh, A., Tambouris, E. (eds.) ePart 2009. LNCS, vol. 5694, pp. 12–23. Springer, Heidelberg (2009)
21. Edelmann, N., Cruickshank, P.: Introducing psychological factors into e-participation research (2011)
22. Macintosh, A., Whyte, A.: Towards an evaluation framework for eParticipation. Transform. Gov.: People Process Policy **2**, 16–30 (2008)
23. Federici, T., Braccini, A.M., Sæbø, Ø.: "Gentlemen, all aboard!" ICT and party politics: reflections from a mass-eParticipation experience. Gov. Inf. Q. **32**, 287–298 (2015)
24. Freschi, A.C., Medaglia, R., Jacob, N.: eParticipation in the institutional domain: a review of research. Analytical report on eParticipation research from an administration and political perspective in six European countries (2009)
25. Grönlund, Å., Susha, I.: A communication genre perspective on e-Petitioning: the case of the citizens' initiative. In: Tambouris, E., Macintosh, A., Sæbø, Ø. (eds.) ePart 2012. LNCS, vol. 7444, pp. 37–48. Springer, Heidelberg (2012)

26. Koussouris, S., Charalabidis, Y., Askounis, D.: A review of the European Union eParticipation action pilot projects. Transform. Gov.: People Process Policy **5**, 8–19 (2011)
27. Panopoulou, E., Tambouris, E., Tarabanis, K.: eParticipation initiatives: how is Europe progressing. Eur. J. ePract. **7**, 15–26 (2009)
28. Panopoulou, E., Tambouris, E., Tarabanis, K.: eParticipation initiatives in Europe: learning from practitioners. In: Tambouris, E., Macintosh, A., Glassey, O. (eds.) ePart 2010. LNCS, vol. 6229, pp. 54–65. Springer, Heidelberg (2010)
29. Prieto-Martín, P., de Marcos, L., Martínez, J.: A critical analysis of EU-funded eParticipation. In: Charalabidis, Y., Koussouris, S. (eds.) Empowering Open and Collaborative Governance, pp. 241–262. Springer, Heidelberg (2012)
30. Susha, I., Grönlund, T.: Context clues for the stall of the citizens' initiative: lessons for opening up e-participation development practice. Gov. Inf. Q. **31**, 454–465 (2014)
31. Tambouris, E., Kalampokis, E., Tarabanis, K.: A survey of e-participation research projects in the European Union. Int. J. Electron. Bus. **6**, 554–571 (2008)
32. Charalabidis, Y., Loukis, E.: Transforming government agencies' approach to e participation through efficient exploitation of social media. Springer, Heidelberg (2011)
33. Dalakiouridou, E., Tambouris, E., Tarabanis, K.: eParticipation and online social networks: The case of the European Institutions. Eur. J. ePract. (2012)
34. Effing, R., van Hillegersberg, J., Huibers, T.: Social media and political participation: are Facebook, Twitter and YouTube democratizing our political systems? In: Tambouris, E., Macintosh, A., de Bruijn, H. (eds.) ePart 2011. LNCS, vol. 6847, pp. 25–35. Springer, Heidelberg (2011)
35. Effing, R., van Hillegersberg, J., Huibers, T.W.: Social media participation and local politics: a case study of the Enschede Council in The Netherlands. In: Wimmer, M.A., Tambouris, E., Macintosh, A. (eds.) ePart 2013. LNCS, vol. 8075, pp. 57–68. Springer, Heidelberg (2013)
36. Effing, R., van Hillegersberg, J., Huibers, T.: Social media indicator and local elections in The Netherlands: towards a framework for evaluating the influence of Twitter, YouTube, and Facebook. In: Sobaci, M.Z. (ed.) Social Media and Local Governments, pp. 281–298. Springer, Heidelberg (2016)
37. Guttormsen, C., Sæbø, Ø.: Municipalities "Like" Facebook: the use of social media in local municipalities. In: Spagnoletti, P. (ed.) Organizational Change and Information Systems. LNCS, vol. 2, pp. 157–166. Springer, Berlin Heidelberg (2013)
38. Johannessen, M.: Genres of participation in social networking systems: a study of the 2009 Norwegian parliamentary election. In: Tambouris, E., Macintosh, A., Glassey, O. (eds.) ePart 2010. LNCS, vol. 6229, pp. 104–114. Springer, Heidelberg (2010)
39. Johannessen, M.R.: Genres of participation in social networking systems: a study of the 2013 Norwegian parliamentary election. In: Tambouris, E., Macintosh, A., Bannister, F. (eds.) ePart 2014. LNCS, vol. 8654, pp. 26–37. Springer, Heidelberg (2014)
40. Johannessen, M.R., Følstad, A.: Political social media sites as public sphere: a case study of the Norwegian labour party. Commun. Assoc. Inf. Syst. **34**, 1067–1096 (2014)
41. Lacigova, O., Maizite, A., Cave, B.: eParticipation and social media: a symbiotic relationship. Eur. J. ePract. **16**, 71–76 (2012)
42. Panagiotopoulos, P., Sams, S., Elliman, T., Fitzgerald, G.: Do social networking groups support online petitions? Transform. Gov.: People Process Policy **5**, 20–31 (2011)
43. Panagiotopoulos, P., Bigdeli, A.Z., Sams, S.: Citizen–government collaboration on social media: the case of Twitter in the 2011 riots in England. Gov. Inf. Q. **31**, 349–357 (2014)
44. Sæbø, Ø.: Understanding Twitter^{TM} use among parliament representatives: a genre analysis. In: Macintosh, A., Bruijn, H., Tambouris, E. (eds.) ePart 2011. LNCS, vol. 6847, pp. 1–12. Springer, Heidelberg (2011)

45. Johannessen, M.R.: "New" vs "old" media a case study of political protest groups' media use in a Norwegian municipality. Int. J. Public Inf. Syst. 11 (2015)

46. Macintosh, A.: E-democracy and e-participation research in Europe. In: Chen, H., Brandt, L., Gregg, V., Traunmüller, R., Dawes, S., Hovy, E., Macintosh, A., Larson, C. (eds.) Digital Government, pp. 85–102. Springer, US (2008)

47. Coleman, S., Blumler, J.G.: The Internet and Democratic Citizenship: Theory, Practice and Policy. Cambridge University Press, Cambridge (2009)

48. Reddick, C., Norris, D.F.: E-participation in local governments. Transform. Gov. People Process Policy 7, 453–476 (2013)

49. United Nation: United Nations E-government Survey 2014: E-government for the Future We Want. UN Publication, New York (2014)

50. Panopoulou, E., Tambouris, E., Tarabanis, K.: Success factors in designing eParticipation initiatives. Inf. Organ. 24, 195–213 (2014)

51. Gulati, G.J.J., Williams, C.B., Yates, D.J.: Predictors of on-line services and e-participation: a cross-national comparison. Gov. Inf. Q. 31, 526–533 (2014)

52. Bohman, S.: Information technology in eParticipation research: a word frequency analysis. In: Tambouris, E., Macintosh, A., Bannister, F. (eds.) ePart 2014. LNCS, vol. 8654, pp. 78–89. Springer, Heidelberg (2014)

53. Dini, A.A., Øystein, S.: The current state of social media research for eParticipation in developing countries: a literature review. Presented at the 2016 49th Hawaii International Conference on System Sciences (HICSS) (2016)

54. Alarabiat, A., Soares, D.S.: Electronic participation through social media. In: Proceedings of the 9th International Conference on Theory and Practice of Electronic Governance, pp. 191–194. ACM, New York (2016)

55. Hoffman, L.H.: Participation or communication? An explication of political activity in the Internet age. J. Inf. Technol. Polit. 9, 217–233 (2012)

56. Grönlund, Å., Horan, T.A.: Introducing e-gov: history, definitions, and issues. Commun. Assoc. Inf. Syst. 15, 39 (2005)

57. Bacon, C.J., Fitzgerald, B.: A systemic framework for the field of information systems. ACM Sigmis Database 32, 46–67 (2001)

58. Alter, S.: 18 reasons why it-reliant work systems should replace "The IT Artifact" as the core subject matter of the IS field. Commun. Assoc. Inf. Syst. 12, 23 (2003)

59. Agarwal, R., Lucas Jr., H.C.: The information systems identity crisis: focusing on high-visibility and high-impact research. MIS Q. 29, 381–398 (2005)

60. Okoli, C., Pawlowski, S.D.: The Delphi method as a research tool: an example, design considerations and applications. Inf. Manag. 42, 15–29 (2004)

61. Van de Ven, A.H.: Engaged Scholarship: A Guide for Organizational and Social Research. Oxford University Press, Oxford (2007)

62. Axelsson, K., Melin, U., Lindgren, I.: Exploring the importance of citizen participation and involvement in e-government projects. Transform. Gov.: People Process Policy 4, 299–321 (2010)

63. Bohman, S., Hansson, H., Mobini, P.: Online participation in higher education decision-making. JeDEM-eJ. eDemocr. Open Gov. 6, 267–285 (2014)

64. Royo, S., Yetano, A., Acerete, B.: E-Participation and environmental protection: are local governments really committed? Public Adm. Rev. 74, 87–98 (2014)

65. Bojovic, D., Bonzanigo, L., Giupponi, C., Maziotis, A.: Online participation in climate change adaptation: a case study of agricultural adaptation measures in Northern Italy. J. Environ. Manag. 157, 8–19 (2015)

Critical Reflections

Success in eVoting – Success in eDemocracy? The Estonian Paradox

Maarja Toots[✉], Tarmo Kalvet, and Robert Krimmer

Ragnar Nurkse School of Innovation and Governance,
Tallinn University of Technology, Tallinn, Estonia
{maarja.toots, tarmo.kalvet, robert.krimmer}@ttu.ee

Abstract. Estonia has acquired the reputation of a successful e-voting country, and perhaps justifiably so. It was the first country in the world to enable remote online voting in nationwide elections in 2005 and the share of e-voters has been on a rise ever since, now reaching one-third of all voters. Against this backdrop of a seemingly flourishing e-democracy, we set out to ask if the country's success in e-voting also implies its success in e-democracy in a broader sense. In a qualitative case study, we compare Estonia's experience in e-voting with the implementation and outcomes of three e-participation projects to demonstrate that considerable discrepancies exist between the take-up and perceived success of e-voting vis-à-vis other e-democracy instruments. In light of these findings the paper further discusses the factors that are likely to account for these differences and highlights the need to look beyond the success of online voting for a holistic evaluation of the state of e-democracy in a given country.

Keywords: e-Democracy · e-Participation · e-Voting · Estonia · Case study

1 Introduction

Throughout time, democracy has continuously evolved and even undergone drastic changes – from face-to-face, via territorial to transnational societies. Most recently, the Internet fosters this transformation as it challenges the concept of state sovereignty and need for representation. Arguably, e-democracy as a transnational, location independent way for citizens to interact with their state and be able to communicate and deliberate in the way of a strong democracy, can be considered the concept for a third transformation following Dahl [1]. Consequently, there is a need for e-democracy instruments that help facilitate and shape such an e-democracy.

Estonia has been a pioneer in developing electronic public services and today all public services include an e-service component. The eID card (the primary identification document for citizens and permanent residents) has enabled digital signing of documents since 2002 and remote e-voting in nationwide elections since 2005. Internet penetration has constantly increased – while in 2005, 58 % of the population used the Internet, today 88 % are internet users [2]. Estonia undertook first steps to develop e-democracy in the early 2000s, creating the first e-participation platform in 2001 and holding electronic elections since 2005. However, while these early efforts placed the

E. Tambouris et al. (Eds.): ePart 2016, LNCS 9821, pp. 55–66, 2016.
DOI: 10.1007/978-3-319-45074-2_5

country among the top ten in the UN e-participation index from 2008 to 2012, Estonia seems to have fallen behind since then, now ranking 22nd out of 193 [3].

While Estonia has acquired the reputation of a successful e-voting country, we set out to ask if Estonia's success in e-voting also implies its success in e-democracy in a broader sense. To answer this, we developed an evaluation framework for the case study of e-democracy instruments in Estonia, by combining some of the success criteria often employed in information systems, e-participation and e-democracy literature, focusing on user acceptance on the one hand and the aspect of democratic legitimacy on the other. Thus, we are looking at the following criteria: (1) level of use; (2) user diversity, (3) stakeholder satisfaction with the system and (4) impact on the political process. While the first and the third category are typical IS success measures, the second and fourth aim to incorporate the component of democratic legitimacy, which is considered the overarching aim of e-democracy projects [4]. The perceived legitimacy and success of a democratic exercise has been associated with not only engaging a sufficient number of participants but also reaching a diverse group of participants [4–7]. Similarly, the actual impact of e-democracy tools on political processes is considered a key measure of their success [5, 6].

The paper is structured as follows. Section 2 gives an overview of our research methodology. Section 3 establishes the theoretical framework for the analysis based on two relevant and complementary literature streams – public sector innovation generally and e-participation literature more specifically. This is followed by a summary of the Estonian e-voting system in Sect. 4 and three major nationwide e-participation projects in Sect. 5. In Sect. 6 we discuss the outcomes of the four e-democracy instruments in relation to the factors that have affected their success, followed by a few concluding remarks on the possible reasons why e-voting has worked more effectively in Estonia than e-participation.

2 Methodology

The aim of this study is to explore the steps that Estonia has undertaken in order to build e-democracy by analyzing the e-democracy instruments, such as TOM, Osale.ee, People's Assembly (*Rahvakogu*), most recently Rahvaalgatus.ee/Citizen OS[1], as well as e-voting, that have been implemented since the transformation of the public sector based on the use of the Internet caught on in the early 2000s. In particular, we are interested in identifying why e-voting works in Estonia and why e-participation does not. The in-depth study of a contemporary phenomenon using multiple sources of evidence in its real-life context is a typical application of case-study methodology. Also, it is an area where there is traditionally – up to today – not enough empirical research [8] undertaken in the IS field.

Yin distinguishes between exploratory, descriptive and explanatory case study types [9]. As we intend to gain new insight in how an e-democracy is (not) being built,

---

[1] Rahvaalgatus.ee is only a very recent development in 2016. It was not further analyzed as part of this study and is only mentioned here for completeness.

the exploratory approach is selected. Due to the unique situation Estonia is in – it is to date the only country in the world that offers e-voting in all its elections without any restrictions to all eligible voters [10], it was abstained from choosing a comparative multiple case study setup and focus solely on the Estonian case. For conducting the actual case study research we follow Yin's three phases (i) define and design; (ii) prepare, collect; and (iii) analyze and conclude [9].

The data for compiling the case study were collected mainly through desk research in 2015, including existing studies, policy papers, reports, press releases, articles in the media, use statistics, legislative acts and government strategies.[2]

3   Conceptual Framework

Driven by the question why some e-democracy instruments, such as e-voting, seem to work better than others, we focused on studying the factors that make for a successful e-democracy tool. As e-democracy instruments can be viewed as a particular kind of public sector innovation, we found some useful guidance in public sector innovation research as well as e-participation and e-democracy literature.

3.1   Key Success Factors in Public Sector Innovation

E-democracy instruments can generally be treated as public sector innovation concerned with "the creation and implementation of new processes, products, services and methods of delivery which result in significant improvements in outcomes efficiency, effectiveness or quality" [12]. The emergence of literature on innovation genuinely attributable to the public sector can be observed since around 2000, with a focus on innovations in public services and governance [e.g., 13, 14–16].

One of the most recent systematic accounts of public sector innovation is a literature review by De Vries et al. [17] that maps influential factors in public sector innovation at different levels and in different stages, from idea-generation to adoption and diffusion. They distinguish key innovation drivers and barriers along four main categories: (1) environmental level, including regulatory pressures, environmental pressures (media attention, political and public demand), participation in networks and

---

[2] For Osale.ee, an important information source was an evaluation report of the usage and usability of Osale.ee published by the Government Office (manager of the system) in spring 2015 (quoted in this paper as [11]), which relied on focus group interviews with Osale's managers and key user groups (ministry officials, civil society organizations, interest groups, and individual citizens). In addition, six semi-structured personal interviews were undertaken with key idea champions, IS managers and active users in April and May 2015, several of whom had also been involved in the creation of Osale's predecessor TOM.

For e-voting the experience as part of the OSCE/ODIHR election related activities on Estonia were of particular importance where one of the authors was able to participate. The opinions put forward in this article are all of the author's alone and should not be attributed to the OSCE/ODIHR or any other institution.

For *Rahvakogu* we were grateful to have had access to a forthcoming study thereon.

inter-organizational relationships; (2) organizational level: resources, leadership styles, risk aversion, incentives/rewards, organizational structures, etc.; (3) characteristics of the innovation itself: ease of use, relative advantage, compatibility, cost, trustworthiness, etc.; (4) characteristics of innovators, including employee autonomy, tenure, mobility, knowledge and skills, creativity, commitment, etc. Some factors, such as leadership, were found to be important in all stages of innovation. The European Commission's report "Powering European Public Sector Innovation" [18], perhaps the most influential policy document on the topic, highlights similar barriers. Some of the key impediments to success are related to scattered competences, lack of coordination, unfavorable administrative and organizational culture, lack of resources, lack of leadership, risk-aversion and failure-avoidance, lack of collaboration and limited knowledge on how to apply and measure the outcomes of innovative processes.

Case studies of e-government innovation support these findings. Political will and innovation acceptance at all levels of the organization have been found to be key drivers of successful e-government innovations, while different stakeholder agendas, political turbulence and resource issues act as barriers [19]. Similarly, a case study of the Estonian e-government evolution identified leadership and public sector competencies, availability of resources, legislative and regulatory support, and the existence of (strategic) IT infrastructure as important drivers. The study also emphasized the importance of frequently underestimated factors: the competencies of the private sector, public-private collaboration and the actual process of technology transfer, including support mechanisms to public procurement of innovation [20].

3.2 Key Success Factors for e-Democracy Instruments

The success and failure of e-democracy instruments has been associated with a variety of factors similar to those outline above for public sector innovation. A key success/failure factor seems to be their level of integration into organizational procedures and political processes [e.g., 5, 6, 21]. E-democracy methods should have a clear mandate [6] and involve decision-makers from the outset [22]. Integration can be seen as a key prerequisite for impact, which to date seems to be limited at best [5, 23]. Another set of factors can be associated with organizational culture, attitudes and political support. In addition to organizational culture, broader cultural preconditions for e-democracy include a developed civil society, social trust and an open political culture [6, 21].

The failure of many e-government initiatives has been attributed to overlooking the demand side and citizen's perspective [24]. Empirical evidence of e-participation tools suggests that their take-up has thus far been globally low [25]. Neither have e-participation initiatives brought more people in decision-making, engaging just a narrow "elite" of politically active citizens [7, 26, 27]. Variables explaining participation include prior interest in politics, internet skills, younger age and high level of education [27], which is very similar to participation patterns in offline contexts [28]. The challenge of attracting users implies the need to reckon with their needs and capabilities by engaging users in designing the e-participation tools [6]. Effective participation in the democratic debate also presumes particular requirements to system design, such as information accessibility and competent moderation [5, 29]. Finally, the acceptance of any ICT-based democracy tool tends to be determined by their perceived usefulness and ease of use, the two central concepts in technology acceptance theories [30]. It is assumed that user acceptance is higher for systems that require less effort, while demonstrating clear benefits for the user.

Either way, the development of an electronic democracy with transnational character [31] needs the further development of e-enabled instruments of democracy, i.e., e-initiatives, e-referenda and of course also e-voting instruments [32]. E-voting takes a special role within this set of e-democracy instruments. Not only is it one of the most visible e-government projects which sometimes receives all the attention of the public, it also is often one of the most discussed and debated [33].

The success of e-voting is often linked with an incremental, step by step, implementation [34], careful consideration of stakeholders' interests [35], as well as a holistic, interdisciplinary, approach [36]. It can be noted that e-voting is more focused on technological issues than other e-democracy instruments, partly due to the inherent paradox between unequivocal identification of voters on the one side and must not being able to establish a link between the vote and the voter, essentially keeping the vote secret and hiding the identity of the voter (preserving anonymity) [37]. Due to the fact that to date most e-voting undertakings do not follow classical experimental setups [38] and are embedded in their national context [39] it is hard to draw comparative conclusions and provide learning to others. We therefore decided to change the approach and conduct an in-depth analysis of a country's efforts around all kind of e-democracy instruments.

4 The Case of e-Voting in Estonia

The Estonian efforts around e-voting started in 2001 with a plan to introduce e-voting, allowing to cast votes remotely via the Internet (often also called "Internet voting") already for the Estonian 2003 parliamentary elections. Following the e-government logic this seemed like the logical next step after e-tax reporting, e-banking and a paperless cabinet meeting of the government's ministers [40]. It took two more years until e-voting become a reality, due to discussion around its constitutionality. With the first ever, countrywide, unrestricted, remote e-voting channel offered in legally binding elections, the 2005 municipal elections, Estonia manifested its narrative of being an e-country. To date it remains the only country with such a universal approach to e-voting.

Several articles have been written about the Internet voting experience in Estonia [41–44], but probably the most comprehensive overview can be found in [45]. Here Vinkel classified the development of Estonian e-voting in three stages: (i) setup period (2002–2005), (ii) growth period (2005–2011), (iii) maturity period (from 2011). In the first period the main technological decisions were taken (usage of the card; double-envelope algorithm). In the second phase, a continuous exponential increase in usage was experienced (see Fig. 1), while the actual application was not changed in functionality, design nor usability. The ongoing third developmental phase was started by a security incident during the 2011 Riigikogu elections[3]. It was followed by an electoral reform with the introduction of individual verifiability as its main result [47].

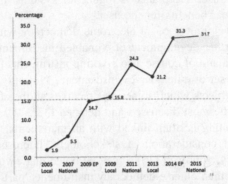

Fig. 1. Share of E-voters out of Voters in Per Cent [48]

5 Estonian e-Participation Projects

5.1 TOM

Estonia's first national-level e-participation project TOM or *Täna Otsustan Mina* (meaning "Today I Decide") was launched at the initiative of Prime Minister Mart Laar and his IT advisor as early as in 2001, possibly making it one of the first of its kind in the world. The online platform, administered by the Government Office, allowed citizens to make proposals for new legislation and policies and discuss and vote upon them. More popular ideas would be forwarded to relevant government officials, who then would have one month to post a formal response.

Despite a relatively lively public interest in TOM, the project soon encountered challenges, such as a limited number of active users, low quality of ideas, limited impact of citizens' proposals and the prevalence of formalistic responses by officials over an open attitude to dialogue [49]. By TOM's third birthday in 2004, e-democracy enthusiasts had declared it a failure [50]. According to interviews with implementers and idea champions of the project, TOM seemed to be ahead of its time. Government institutions lacked an understanding of how to integrate TOM-generated ideas into their work process and citizens lacked the knowledge and skills to formulate their ideas in sufficient quality and formats that officials could work with. According to TOM's administrator, there was a gap in the regulatory, strategic and political context – as government-wide discussions on citizen engagement policies only started around 2004–2005, the ground for e-participation was not yet fertile [51].

---

[3] A student managed to program a Trojan horse that would cast a different vote than the one intended by the voter. He consequently filed a complaint to the election management body but this was eventually turned down [46].

Citizens were equally dissatisfied. In a survey involving 25 active users, a number of ideas for improvement were voiced, such as the need for more active promotion of the project, improved information accessibility (e.g. systematizing citizens' ideas according to topics), design updates, involvement of experts and moderators to increase the quality of debate, and integration with other government information systems [52]. However, instead of re-designing TOM, the government decided to build a new e-participation tool (later named Osale.ee) and migrate TOM to the new platform. By that time, TOM had more than 7,000 registered users, who had generated 1187 ideas in total [53] out of which no more than 1 % were actually implemented by the government [49].

5.2 Osale.ee

The idea for developing Osale.ee (www.osale.ee) emerged around 2004–2005 during the process of designing a government-wide policy for citizen engagement. The process brought together government officials and civil society activists and led to ideas for a new e-participation tool, which would address the shortcomings of TOM by better integration into formal rule-making processes [51, 54]. Consequently, the Government Office took the decision to develop a new e-participation portal which would enable officials to engage civil society in legislative drafting. The goal of the portal was to enhance the transparency, openness, quality and legitimacy of decision-making [55].

Osale.ee was launched in 2007 as a platform for public consultations on legislative drafts. A year later, the system was upgraded with the functionality of an "improved TOM", which allowed citizens to propose ideas to the government, and gather comments and votes in support. Despite all the criticism of TOM, its functionality was preserved in Osale.ee because of TOM's high symbolic value, pressure from civil society and the wish to signal that the government had not lost interest in citizens' ideas [51]. Osale.ee also included a third function – a search engine of government documents. It thus aimed to enable all three types of government-citizen interaction: information, consultation and active participation [56].

Osale.ee intended to engage three kinds of users: officials of government institutions (mostly of the executive branch), individual citizens and their institutionalized representatives. In practice, however, the tool soon became criticized for failing to attract users and lack of impact [57, 61]. The portal is still operational today but largely considered failed in terms of adoption and outcomes [11].

5.3 People's Assembly

In 2013 Estonia experimented with a post-Parliamentary democracy tool, the People's Assembly (*Rahvakogu*). The initiative came from the President of Estonia and several civil society organizations as a response to a public trust crisis. It consisted of an online platform for crowdsourcing proposals to amend Estonia's electoral laws, political party law, and other issues related to the future of democracy in Estonia. After three weeks of online crowdsourcing, the ideas were debated during a one-day 'deliberation day' involving a stratified random sample of members of the public to proportionally represent different regions, age groups and gender [58]. The process resulted in 15 proposals that were presented to the parliament.

A year later, three proposals out of the 15 became laws and several more have by now been partly implemented or re-defined as commitments in the government coalition program. However, as the organizers admitted, the exercise failed to achieve its main goal – to increase trust in institutions of representative democracy [59].

6 Discussion

The four e-democracy instruments that have been implemented in Estonia – e-voting, TOM, Osale.ee and People's Assembly – have met mixed success. E-voting, despite some initial barriers, has by now been adopted by a considerable share of voters (close to 32 % in the latest elections) and is generally regarded as an effective tool [48]. At the same time, the e-participation projects have only been able to engage a narrow group of active users and are largely perceived as lacking impact. Although TOM had close to 7,000 registered users, only 9 % of them actually posted an idea [49]. Osale.ee, the only ongoing e-participation project, has been reported to have no more than 5–10 committed active users [11]. While the People's Assembly online platform succeeded in attracting a high number of proposals and comments (close to 4,800) it was still heavily dominated by a homogenous user group – middle-aged well-educated ethnic Estonian men [59]. It is therefore fair to conclude that none of the e-participation projects has been particularly successful in enhancing e-democracy in the sense of fostering an active engagement of all parts of society in shaping public decisions.

Based on theoretical and empirical literature, e-democracy innovations are challenged by various barriers. These include a lack of administrative and political championing, poor integration into organizational procedures and broader political processes, lack of easily demonstrable impact, unfavorable cultural context, hostile attitudes to citizen engagement, and the difficulty of matching different expectations and capabilities in designing systems intended to engage diverse user groups. Therefore, the success of e-voting compared to e-participation projects could at least partly be associated with its inherently high integration into policy processes and administrative routines, high political interest and support to the instrument, its immediate and easily demonstrable impact on the constitution of elected bodies, clear mandate and a clear procedure for translating input to outcomes.

E-voting has demonstrated clear benefits related to convenience to users – if voting on paper would take more than half an hour, voters are more likely to prefer the electronic channel over the traditional one [48, 60]. Looking more closely at the development path of e-voting, one can identify that the service has been characterized by a relative stability as the application remained relatively unchanged within the first six years of operation – and this change only happened due to external pressure (an attack) [45]. Initially the take-up of e-voting was relatively low (only 2 % of the voters chose the electronic channel in the 2005 municipal elections first offering e-voting) and focused on early adopters of the ID card, similar to e-banking. There was thus in fact a high barrier of learning to be overcome. Once this barrier was mastered, the immediate return was incurred: convenience. With e-voting people potentially save time, while with other e-democracy instruments the actual impact has often not been clearly visible.

Unlike e-voting, Estonian e-participation projects have never achieved true integration with existing political processes and their mandate has remained unclear. In the case of TOM and Osale.ee, government institutions do not seem to have found a way to accommodate unsolicited ideas from citizens into their daily routines. Although Osale. ee aimed to fix the shortcomings of TOM by better integration into the policy-making process, it largely seems to have failed in this respect. Part of the problem has been the ambiguity of the concept of public consultations, which is undefined in legislation [11, 62]. Hence, the extent to which the government should take citizens' input into account has remained unclear. Similarly, as the Parliament's policy-making routine included no procedures for working with crowdsourced proposals, the Parliament was generally reluctant to discuss the ideas put forward by the People's Assembly [59].

The latter also has to do with political interest, which seems to have been relatively low for all e-democracy instruments but e-voting. As the Prime Minister's project, TOM clearly had political backing at the highest level, albeit limited to the Prime Minister's office, while its successor Osale.ee never saw any political champions [54, 62]. Political interest was more mixed for People's Assembly – although the process was formally initiated by the President, it did not meet similar interest on the part of the Parliament, the group of politicians whose support would have been key to the project's impact.

Due to loose integration and low political interest, all three e-participation projects have lacked the expected impact. The actual implementation of citizens' ideas proposed through TOM and Osale.ee has remained marginal [49]. Public consultations on Osale. ee have not yielded better outcomes – both government officials and interest groups criticize the platform for low usefulness [11]. The People's Assembly, despite several positive effects, did not bring the government closer to citizens and failed to stimulate a fundamental reform of political institutions it originally intended to [59]. Therefore, considering the effort that is required from citizens, administrators and politicians to engage in a complex political dialogue and the absence of immediate benefits such as time savings, it might well be argued that it is inherently more difficult for e-participation projects to repeat the success story of e-voting.

7 Conclusions

Estonia's success in e-voting does not mean the country has been successful in promoting and enabling e-democracy in general. Somewhat paradoxically, the country that has been a champion of e-government and a pioneer in e-voting has not quite been a success story in e-participation and has consequently failed to develop a full-fledged e-democracy as some had initially hoped.

However, it is not only that the politicians lack out on supporting this transformation (which could be due to the fear of losing power; compare [63]) but also citizens themselves. Contrary to the hopes of many early Internet enthusiasts, citizens do not appear to be particularly interested in taking advantage of all the opportunities for direct access to decision-making that contemporary technologies can offer, especially if the benefits are not immediately evident. As it seems, the third transformation of democracy towards a fully developed e-democracy still has to happen and not even Estonia can help out with this one – for now.

Acknowledgements. This work was supported by the European Commission (OpenGovIntelligence H2020 grant 693849), Estonian Research Council (grants IUT19-13, PUT773) and Tallinn University of Technology Project B42.

References

1. Dahl, R.A.: Democracy and Its Critics. Yale University Press, New Haven (1989)
2. Statistics Estonia: IC321: computer and internet users aged 16-74 by place of residence (2016)
3. United Nations: E-Government survey 2014. E-Government for the future we want (2014)
4. Prosser, A.: eParticipation – did we deliver what we promised? In: Kö, A., Leitner, C., Leitold, H., Prosser, A. (eds.) EDEM 2012 and EGOVIS 2012. LNCS, vol. 7452, pp. 10–18. Springer, Heidelberg (2012)
5. OECD: Promise and Problems of E-democracy. Challenges of Online Citizen Engagement (2003)
6. Council of Europe (2009, 11-20): Recommendation CM/Rec(2009)1 of the Committee of Ministers to member states on electronic democracy (e-democracy)
7. Karlsson, M.: Democratic legitimacy and recruitment strategies in eParticipation projects. In: Charalabidis, Y., Koussouris, S. (eds.) Empowering Open and Collaborative Governance, pp. 3–20. Springer, Heidelberg (2012)
8. Benbasat, I., Goldstein, D.K., Mead, M.: The case research strategy in studies of information systems. MIS Q. **11**, 369–386 (1987)
9. Yin, R.K.: Case Study Research. Design and Methods, 3rd edn. Sage Publications, Thousand Oaks (2003)
10. Krimmer, R.: The 2016 World-Map of E-Voting Activities, Sulz: E-Voting.CC (forthcoming)
11. Praxis Center for Policy Studies and Pulse: "Osalusveebi ja valitsuse eelnõude infosüsteemi kasutatavuse analüüs," Lõpparuanne (2015)
12. Albury, D.: Fostering innovation in public services. Public Money Manag. **25**, 51–56 (2005)
13. Hartley, J.: Innovation in governance and public services: past and present. Public Money Manag. **25**, 27–34 (2005)
14. Verhoest, K., Verschuere, B., Bouckaert, G., Peter, G.B.: Innovative public sector organizations. In: Campell, C., et al. (eds.) Comparative Trends in Public Management, pp. 106–118. Canada School of Public Service, Ottawa (2006)
15. Moore, M., Hartley, J.: Innovations in governance. PMR **10**, 3–20 (2008)
16. Pollitt, C., Bouckaert, G.: Public Management Reform: A Comparative Analysis: New Public Management, Governance, and the Neo-Weberian State. Oxford University Press, Oxford (2011)
17. De Vries, H., Bekkers, V., Tummers, L.: Innovation in the public sector: a systematic review and future research agenda. Public Adm. **94**, 146–166 (2015)
18. European Commission: "Powering European Public Sector Innovation," Directorate General for Research and Innovation, Innovation Union. European Commission, Brussels (2013)

19. Angelopoulos, S., Kitsios, F., Kofakis, P., Papadopoulos, T.: Emerging barriers in e-government implementation. In: Wimmer, M.A., Chappelet, J.-L., Janssen, M., Scholl, H. J. (eds.) EGOV 2010. LNCS, vol. 6228, pp. 216–225. Springer, Heidelberg (2010)
20. Kalvet, T.: Innovation: a factor explaining e–government success in Estonia. Electron. Gov. 9, 142–157 (2012)
21. Freeman, J., Quirke, S.: Understanding e-democracy: government-led initiatives for democratic reform. JeDEM 5, 141–154 (2013)
22. Scherer, S., Wimmer, M.A., Ventzke, S.: Hands-on guideline for e-participation initiatives. In: Janssen, M., Lamersdorf, W., Pries-Heje, J., Rosemann, M. (eds.) EGES 2010 and GISP 2010. IFIP AICT, vol. 334, pp. 49–61. Springer, Heidelberg (2010)
23. Scherer, S., Wimmer, M.A., Schepers, J.: Regional participation model to engage citizens in distant decision-making. In: Charalabidis, Y., Koussouris, S. (eds.) Empowering Open and Collaborative Governance, pp. 139–155. Springer, Berlin (2012)
24. Hsiao, C.-H., Wang, H.-C., Doong, H.-S.: A study of factors influencing e-government service acceptance intention: a multiple perspective approach. In: Kö, A., Leitner, C., Leitold, H., Prosser, A. (eds.) EDEM 2012 and EGOVIS 2012. LNCS, vol. 7452, pp. 79–87. Springer, Heidelberg (2012)
25. Edelmann, N., Höchtl, J., Sachs, M.: Collaboration for open innovation processes in public administrations. In: Charalabidis, Y., Koussouris, S. (eds.) Empowering Open and Collaborative Governance, pp. 21–37. Springer, Heidelberg (2012)
26. Hindman, M.: The Myth of Digital Democracy. Princeton University Press, Princeton (2009)
27. Lidén, G.: Qualities of e-democracy: examples from Sweden. In: Geißel, B., Joas, M. (eds.) Participatory Democratic Innovations in Europe, pp. 225–248. Budrich, Opladen (2013)
28. Navarro, C., Font, J.: The biased inclusiveness of local democratic innovations: vehicles or obstacles for political equality? In: Geißel, B., Joas, M. (eds.) Participatory Democratic Innovations in Europe, pp. 95–122. Opladen, Budrich (2013)
29. Talpin, J.: When deliberation happens. Evaluating discursive interactions among ordinary citizens in participatory budgeting institutions. In: Geißel, B., Joas, M. (eds.) Participatory Democratic Innovations in Europe, pp. 73–93. Barbara Budrich Publishers, Opladen (2013)
30. Venkatesh, V., Morris, M.G., Davis, G.B., Davis, F.D.: User acceptance of information technology: toward a unified view. MIS Q. 27, 425–478 (2003)
31. Held, D.: The transformation of political community: rethinking democracy in the context of globalization. In: Shapiro, I., Hacker-Cordón, C. (eds.) Democracy's Edges, pp. 84–111. Cambridge University Press, Cambridge (1999)
32. Heindl, P.: Elektronische Demokratie-"Dienstleistungen" des Staates: E-Voting, E-Legislation und E-Participation. In: Prosser, A., Krimmer, R. (eds.) E-Democracy: Technology, Law and Politics, vol. 174, pp. 175–188. OCG Verlag, Vienna (2003)
33. Krimmer, R., Ehringfeld, A., Traxl, M.: Evaluierungsbericht: E-Voting bei den Hochschülerinnen- und Hochschülerschaftswahlen 2009. BMWF, Vienna (2010)
34. Caarls, S.: E-Voting Handbook: Key Steps in the Implementation of E-Enabled Elections. Council of Europe, Strasbourg (2010)
35. Council of Europe (2011, 06-13): Guidelines of the Committee of Ministers of the CoE on Transparency of E-enabled Elections (2011)
36. Krimmer, R.: The evolution of e-voting: why voting technology is used and how it affects democracy, Tallinn (2012)
37. Krimmer, R.: e-Voting.at: Elektronische Demokratie am Beispiel der österreichischen Hochschülerschaftswahlen. WU Vienna University of Economics and Business, Vienna (2002)
38. Alvarez, R.M., Hall, T.: Point, Click, & Vote. Brookings Press, Washington, D.C. (2004)

39. Svensson, J., Leenes, R.: E-voting in Europe: divergent democratic practice. Inf. Polity **8**, 3–15 (2003)
40. Drechsler, W., Madise, Ü.: Electronic voting in Estonia. In: Kersting, N., Baldersheim, H. (eds.) Electronic Voting and Democracy, pp. 97–108. Palgrave, Basingstoke (2004)
41. Alvarez, R.M., Hall, T.E., Trechsel, A.H.: Internet voting in comparative perspective: the case of Estonia. PS: Polit. Sci. Polit. **42**, 497–505 (2009)
42. Kalvet, T.: Management of technology: the case of e-Voting in Estonia. In: ICCTD 2009, pp. 512–515. IEEE Computer Society (2009)
43. Drechsler, W.: (2006, 04-12). Dispatch from the Future, Issue 5 11 2006. Washington Post
44. Madise, Ü., Martens, T.: E-Voting in Estonia 2005. The first practice of country-wide binding Internet voting in the world. In: Krimmer, R. (ed.) EVOTE2006, pp. 27–35. GI, Bonn (2006)
45. Vinkel, P.: Remote electronic voting in estonia: legality, impact and confidence. Ph.D., Tallinn University of Technology, Tallinn (2015)
46. OSCE/ODIHR (2011, 04-01): Election Assessment Mission Report on the 6 March 2011 Parliamentary Elections in Estonia. http://www.osce.org/odihr/77557
47. Vinkel, P.: Presentation to the OSCE Human Dimension Committee, Vienna (2012)
48. Solvak, M., Vassil, K.: E-voting in Estonia: technological diffusion and other developments over ten years (2005–2015). Johan Skytte Institute of Political Studies, Tartu (2016)
49. Glencross, A.: E-participation in the legislative process. eJ. eDemocr. Open Gov. **1**, 21–29 (2009)
50. Postimees: "Eesti e-riigi kuulsamaid lipulaevu kukkus läbi," Tallinn, 19 June 2004
51. Rugam-Rebane, E.: Interview on 2015-05-15. Written notes (2015)
52. TOM Survey: TID+ website (2008)
53. Simson, K.: Saada parimad ideed valitsusele. Maaleht, 04 June 2008
54. Hinsberg, H.: Interview on 2015-04-30. Audio record (2015)
55. Hinsberg, H.: Osalusdemokraatia veebi kaudu. Infotehnoloogia avalikus halduses (2007)
56. Gramberger, M.: Citizens as Partners. OECD Handbook on Information, Consultation and Public Participation in Policy-Making. OECD, Paris (2001)
57. Runnel, P., Pruulmann-Vengerfeldt, P., Reinsalu, K.: The Estonian Tiger Leap from post-communism to the information society. J. Baltic Stud. **40**, 29–51 (2009)
58. Rahvakogu: People's Assembly. www.kogu.ee/en/activity/peoples-assembly/
59. Hinsberg, H.: Rahvakogu tulemus: võim kaotas, kuid inimesed lähenesid, Mõttehommik (2014). mottehommik.praxis.ee/rahvakogu-tulemus-voim-kaotas-kuid-inimesed-lahenesid/
60. Kalvet, T., Kaldur, K.: E-hääletamine (e-voting). In: Kalvet, T., Tiits, M., Hinsberg, H. (eds.) Impact Assessment of the Estonian E-government Services. Institute of Baltic Studies & Praxis Center for Policy Studies, Tallinn (2013)
61. e-Governance Academy: Eesti valitsusasutuste e-kaasamispraktikate analüüs (2012)
62. Hänni, L.: Interview on 2015-04-02. Written notes (2015)
63. Mahrer, H., Krimmer, R.: Towards the enhancement of e-democracy: identifying the notion of the 'middleman paradox'. Eur. Inf. Syst. J. **15**, 27–42 (2005)

Citizens' Deliberation Online as Will-Formation: The Impact of Media Identity on Policy Discourse Outcomes in Russia

Andrei Chugunov[1], Olga Filatova[2], and Yuri Misnikov[1(✉)]

[1] ITMO University, St. Petersburg, Russia
chugunov@egov-center.ru, yuri.misnikov@gmail.com
[2] Saint Petersburg State University, St. Petersburg, Russia
filatovo@gmail.com

Abstract. The paper examines linkages between the type of the digital media resources that host internet discussions on publicly important issues and the outcomes of such debates viewed from the perspective of online deliberation theory and practice. The presented case-based study analyses seven online discourses that debated the destruction of western agricultural products imported to Russia after the embargo imposed by the Russian government on such food in August 2015. The study hypothesized that the digitally enabled discussions would be similar to face-to-face deliberation practices that tend to attract the like-minded people and thus reinforce the already established beliefs and worldviews among discourse participants. Specifically, it was assumed in this context that the attitude towards the policy of food destruction would differ across the media and depend on its public identity viewed from the perspective of political allegiance. The paper presents empirical evidence that supports – with some caution – the postulated assumption.

Keywords: Online deliberation · e-Participation · Media identity · Policy discourse · Validity claims · Russia · Food destruction · e-Petitions · Jürgen Habermas

1 Introduction

The notion of media's public identity – understood by this paper as a real or perceived image of a particular media resource – is not necessarily included into the process of examining and explaining deliberation practices online. As far as the public politics and will-formation are concerned, the endless proliferation of media resources that enable public conversations demands greater clarity about the impact of their political allegiances on discourse outcomes. In this paper we attempt to investigate whether position-taking by discourse participants is linked to the media type, especially in terms of endorsing or rejecting government policies. It is assumed that the process of political participation requires taking sides and thus forming (joining) certain solidarities among participants. Being a member of a political party or any other organised entity pursuing

E. Tambouris et al. (Eds.): ePart 2016, LNCS 9821, pp. 67–82, 2016.
DOI: 10.1007/978-3-319-45074-2_6

certain public goals typically means solidarity with the like-minded peers, particularly in the face-to-face setting. However, participation in online discourses, often anonymous, is a different type of social and personal experience providing more flexibility in choosing a preferred debating community. It is assumed that core political preferences, allegiances and motivations do not change quickly. Yet, ideally, the virtual environment of online conversation may help citizens compare differences, fine-tune the established positions and change them altogether, as a result of talking to the peers. It also implies that when a participant articulates a similar opinion on something that has already been uttered by someone else, he or she joins a virtual 'solidarity' with that participant at this discourse moment; this is something that Jürgen Habermas defines – within the framework of his discourse ethics theory – 'inter-subjective solidarities' built to share the common values expressed in the public sphere.

2   Research Context

We consider online discussions among ordinary Russian citizens as distinctive policy discourses in relation to whether or not the Russian authorities are right to destroy the embargoed food imported from the West.[1] Many digital discourses have emerged on the internet debating both the relevance and morality of food destruction policy, with many of them aiming to stop or amend this policy by, for example, launching e-petitions [1]. The latter have become an especially popular e-participation tool in Russia after the start of the official Russian Public Initiative [2, 3] following in the footsteps of the European Citizen Initiative. We view the act of joining any e-petition or contributing to online discussions as a manifestation of political participation – a public activity undertaken by ordinary citizens voluntarily to influence political authorities and decision-making [4: p. 2], [5: p. 120]. Given the growing accessibility of digital networking for ordinary citizens, opportunities for their political activism increase as well. In addition to the importance of studying policy discourses as such through the lens of public deliberation in order to understand their course and outcomes, the expanding diversity and richness of new digital media suggests taking a closer look at the impact of the media itself on discourse outcomes; that is to say, whether certain solidarities formed on certain issues differ across different media? Whether or not discourse participants prefer those media that are closer to their worldviews? Whether or not participants could be encouraged rather than discouraged joining alternative discourses advocating other, opposing views? Knowing answers to these questions may help lower the level of political polarization that inevitably increases when people prefer talking to their like-minded peers and thus further strengthen the beliefs they already have instead of enlarging the space for potential compromise and dialogue.

---

[1] President Putin's Executive Order of 29 July 2015; the embargo is set to last until 6 August 2016 – more is **here**.

Judging by high approval ratings of President Putin by the public,[2] Russia does not seem to be a politically polarized society. However, the lack of competitive politics coupled with a short and not always fair history of political representation does not mean that the ordinary citizen is uninterested in public life and policy-related issues. Despite the limitations of official politics, informal citizen initiatives based on social networking are as vibrant in Russia as anywhere in the connected to the internet world.[3] It is assumed that political cultures dwell on prevailing civic cultures and comprise inseparably both individual competencies (such as knowledge, beliefs, feelings, judgements) that reflect the society's prevailing norms and values and the personalized attitudes towards the official political system (political allegiances and preferences) that citizens articulate in the course of civic activism and political participation [6].

3 Theoretical Foundations

3.1 Deliberation as Civic Culture

Just as civic and political cultures overlap, the conceptualization of public deliberation is linked with the concept of political participation and democratic legitimacy of liberal democracy. However, Jürgen Habermas viewed the public sphere as a common communication space exclusively for citizens' life-world which is separate from the state's 'system' occupied with its strategic communication mission (i.e. propaganda), as opposed to free and uncoerced communication flow among equal members of the public. Yet the even highly idealized public sphere concept has a distinctive civic character free from the state influence (e.g. a need for independent media) as a condition to realise democratic deliberation. For Habermas, (rational) deliberation constitutes the core of deliberative democracy. Governing regimes can only be morally and ethically justified if citizens are engaged in truth-tracking moral discourses to understand others [7: p. 52]. The role of public discourse is to 'uncover topics of relevance to all of society, interpret values, contribute to the resolution of problems, generate good reasons, and debunk bad ones' [8: p. 452]. Such discoveries are realized discursively, i.e. communicatively and collectively in the course of public discussion by making three types of basic claims to: (a) objective (propositional) truths, i.e. when the speaker refers to the 'totality of objects or existing states of affairs' in the objective world; (b) shared values (intersubjective normative rightness), i.e. when the speaker refers to the totality of shared interpersonal relationships of social groups; and (c) individual experiences (subjective truthfulness), i.e. when the speaker refers to the totality of his or her personal world [9: pp. 313–314], [10: p. 52]. These are the explicit speech acts carrying certain intentions. Using the real case of The Jerry Springer Show [11: p. 393], Habermas demonstrates how through claim-making a communicative action becomes 'meaningful when it engages with high moral standards'.

---

[2] Approval ratings reach 80 % and above which is highly unusual for a functioning liberal democracy.

[3] For example, the web site of the **Beautiful Petersburg movement** engages the public in local affairs to improve the city's environment entirely depends on active citizens.

Such discursive practices are not only defined as communicative – because participants coordinate their actions consensually via validity claims; they are also rational, because communication actors seek to motivate reciprocal discursiveness instead of influencing each other through less honest 'strategic communication' actions that are often accompanied by threat or coercion rather than consensual communication intentions [7: p. 58]. Being a rational discourse participant means being a responsible, reciprocal discussant. Rationality is not necessarily a formulaic robot-style exchange of arguments and reasons. It is also emotions, values and motivation. By claiming values and truths as they understand them, citizens demonstrate their communicative rationality 'in the form of uncoerced and undistorted interaction among competent individuals' [12: p. 12].

While many agree that citizens as discourse participants should cooperate in pursuing together the morally justified common good, the terms of such cooperation are not always clear [13: p. 9, p. 27]. For example, there is a lack of clarity with regard to the role of consensual practices. Gutmann and Thompson [13, 14] resist the traditional Habermasian emphasis on the discursively accomplished consensus. They believe that there are instances when participants cannot agree, 'no matter how respectfully they deliberate with their opponents', and no matter how morally strong the opponents' positions may be [13: p. 20]. There could be 'deliberative disagreements' that despite, for example, moral differences, discussants still can find a mutually acceptable solution by disputing one another's position in a reciprocal manner; but there could also be 'nondeliberative disagreements', when positions are mutually exclusive and could not be reconciled through reciprocal discourse. In many cases, people will not change their opinion, and therefore discussions will not 'always or even usually' end in agreement [13: p. 7].

3.2   Rules and Principles of Deliberation

Internet-based discussions this paper investigates are viewed through the concept public deliberation. There are two main notions of deliberation. The 'procedural' concept argues that for a discussion to be qualified as deliberative certain strict conditions must be met as far as the course of deliberation is concerned [13, 15]. The other position does not prescribe any specific rules that the discussion should follow in order to be counted as deliberative [16–19]. Joshua Cohen [15, 20] represents a more cautious position by emphasising certain conditioning principles for deliberative politics such as: (a) independence (from authorities) and continuous character; (b) equality of participants, who must agree on the ground rules of deliberation; (c) commitment to mutual cooperation; (d) diversity of participants and pluralism of opinions, but excluding pronounced political or ideological biases; (e) respect for internal deliberative procedures (as the source of legitimacy); (f) ability to deliberate competently; (g) use of reason and better argument; and (h) adherence to decisions by rationally-motivated consensus (voting is accepted if no consensus is possible). Gutmann and Thompson [13] also add the importance of deliberation scale and agenda, since only large-scale public debates discussing publicly important policy issues could count as deliberations.

In contrast, a more loosely defined approach toward deliberation admits the inclusion of smaller-scale discussion events, such as 'deliberative polls' that can discuss any issue relevant to a particular community of citizens [17]. Such discussions are usually moderated and short in duration. Diana Mutz [19] supports a more flexible interpretation of deliberation and objects Cohen's procedural model as too 'all-encompassing'. She argues that such an idealized and strictly conditioned deliberation would be virtually impossible to realize in practice as, for example, routine political conversations between neighbours, family members or co-workers would be unjustly excluded [18, 19]. For Bohman [16], one of the major weaknesses of procedure-based deliberation lies in the lack of genuine interest in debate, which would demand the demonstration of strong commitment on the part of prospective discussants. The bias toward the procedural side of deliberation may, for example, lead to the rationally produced argumentation that is non-dialogical and lacking the potential benefits of knowledge sharing and mutual learning. Hardly the focus on deliberation at the expense of the reciprocal 'mutual understanding' could result is a successful discourse, for deliberation should be viewed as a 'particular social activity that can be performed only through public discourse', and hence is 'imbedded in the social action of dialogue' [16: p. 32]. In this respect, Gutmann and Thompson [13: p. 3] agree that deliberation can be both procedurally strict and dialogic. The main challenge, however, is striking the right balance between the both sides of deliberation.

This paper supports a more flexible idea of deliberation as a civic and political activity, since it fits better the nature and character of online discussions among ordinary citizens. Through discursive interaction, they are capable of assuming the role of rational discussants who are willing to debate difficult and sensitive public issues in a dialogical manner. The typical participant is also often emotional and sometimes uncivil. Expressiveness is not necessarily a drawback in peer-to-peer discussions; it is rather an objective discourse trait helping to maintain communication and overcome disputes in a casual conversational manner. Citizens are well aware of what and how they are communicating. They also appreciate the importance of public debate and take participation seriously as a special civic activity and at the same time as a political participation act.

4 Research Design

4.1 Research Assumptions and Objectives

As mentioned above, the study's main research question is to assess the role of the media in will-formation by hosting online discussions; that is, whether a particular media identity – its type, public status, ownership, political allegiances – has an impact on the quality and outputs of online discources. Indirectly, knowing the answer to this question could provide some insights into (a) the degree of awareness of discourse participants about the media's role and hence their decision to choose a certain media outlet (e.g. in order to further strengthen the already existing personal political preferences among the like-minded people); (b) knowing more about whether such an awareness might prevent them from participating in discourses that advocate opposite points of view on the publicly important issues that divide and polarize citizens? The topic of food destruction was found a highly dividing issue in August 2015 among the public in Russia and abroad.

The concept of public deliberation refers primarily to the pre-digital, offline context when participants debate issues in the face-to-face mode which is highly different from the anonymous environment of internet discussions. Face-to-face public discussions were championed by James Fishkin [17, 22] in the form of 'deliberative polls' in the United States. But Diana Mutz [19] asks in this regard whether routine, real-world political activism can be truly deliberative, since people usually prefer to be 'surrounded by those who agree with them (and) thus reinforce... their own political views' since such an agreeable environment does not necessarily encourage political discussion [19: p. 3]. Bohman [16: p. 25] believes that genuine deliberation requires a more diverse and heterogeneous setting to become meaningful; in addition, it should be impersonal to be truly public (and thus more democratic). Individuals tend to exchange their opinions more eagerly if they are unaware of other participants' social identities. It is then assumed that in online debates citizens may prefer 'to debate with diverse others' [21: pp. 2–3, p. 31], contrary to face-to-face discussions. If so, the very deliberation context might be crucial for determining its outcomes. Settings where participants are anonymous might diminish possible intimidation or confusion created by status, appearance or group pressure. Another important question that arises in this context is whether discussion can help change established opinions through a more flexible mode of side-taking.

Drawing on these considerations, the research hypothesised that in an online environment, discourse participants would tend to choose that media resource which has a distinguishable identity in terms of whether it supports or opposes their own views regarding government policies. The logic behind such a hypothesis was grounded in the assumption that people would like to see their beliefs and opinions – for example, a position supporting the government's policy of food destruction – reinforced by other like-minded peers rather than diverse others; that discussions on pro-government media would approve of destroying the embargoed food, whilst the discources hosted by independent media would instead say "No" to such policies.

4.2   Research Sample

According to Denis McQuail, there are no commonly agreed media typology [23: p. 29]. As a general entry point, this study considers three main types of media by applying the following criteria of audience and thematic focus: (a) partisan, political media, (2) elitist media, and (3) the mass media. Pippa Norris [24] also mentions such characteristics, as coverage (national, regional, local), publishing frequency (daily, evening/Sunday), content quality. Media ownership plays a key role in determining thematic orientation and political allegiance. A clear focus on promoting specific content and involving particular contributors determine to a large degree the main target audience and dominant topics [38: p. 238]. Loyalty to the current political order and governing elite – either openly when the media is owned by the government or implicitly when it controls the owners – has a direct impact on the media's editorial policy and target audience

[39: p. 405]. That is especially important for a democratically immature society where the insufficient representation of certain groups in government and hence their inadequate participation in decision-making may demand additional and often informal communication channels to express their views. Digital media, with its many-to-many communication capabilities, provides such channels and somewhat offsets the democratic deficiency of the official public communication system [25]. Even for a more democratic western society, there is a challenge of overcoming the excessive reliance on mediated politics that diminishes the participatory potential of public communication instruments [26–29]. Based on the above considerations, as well as taking into account the research focus on examining the will-formation process as citizens' reaction to government's policy of food destruction, the presented study was designed to examine the following seven internet discussions that formed the research sample, namely:

1. E-Petitions site Change.org, part 1 e-Petition '#Don'tCrushFood'; 100 first posts coded; 7 August 2015; media identity type – international, independent, language; Russian.
2. E-Petition site Change.org, part 2 'e-Petition Don'tCrashFood Update: We will achieve our goal! Preparing a conference (*Мы добьемся результата! Готовим конференцию*); 77 last posts coded (out of 77); 30 August 2015; media identity type – international, independent, language: Russian.
3. Web site Business newspaper Vzglayd (*Деловая газета "Взгляд"*). Lead article title: Polish Minister writes to Putin calling food destruction a sin (*Польский министр в обращении к Путину назвал уничтожение продуктов «грехом»*); 7 августа 2015; 100 posts coded (out of 240); media identity type – Russia, openly pro-government; language: Russian.
4. Russia Today TV channel (*Россия Сегодня*, in Russian). Lead article: Dmitry Peskov (President Putin's press representative) commented on the reaction following the destruction of embargoed food (*Дмитрий Песков прокомментировал реакцию на уничтожение санкционных продуктов*); 5 August 2015; 97 first posts coded (out of 344); media identity type – Russia, government-owned; language: Russian.
5. Novaya Gazeta (*Новая газета*). Lead article: Authorities staged a risky experiment by publicly destroying food in a country whose people are still following a food cult (*Осытенели. Власти поставили рискованный эксперимент с публичным уничтожением еды в стране, население которой всё еще поклоняется культу жрачки*); 6 August 2016; 100 first posts coded (out of 544); media identity type – Russia, independent, language: Russian.
6. Playground – gamers' forums (Playground, *Болталка/Общество*). Lead article: Destruction of embargoed food. Your opinion (*Уничтожение санкционных продуктов. Ваше мнение*); 8 August 2015; 73 first posts coded (out of 74); media identity type – Russia, independent, language: Russian.
7. The Guardian. Lead article: Russians despair at food destruction as Moscow says it is having desired effect; 7 August 2015; 100 first posts coded (out of over 2,000); media identity type – UK, independent, language: English.

The sample was randomly selected by searching the internet. The main selection criteria were as follows: (a) the dominant discussion topic must be food destruction;

(b) there must be at least 70 messages posted by users after the reports; (c) at least one discussion must take place in a western country (in English); (d) presence of independent, pro-government and government-owned media outlets hosting the food destruction discussions; (e) at least one media outlet must not be connected with public politics in any obvious way.

In total, 647 messages posted by 417 unique participants on seven discussion threads were coded and analyzed to reveal the implicitly or explicitly expressed positions either supporting or rejecting government policy of destroying the embargoed food imported from the West.

4.3   Content Coding Methodology

The content coding method aimed at discovering the dominant positions expressed by discourse participants in their assessment of the government policy of food destruction. Specifically, the content analysis looked at the presence of the mutually excluding statements 'For food destruction' and 'Against food destruction'. The important aspect of the validity-based method is that it requires to disclose the intended meaning contained in the uttered message, i.e. to reveal its illocutionary force in terms of the Austian and Searlean notions of intentional 'speech acts'. The notion of the illocutionary speech act is borrowed from linguistics pragmatics as part of the philosophy of language and communication [30, 31]. For Searle [31: p. 16; 32: p. 45], just as for Habermas, 'speaking a language is performing speech acts, acts such as making statements, giving commands, asking questions, making promises and so on'; this is done according to certain rules as an attempt to communicate an intention to obtain the hearer's recognition of a certain assertion or to convince in the truth of a particular proposition. Illocutionary acts are based on the fundamentally dialogical relationship of mutual recognition between the speaker and the hearer.

The Habermasian claims to validity have a lot in common with the Searlean illocutionary force. The latter is increasingly applied in the argumentation and artificial intelligence (AI) research. The focus on argumentation underpins much of the existing scholarship on the topic of deliberation (both offline and online). In effect, argumentation is considered as deliberation itself according to Frank Fischer and Gerber Gottweis for whom deliberation is a 'procedurally governed form of collective argumentation' [33: p. 9]. They further argue that argumentation drives social relations and practices when 'concepts and ideas...shape argumentation' and turn discourse participants into knowledge agents 'to give meaning to physical and social relations' through which 'people experience the world' [33: pp. 10–11]. The AI research domain 'argument and computation' aims at establishing 'inferences between propositions in the domain of discourse' that should be revealed and recorded in the spoken utterances (speech acts) along with the understanding of the 'means of persuasion used by discourse participants' [34]. Argumentation is viewed – and analyzed – here as a special type of speech act which usually contain implicit inferences by which discourse participants influence and persuade one another in a dialogical manner. As a consequence, online deliberative processes are viewed as a series of argumentative dialogues that can be examined to map arguments by 'argument structures' created with the help of argument mapping software tools [35].[4]

Argumentation aspects are important for understanding the value of policy discourses for decision-making. In the similar vein, the claim validation method also includes revealing and documenting factual evidence and other forms of argumentation presented by discourse participants to make their claims more convincing. Such evidence has been collected and recorded in the process of content coding to ensure that the expressed statements and positions were indeed validated by discourse participants. However, the argumentation aspect of discourse analysis presented in this paper has not been its main objective. Moreover, this paper does not tend to support the view that exchanging arguments in a rational manner would be the main motivational factor of online discourses among ordinary citizens (that might be the case, though, in procedural debates among experts). Being a knowledge agent would entail more than presenting arguments. Citizens' discourses are moral conversations in the first place. Studying the claims to normative rightness helps maintain the emphasis on morality and social values underpinned by the Habermasian 'intersubjective solidarities'. It is believed that citizens judge government policies on ethical grounds as well, in addition to looking at the rational and argumentative sides of policy decisions.

5 Research Results

5.1 Coding Steps

Each discourse was analyzed by coding the content of its messages as they were posted on discussion threads in a chronological order. As explained earlier, the coding aimed at identifying the Habermasian claims for validity of the second type, i.e. claiming the normative rightness of certain worldviews and positions. The coding process comprised the following steps. Firstly, each post was assigned a unique ID so as to connect it to the post's author.[5] The second step included identification of the content type which would point at the presence of one of three basic claims to validity, i.e.: content about fact-based objective lifeworld known for all, something that is hard to dispute – validity claim type 1; content revealing value/morale-based statements about social worlds for some, not for all, something that is disputable – validity claim type 2; content about personal sincerity, something that is deeply individuals shared with others, a proof of openness – validity claim type 3. Types 1 and 3 were needed to be identified in order to discern more clearly type 2 – the main aim of content coding. The next, third step, focused on the validation of the claims made, i.e. to separate those that were actually responded via agreement or disagreement. As argued above, the presence of arguments was essential as part of the validation act. The latter did not mean direct responses alone, since the objective was to validate – by supporting or rejecting – the intended and often hidden meaning, its propositional (illocutionary force) the posts

---

[4] For example, the OVA analysis tool and Arvina dialogue system were used to examine large-scale deliberation and politically complex decision-making in Scotland.

[5] On the content coding steps and method see more in [36].

could contain. Posts with uncertain content were removed from the analysis, just as were personal messages that had little to do with the main discourse theme of food destruction. At the fourth stage, the validated claims were summarized to look like the moral statements about food destruction that were either disputed or agreed with by others. The list of such statements could be rather long depending how focused the discussion was. Behind each statement was a certain number of supporters exemplifying a 'social weight' attached to such statements as a measure of the statement's public significance shared by other discourse participants. The final fifth step included further aggregation of the agreed-disagreed statements into a shorter list of the broader "For" and "Against" positions.

5.2 Dominant "For" and "Against" Positions

Tables 1 and 2 below summarize the aggregated position statements represented in *The Guardian* newspaper discourse (as an example).

In the case of the *Guardian* discourse, there were a total of 54 distinctive statements identified, of which 25 were articulated via agreement and 29 – via disagreement. The most prominent was a position against food destruction which supported by 11 validated claims. The most popular "For" statement was exemplified by eight validated claims supporting the government policy of food destruction. Each "For" and "Against" side supplied different sets of argumentation to substantiate their claims. Discourse participants touched upon a wider range of issues that were not necessarily related to the theme of food destruction alone; in fact, many of them did not discuss the main topic of the lead article that opened the discussion. While it is not the best example of online deliberation quality, nonetheless it is a telling case for this particular media resource.

5.3 Position Differentiation Across Media Type

Other discourses were analyzed in a similar way to reveal the dominant position statements on which discourse participants agree and disagree when discussing the government policy of food destruction and to determine the scale of such support and rejection. Table 3 contains the coding results across the entire discourse sample. These data reveal, first of all, that discourses on the pro-government media outlets Vzglyad and the Russia Today TV channel clearly supported food destruction (55 % and 72 % of all validated positions accordingly), whereas the discourses hosted by independent media rejected food destruction (with the rate of 80 % and above). This is an interesting case of opinion polarization suggesting that the media identity itself can be a dividing factor and can significantly, although not decisively, influence discourse outcomes. People indeed tend to participate in those discussions that generate positions similar to their own preferences, as it would happen in face-to-face discussions (according to [19]). On the other hand, these analytics also reveal that, in general, apart from the Russia Today TV channel (which was expected), the support to food destruction policies was rather low; even on the pro-government resources such support

Table 1. Side-taking in the Guardian discourse – 10 most common "For Positions" (FP)

FP-1: For food distribution among the poor	**FP-2: For food destruction**	FP-3: For accusing Russia in not caring about its people	FP-4: For Putin's policies	FP-5: For defending the truthfulness of the article	FP-6: For viewing Russia as a corrupted country	FP-7: For considering food embargo as Putin's revenge against anti-Russian sanctions	FP-8: For defending the West and its anti-Russian sanctions as justified (blaming Russia for changing international borders) and not responsible for confrontation	FP-9: For viewing Russia as a threat responsible for confrontation with a need to contain it to prevent more aggression	FP-10: For blaming the West and its anti-Russian sanctions responsible for confrontation and food embargo
3	**8**	1	1	2	2	3	1	2	1
6 %	**15 %**	2 %	2 %	4 %	4 %	6 %	2 %	4 %	2 %

Table 2. Side-taking in the Guardian discourse – 9 most common "Against Positions" (AP)

AP-1: Against food distribution among the poor	**AP-2: Against food destruction**	AP-3: Against accusing Russian government for not caring about its people	AP-4: Against Putin's policies	AP-5: Against the truthfulness of the article	AP-6: Against viewing Russia as a corrupted country	AP-7: Against the West and its anti-Russian sanctions that are responsible for confrontation and food embargo	AP-8: Against viewing Russia as a threat responsible for confrontation with no need to contain it	AP-9: Against blaming the West and its anti-Russian sanctions responsible for confrontation and food embargo
4	**11**	1	1	4	1	3	1	3
7 %	**20 %**	2 %	2 %	7 %	2 %	6 %	2 %	6 %

Table 3. Differentiation of For/Against position statements regarding food destruction policy by media type

Media resource		All posts	All unique participants	Side-taking via claim validation (solidarity building)							
				All validated positions - all topics		Food destruction related topics					
						including					
						All FOR/AGAINST validated positions		Position "Against food destruction" (including position "For food distribution/sale")		Positions "For food destruction" (including position "Against food distribution/sale")	
Name	Country/type			#	% in all posts	#	% in all positions	#	% in all FOR/AGAINST positions	#	% in all FOR/AGAINST positions
The guardian	UK, independent (first posts)	100	68	54	54 %	26	48 %	14	54 %	12	46 %
Vzglyad (Delovaya Gazeta)	Russia, pro-government (first posts)	100	70	92	92 %	42	46 %	19	45 %	23	55 %
Russia today	Russia, pro-government (first posts)	97	58	68	70 %	53	78 %	15	28 %	38	72 %
Change.org-1	International, independent (first posts)	100	72	69	69 %	64	93 %	55	86 %	9	14 %
Change.org-2	International, independent (last posts)	77	69	52	68 %	47	90 %	37	79 %	10	21 %
Novaya Gazeta	Russia, independent (first posts)	100	47	68	68 %	34	50 %	33	97 %	1	3 %
Gamers' forum	Russia, independent (first posts)	73	33	36	49 %	35	97 %	32	91 %	4	11 %
		647	417	439		301					

just slightly exceeds 50 %, while on the Playground Gamers' forum is as low as 3 %. Otherwise speaking, the impact of media identity has its limits and should not be over-emphasized. The Playground Gamers' discourse is especially interesting, as it is an apolitical media resource by design. Still its participants were unanimous in being against food destruction. One of the explanation of that could be the stronger presence of presumably young gamers than on other resources (it is also presumed that young people might be more critical towards authorities). This case also points at the earlier discussed close connection between civic and political activism.

These discourse outcomes point at a number of other essential for online deliber-ation factors, such as the focus on the discourse main topic which is measured by (a) deliberation reciprocity ("dialogicality") – a percentage of all validated positions on all topics to all posts, and (b) deliberation consistency – a percentage of all validated positions related to the topic of food destruction in the total number of all positions on all topics. According to these measures, all discourses (with some exception of the discussions run on the Guardian and Gamers' Forum) were dialogical and reciprocal, while the e-petitions Change.org media, the Russia Today TV channel and the Gamers' Forum hosted the most focused on the main theme discussions displaying little "de-liberation noise".

On surface, media identity, both objectively and as perceived by participants, seems to determine the discourse outcome. However, in reality, it might be the case that discourse participants simply prefer a particular media outlet that they are comfortable with, that generates statements and positions close to their own worldviews. It is not clear, therefore, what would be the discourse outcome on other media were the par-ticipant audiences as heterogeneous as possible. That doubt leaves the study's main research question not fully answered. More research would be needed to deeper examine the role of media in online policy discourses attracting a more diverse range of participants.

6 Conclusions

As argued above, the media type and its identity does have a role to play in determining deliberation outcomes. That is, the pro-government and openly government media outlets host discussions that are supportive to government policies and actions. In the same manner, independent from government control media is more critical towards authorities. However, the impact of media identity has its limits. The study results support the conclusions of those researchers who argue that, when it comes to a political conversation, citizens prefer talking to their like-minded peers than diverse others. Hence, those who support the government on some principled and moral basis – say for patriotism reasons – would turn to the media which identity is known to be, for example, pro-government. Participation in the discourses hosted by such media outlets would reinforce the already existing beliefs in favour of the authorities' actions, even if they might seem unusual, such as food dumping into the soil by tractors. On the other hand, those who are critical towards the government on the differently understood moral grounds would more likely contribute to the discourses that reflect best upon their own worldviews. However, these are only the general observations. The discussion on the politically neutral Gamers' Forum illustrates suggests that at least the spectrum of those criticizing the government is rather broad. We still don't know what would be the discourse outcome on the media resources that are equally attractive for the bearers of opposing positions and whether, as a result, their positions would be swayed.

Additional studies are needed on other topics and more diverse media samples, including via focus groups and surveys, to examine the motivational side of participation in online policy discourses versus offline deliberation. Understanding better the relationships between civic and political activism in the digital realm remains an essential research agenda too.

This study has not been able to answer a great deal of other important questions, such as: how entrenched and unchangeable the articulated position statements are at the participant level; and to which extent participants themselves see their positions changeable and under which conditions they are ready to change them. Inability to answer these and other questions was a major limitation of the study. Yet we believe that the presented study contributes to the scholarship concerning online deliberation theories and practices by arguing that citizens' casual conversations online represent legitimate policy discourses that can radically expand the level and scope of public knowledge (and specific expertise) needed for better policy-making [37].

Acknowledgements. This research was supported by Russian Fund of Humanities, Grant 15-03-00715. The paper also draws on the doctoral (PhD) dissertation of Yuri Misnikov (University of Leeds, UK).

References

1. Chugunov, A., Filatova, O., Misnikov, Y.: Online discourse as a microdemocracy tool: towards new discursive epistemics for policy deliberation. In: Proceedings of the 9th ICEGOV2016 International Conference on Theory and Practice of Electronic Governance, Uruguay, Montevideo, 1–3 March 2016. ACM Press, New York (2016, forthcoming)
2. Bershadskaya, L., Chugunov, A., Golubtsova, E.: Measurement techniques for e-participation assessment: case of russian e-petitions portal. In: Proceedings of the 8th ICEGOV2014 International Conference on Theory and Practice of Electronic Governance, Guimarães, Portugal, 27–30 October 2014, pp. 395 – 398. ACM Press, New York (2014)
3. Bershadskaya, L., Chugunov, A., Filatova, O., Trutnev, D.: e-Governance and e-Participation services: an analysis of discussions in Russian social media. In: Parycek, P., Edelmann, N. (eds.) Proceedings of the International Conference for e-Democracy and Open Government, CeDEM 2014, pp. 573–578. Danube University, Krems (2014)
4. Verba, S., Nie, N.: Participation in America: Political Democracy and Social Equality. University of Chicago Press, Chicago (1987)
5. Dryzek, J.S.: Deliberative Democracy and Beyond: Liberals, Critics, Contestations. Oxford University Press, Oxford (2000)
6. Almond, G., Verba, S. (eds.): The Civic Culture Revisited. Sage, Newbury Park (1989)
7. Habermas, J.: Moral Consciousness and Communicative Action. Polity Press, Cambridge (1992)
8. Habermas, J.: Concluding remarks. In: Calhoun, C. (ed.) Habermas and the Public Sphere, pp. 462–479. The MIT Press, Cambridge (1992)

9. Habermas, J.: The Philosophical Discourse of Modernity. Polity Press, Cambridge (1987)
10. Habermas, J.: The Theory of Communicative Action. Reason and the Rationalization of Society, vol. 1. Beacon, Boston (1984)
11. Richardson, K.: Specific debate formats of mass media. In: Ruth, W., Koller, V. (eds.) Handbook of Communication in the Public Sphere, pp. 383–400. Mouton de Gruyter, Berlin (2008)
12. Dryzek, J.S.: Discursive Democracy: Politics, Policy, and Political Science. Cambridge University Press, Cambridge (1990)
13. Gutmann, A., Thompson, D.: Why Deliberative Democracy? Princeton University Press, Princeton (2004)
14. Gutmann, A., Thompson, D.: Democracy and Disagreement. Cambridge University Press, Cambridge (1996)
15. Cohen, J.: Procedure and substance in deliberative democracy. In: Benhabib, S. (ed.) Democracy and Difference: Contesting the Boundaries of the Political, pp. 95–119. Princeton University Press, Princeton (1996)
16. Bohman, J.: Public Deliberation: Pluralism, Complexity and Democracy. MIT Press, Cambridge (1996)
17. Fishkin, J.S.: Democracy and Deliberation: New Directions for Democratic Reform. Yale University Press, New Haven (1991)
18. Gastil, J.: Political Communication and Deliberation. Sage, Los Angeles (2008)
19. Mutz, D.: Hearing the Other Side: Deliberative Versus Participatory Democracy? Cambridge University Press, Cambridge (2006)
20. Cohen, J.: Democracy and liberty. In: Elster, J. (ed.) Deliberative Democracy, pp. 185–231. Cambridge University Press, Cambridge (1998)
21. Kelly, J., Fisher, D., Smith, M.: Debate, division, and diversity: political discourse networks in USENET newsgroups. Conference Paper. Second Conference on Online Deliberation: Design, Research, and Practice, DIAC 2005, 20–22 May 2005. Stanford University (2005). http://www.online-deliberation.net/conf2005/viewabstract.php?id=27)
22. Fishkin, J.S.: When the People Speak: Deliberative Democracy and Public Consultation. Oxford University Press, Oxford (2009)
23. Quail, D.: McQuail's Mass Communication Theory. Sage, London (2005)
24. Norris, P.: A Virtuous Circle: Political Communications in Postindustrial Societies. Cambridge University Press, Cambridge (2000)
25. Etling, B., Alexanyan, K., Kelly, J., Faris, R., Palfrey, J., Gasser, U.: Public Discourse in the Russian Blogosphere: Mapping RuNet Politics and Mobilization. The Berkman Center for Internet & Society at Harvard University. Berkman Center Research Publication No. 2010–11. http://cyber.law.harvard.edu/sites/cyber.law.harvard.edu/files/Public_Discourse_in_the_Russian_Blogosphere_2010.pdf
26. Blumler, J., Gurevitch, M.: The Crisis of Public Communication. Routlege, London (1995)
27. Entman, R.M., Bennett, W.L.: Communication in the future of democracy: a conclusion. In: Bennett, W.L., Entnam, R.M. (eds.) Mediated Politics: Communication in the Future of Democracy, pp. 468–480. Cambridge University Press, Cambridge (2001)
28. Hallin, D.C., Mancini, P.: Americanization, globalization, and secularization: understanding the convergence of media systems and political communication. In: Pfetch, B., Esser, F. (eds.) Comparing Political Communication: Theories, Cases, and Challenges, pp. 25–44. Cambridge University Press, Cambridge (2004)
29. Hallin, D.C., Mancini, P.: Comparing Media Systems: Three Models of Media And Politics. Cambridge University Press, Cambridge (2004)
30. Austin, J.L.: How to Do Things with Words. The William James Lectures Delivered at Harvard University in 1955. Oxford University Press, Oxford (1962)

31. Searle, J.R.: Speech Acts: An Essay in the Philosophy of Language. Cambridge University Press, Cambridge (1969)

32. Searle, J.R.: What is a speech act? In: Searle, J.R. (ed.) The Philosophy of Language, pp. 39–53. Oxford University Press, Oxford (1971)

33. Fischer, F., Gottweis, H.: Introduction. In: Fischer, F., Gottweis, H. (eds.) The Argumentative Turn Revisited: Public Policy as Communicative Practice, pp. 1–30. Duke University Press, Durham (2012)

34. Budzynska, K., Reed, C.: Speech acts of argumentation: inference anchors and peripheral cues in dialogue. In: Computational Models of Natural Argument: Papers from the 2011 AAAI Workshop (WS-11-10) (2011). https://www.aaai.org/ocs/index.php/WS/AAAIW11/paper/viewFile/3940/4244

35. Snaith, M., Lawrence, J., Reed, C.: Mixed initiative argument in public deliberation. In: De Cindio, F., Macintosh, A., Peraboni, C. (eds.) From e-Participation to Online Deliberation, Proceedings of the Fourth International Conference on Online Deliberation, OD 2010, pp. 2–13. University of Leeds and Universita Degli Studi Di Milano (2010)

36. Misnikov, Y.: How to read and treat online public discussions among ordinary citizens beyond political mobilisation: empirical evidence from the Russian-language online forums. Digit. Icons: Stud. Russ. Eurasian Central Eur. New Media 7, 1–37 (2012). http://www.digitalicons.org/issue07/yuri-misnikov

37. Noveck, B.: The rise of the citizen expert: how can data-rich technology drive better citizen engagement and make government more effective? Policy Netw. (2016). http://www.policy-network.net/pno_detail.aspx?ID=5056&title=The-rise-of-the-citizen-expert

38. Массмедиа российского мегаполиса: типология печатных СМИ/под общ. ред. М.А. Шишкиной. СПб: Роза мира (2009)

39. Соловьев А.И. Политология: Политическая теория, политические технологии. М. (2003)

Will e-Participation Bring Critical Citizens Back In?

Joachim Åström and Martin Karlsson(✉)

Department of Political Science, Örebro University, Örebro, Sweden
{joachim.astrom, martin.karlsson}@oru.se

Abstract. This paper sets out to critically examine the mobilizing potential of e-participation. The extent to which citizens beyond the usual suspects are engaged is studied by way of survey data from two novel e-participation case studies: one Swedish, one Finnish. Besides from the traditional socio-demographic variables, the analyses highlights cultural attitudes and ask: Do e-participation processes succeed in mobilizing citizens dissatisfied with the way democracy works? Can e-participation bring critical citizens back in? Certainly, the empirical analysis indicates critical citizens are clearly overrepresented in these two cases.

Keywords: e-Participation · Mobilization · Critical citizens · Political culture · Democratic satisfaction

1 Introduction[1]

The nature of civic engagement has changed from participation in political parties and other traditional organisations to more direct and individualised forms. 97 % of Swedes and 92 % of Finns are not members of one of the eight political parties currently in parliament. In Sweden over 70 % do not feel affiliated to any one political party [1, 2]. At the same time, campaigns in favour of individual political issues often draw widespread involvement, not the least online and on social media [3].

To accommodate this development many parliaments, governments, and municipalities have begun adopting 'democratic innovations', an umbrella term for several new methods of participation used by a representative democracy to bolster diminishing civic engagement and to bring citizens closer to the decision-making process. The myriad methods available include: citizen panels, councils, participatory budgeting, and e-participation.

One of the goals ascribed to e-participation is to increase civic engagement in the representative democracy's institutions. But even if e-participation, by virtue of having lower barriers for entry, often do increase civic engagement, it is far from certain that the higher level of participation corresponds to a less unequal division of political activity. If e-participation mostly mobilizes already politically active individuals, groups, and organisations, the consequence instead is that it replicates, or intensifies, existing inequalities. For this reason it is important to assess who participates [4].

---

[1] This work was supported by The Swedish Research Council Formas.

E. Tambouris et al. (Eds.): ePart 2016, LNCS 9821, pp. 83–93, 2016.
DOI: 10.1007/978-3-319-45074-2_7

This paper sets out to critically examine the mobilizing potential of e-participation by investigating whether or not citizens beyond the usual suspects are engaged in e-participation processes. In addition to investigating the socio-demographic characteristics of participants in two e-participation cases, we engage in empirically analysing an often forgotten but arguably important dimension of political inclusion: the cultural attitudes of participants. Do e-participation processes succeed in mobilizing citizens dissatisfied with the way democracy works? Can e-participation bring critical citizens back in?

2 Political Culture in Change

Over the course of recent decades, major challenges to representative institutions have offered a breeding ground for reflection on the future of democratic governance. Concerns usually relate to the very low levels of political support. There is no evidence that publics in established democracies are expressing diminishing levels of support for the ideals and aims of democracy. People agree on democracy being the best form of government, but are increasingly critical towards how current regimes meet public expectations in practice [3, 5].

Although there are different trends in different countries and fluctuations rather than secular trends in individual countries, many commentators now argue that levels of trust are dramatically low [6, 7]. In the 2012 European Social Survey, where trust was measured on a scale from 0 ('no trust at all') to 10 ('complete trust'), the mean trust score for politicians across all 23 countries was 3.2 [8]. Sizeable proportions of mass publics thus lean towards the view that representative institutions and actors are failing to accurately reflect public values and preferences. An even more generalized attitude of support is the degree to which people feel satisfied with how democracy works in their country. The fact that fewer than half of the citizens in many European countries are now satisfied with democracy have drawn further attention to the need to better understand how and why support for the functioning of democracy varies [7].

The prevailing assumption has been that we should look at outcomes rather than processes [9]. However, due to evidence of shifting patterns of political participation, this view has been increasingly challenged. Political parties are commonly regarded as faced by one of the most profound crises in their history, in terms of their ability to attract members and provide meaningful cues to voters [10]. Moreover, a clear rise in non-institutionalised forms of political participation can also be identified. Political participation is not necessarily declining, but it is changing, from the narrow domain of party politics and electoral campaigns to increasingly autonomous, issue-specific forms of expression. Interestingly, empirical research reveals a relationship between political support and patterns of participation: namely, that support for representative institutions and actors is positively associated with conventional participation, and negatively associated with newer forms of participation [5, 11].

The establishment of a link between participation and support has fuelled the debate on how various decision-making processes actually match citizens with different attitudinal predispositions. The classification and interpretation of these predispositions is done in various ways, but they often relate to political support as well as to political interest. Christensen distinguishes four predispositions commonly found in the literature: Traditional Ideal Citizens, Stealth Citizens, Critical Citizens, and Disenchanted Citizens [12]. The first of these corresponds to traditional understandings of what an ideal citizen should be like in a representative democracy [13]. Traditional Ideal Citizens are supportive of political institutions and actors and politically active, preferably in conventional forms of participation. Stealth Citizens [14], though, tend to support political institutions but do not (nor want to) participate in politics beyond the vote. As Bengtsson and Christensen rightly point out, formal representative structures still have many supporters satisfied merely by choosing their leaders on Election Day. Although this group is detached from the political sphere, it is quite happy leaving the dirty work to the authorities, who are held in rather high esteem.

Yet when it comes to dissatisfied citizens, very much at the centre of current debate, it is necessary to differentiate between Critical Citizens [3, 5] on the one hand, and Disenchanted Citizens [6, 15] on the other. Pippa Norris argues that positions of distrust and dissatisfaction sometimes aim to improve the political system [3]. Criticism, in this variant, does not imply disengagement. On the contrary, critical citizens are widening their repertoire of political intervention and appear to favour a more direct participatory relationship with rulers. Other citizens, however, grow disenchanted with politics and abstain from political activity altogether [6, 15].

How do these various predispositions – ideal, stealth, critical, and disenchanted – affect who (e-)participates?

3 Method and Measurements

The empirical analyses of this article are conducted on survey data from two e-participation case studies. A survey of participants in the *Malmö Initiative*, an e-petitioning system used in the city of Malmö, Sweden, was conducted as an online survey, and collected 1,470 responses in total. As sample selection targeted all citizens who had participated in the system, the total number of contacted citizens was 7,024, which produced a moderate response rate of 21 %. While a low response rate is problematic, it is important to stress that the survey was based on a census selection and not a sample of participants.

A survey to participants of *Täsä*, a mobile participation process hosted in the city of Turku, Finland, was distributed through the mobile participation app used in the project and hence distributed to all 780 registered participants in the project. The survey received 186 answers equal to a response rate of 24 %. Again, a very low response rate, yet based on a census of all participants in the participatory process.

Pre-existing large scale survey studies were consulted in order to gather comparative data on the general public in the two contexts of the participatory processes that make up the cases of this study. In the case of the *Malmö Initiative,* extensive survey data was available on a random sample of residents of the county of Skåne in which the city of Malmö is located through the SOM-survey studies [16]. In the case of *Täsä,* no corresponding regional or local survey data was available, compelling us to turn to surveys covering the whole nation of Finland. The European Values Study (wave four) was used to get information about the political participation and satisfaction with democracy among Finnish citizens [2].

In order to investigate the potential of these e-participation cases to mobilize participants beyond the "usual suspects", comparative descriptive analyses were conducted where the characteristics of e-participants were compared to the characteristics of the general public in the respective contexts. Comparable data was analysed regarding the age, gender, education, and satisfaction with democracy and interest in politics of the participants, as well as the general public. Descriptive data is presented and compared between the groups, as well as confidence intervals calculated through bootstrapping (with 1000 samples) in order to produce statistical significance measures of the differences between groups.

The measurements used in the analyses are described in Table 1 below.

Table 1. Measurements.

Item	Survey question	Scale	Categorization
Age	What year were you born?	-	0–43: low, 44 or higher: high
Gender	What is your legal gender?	-	Male/female
Education	What is your highest completed level of education	[Dependent on the education system in the country]	<Bachelor degree: low, Bachelor degree or higher: high>
Interest in politics	To what extent do you agree with the following statement: "I am interested in politics"?	1 (fully disagree) –4 (full agree)	1–2: low, 3–4: high
Satisfaction with democracy	How satisfied are you with the way that democracy works in [country]?	1 (not at all satisfied) –4 (fully satisfied)	1–2: low, 3–4: high

4 Analysis and Results: Who Participates?

In this section the results of the analyses are presented, discussed, and compared to earlier studies in two separate sections. The first section focuses on resources and socio-demographic characteristics, the second on cultural attitudes.

4.1 Resources and Socio-Demographic Characteristics

What we know about civic engagement is that, generally speaking, it is higher among the better educated middle class, and also generally higher among men and older people than among women and the young [4]. One explanation for this involves socio-economic resources in terms of education, income, and social status.

Resources are important, as civic engagement carries with it certain costs for individuals. Citizens need to be assured the gains of participating are greater than the

Table 2. Characteristics of e-participation participants in comparison with the general public.

Sources: Statistics for the general public in Finland were collected from the European values survey wave 4. Statistics for the general public in the Skåne region of Sweden were gathered from the SOM-survey of 2011. Statistics for the participants in Täsä and the Malmö Initiative were gathered from surveys conducted by the authors.

	Täsä				The Malmö Initiative			
	General public	Participants	Difference	Sig.	General public	Participants	Difference	Sig.
Socio-demographic characteristics								
Age (44 or older)	46 %	36 %	−9 %	***	51 %	42 %	−8 %	***
Gender (female)	51 %	40 %	−10 %	**	54 %	52 %	−2 %	-
Education (bachelor degree or higher)	56 %	61 %	+5 %	-	33 %	59 %	+26 %	***
Political interest								
Interested in politics	40 %	72 %	+32 %	***	57 %	87 %	+30 %	***
Satisfaction with democracy								
Satisfied with how democracy works	53 %	56 %	+3 %	-	81 %	56 %	−25 %	***

Notes: Confidence intervals were produced using bootstrapping with 1000 samples at 90 %, 95 %, and 99 % levels of statistical significance.

costs; if not, they refrain from engaging. Therefore, the belief in the potency of the specific method is important, while it is also equally important that the form of participation is not too demanding. The challenge facing political institutions lies in developing forms of civic engagement that both enables citizens to influence politics in a meaningful way and that takes into account the limitations of their individual situations.

E-participation processes are often shaped in a way that makes participation easier, but it is unclear how this affects different individuals. Some scientists argue that the internet can contribute to mobilising previously inactive citizens. Digital resources can reduce the significance of traditional resources, while digital social networks can contribute to redistributing political engagement between various social groups. It is often younger citizens who catch the interest of researchers in this field. They are the group with the most developed digital abilities and take part in most digital social networks, which could spill over into political engagement. More knowledge in navigating the online environment enables these users to effectively search for information on topics of interest and get in contact with other users with similar interests. This increases the likelihood of a user being stimulated into participating in politics online.

Other researchers, however, argue that e-participation will primarily only activate those who are already politically interested, rather than mobilising previously inactive citizens. When it becomes easier to take part in political information, and more convenient forms of online participation are developed, it becomes clear that it is mostly those already involved and motivated that are attracted to them. Resources are also considered important. Higher education levels are expected to provide a greater understanding of political issues and societal problems.

The pattern emerging from our empirical studies seems to suggest continued inequalities (see Table 1 below). Based on our own studies of the *Malmö initiative* and *Täsä*, it seems there is a lasting socio-economic imbalance in relation to education as participants have a higher level of education than the general population. However, women and men participate in largely equal numbers, and the average age is notably lower than among the general population. Hence young citizens are finding an attractive form of political engagement in these e-participation processes, corresponding to what the many earlier studies of e-participation have also shown.

While e-participation arguably makes participation easier, these results support the idea that resources still play an important *indirect* role. In a Spanish study, Anduiza et al. showed that digital competency is significantly more important than traditional socio-economic factors in terms of explaining participation in the e-participation processes [17]. If everyone had the same digital competency, then socio-economic status would matter, but since socio-economically strong groups have greater access to the internet (and thereby can develop their digital competency), they still play an indirect role.

Similarly, Carman's studies of the Scottish parliament's e-petition system shows that socio-economically strong groups have a significantly higher degree of knowledge about how to participate compared to weaker groups [18]. Age also plays a part. Middle-aged people tend to be more aware of the opportunities available in comparison to both younger and older respondents. These differences in awareness, in turn, determine the likelihood of signing and writing petitions. Among people with very good awareness of how to participate in Scottish politics, the likelihood of participating was more than ten times higher than it was for those less aware. If the awareness of available opportunities for participating were equal, then socio-economic factors would be insignificant in terms of who would participate.

That the effects largely seem to be indirect suggests there is long-term mobilisation potential if the information regarding new forms of participation and digital competency were spread further. But the imbalance that arises still poses a relevant inequality issue today.

4.2 Motivation and Cultural Attitudes

Interest in Politics. Although the results presented above indicate that socio-demographic characteristics, not least level of education, play an important role in e-participation engagement, the striking difference between the participants of the two cases and the general public instead concerns the level of interest in politics among participants in e-participation processes.

As is evident from Table 1 (below), the share of participants in the two e-participation cases that declare to be interested in politics far exceeds the corresponding share in the general public in each context. Among the *Täsä* participants, 72 % are interested in politics, compared to about 40 % of the general Finnish public (+32 %, p < .01). A staggering 87 % of the participants in the *Malmö Initiative* are politically interested, compared to 57 % of the general public (+30 %, p < .01). Hence, these e-participation projects do not seem to be able to mobilize the politically disengaged to a very large extent. Rather, the previously engaged, politically interested citizens dominate participants in the two cases.

This bias was also highlighted in a previous study in which the participants in the Malmö initiative were compared to the general population with regard to experiences of political participation. The first group has significantly more often contacted politicians and civil servants, discussed politics online, and worked in political parties and NGOs. The majority of the population of Skåne, Sweden's southernmost province where Malmö lies, has not participated in any of these types of activities during the last year, while more than nine out of ten of those participating the Malmö initiative had [19].

Satisfaction with Democracy. When looking at who participates in e-participation processes, it is interesting to note their dual nature. On the one hand, e-participation exists as an informal process dependent on activities among citizens and civic society (from below). On the other hand, they exist as a more formalised process created by institutions to encourage civic engagement (from above). The first category makes up part of a broader set of mobilisation channels and protest movements on the internet, without mechanisms guaranteeing a response from the authorities. This variant of e-participation is often seen as the archetype for the individualising, anti-establishment, and independent forms of civic engagement used by "critical citizens" in order to, as Inglehart and Welzer expressed it, "organize resistance and mobilize people power" [20]. These independent forms of civic engagement are considered especially compatible with the new generations' demands and wishes: they would rather spend money than time and support democratic principles but are critical of how democracy currently works, and they engage in politics but are not fond of party politics and joining traditional organisations.

Institutionalised forms of civic engagement, such as voting in elections, being a member of a political party, or contacting politicians has traditionally been more connected to the electoral process. Participants have "become a part of the system" in a different way than when independent platforms, which offer critical distance, are used. For this reason, institutionalized forms have foremost engaged citizens who are already relatively satisfied with the way the democratic system currently works. Some newer "democratic innovations" have similarly been biased towards already satisfied citizens. Curato and Niemeyer have shown, for example, that those who agree to participate in deliberative consultation meetings tend to be less critical of political institutions than the public in general. Because of their dual nature, e-participation processes can therefore be seen as a critical case: if a form of civic engagement with its roots in protest movements on the internet is not able to engage critical citizens, how will institutionalised forms of civic engagement succeed?

Our analysis shows that participants in the Malmö Initiative are significantly less satisfied with the way democracy currently works in Sweden than the general public. Among the public, 81 % are fairly or very satisfied, while the corresponding number for our respondents is 56 % (−25 %, p < .01). In the same spirit, Schmidt and Johnsen have shown that, compared with the general public, the participants in the German Parliament's e-petitions system tend to be relatively sceptical towards politicians, and that a significant portion have participated in demonstrations and other protests. To this can be added that those who participated in the Scottish parliament's e-petition system, to a much greater extent than the general public, reported having no party affiliation. While 13 % of the general public where not affiliated with a political party, the equivalent number for participants was 35 %.

The same pattern is not apparent in the Finnish context. While the *Täsä*-participants share the same level of discontent with the state of democracy (56 % of participants in both cases are dissatisfied with how democracy works), these participants share this evaluation of the state of Finnish democracy with the general public (+3 %, p > .1). Hence, there is no statistically significant difference in the values of the e-participants and the general public. Still, it is evident that the *Täsä* case also succeeds in mobilizing critical citizens.

These result, therefore, suggests that critical citizens did not abandon these institutionalized e-participation processes. Rather, it seems that e-participation have been able to attract some of those with weak connections to the party system and who feel there is a discrepancy between how democracy should work and how it actually works. Even if those using e-petitions were already politically active critics, this raises, as Schmidt and Johnsen put it, a hope that e-participation "can bring people who are critical towards politics closer to the parliamentary system and thus prevent them from becoming political cynics or even politically apathetic citizens."

Combining Political Interest and Satisfaction with Democracy. Following the previous research presented above, the attitudinal predispositions of citizens can be combined to produce a division into four divergent types of political cultural ideal types: (1) *Disenchanted citizens,* who are neither interested in politics nor satisfied with democracy; (2) *Stealth citizens,* who, despite having low political interest are satisfied with how democracy works; (3) *Critical citizens,* who combine high political interest with dissatisfaction with democracy; and, finally, (4) *Traditional ideal citizens,* who are both politically interested and satisfied with democracy.

Table 3. The political culture of e-participation participants and the general public.
Sources: see Table 1 above.

	General public	Participants	Difference	Sig.
Täsä				
Disenchanted	27 %	12 %	−15 %	***
Critical	20 %	32 %	+12 %	**
Stealth	29 %	14 %	−15 %	***
Traditional ideal	24 %	42 %	+18 %	***
The Malmö Initiative				
Disenchanted	8 %	5 %	−3 %	*
Critical	10 %	39 %	+29 %	***
Stealth	34 %	7 %	−27 %	***
Traditional ideal	48 %	49 %	+1 %	-

Notes: Confidence intervals were produced using bootstrapping with 1000 samples at 90 %, 95 % and 99 % levels of statistical significance.

When this typology is used to compare the participants in the two e-participation cases with the general public (see Table 3 above) we find that participants are less often *disenchanted* or *stealth citizens*. Hence, citizens that have opted out of politics are not getting engaged in e-participation, regardless of whether they are satisfied (Stealth) or dissatisfied (Disenchanted) with the state of democracy. This is the case in both contexts although the underrepresentation of *disenchanted citizens* is much less flagrant in the *Malmö Initiative* compared with *Täsä* (−3 %, p < .1 compared with −15 %, p < .01). Further the underrepresentation of *Stealth citizens* is stronger in the *Malmö Initiative* (−27 %, p < .01, compared to −15 %, p < .01 among *Täsä* participants). These results confirm the difference between the two e-participation processes explicated above: level of satisfaction with democracy is a much stronger predictor for participation in the Swedish case, as participants in the Malmö initiative are much more dissatisfied with the workings of democracy than the general public.

One prominent difference between the two e-participation cases relates to the representation of *traditional ideal citizens*, the group that most prominently represents the "usual suspects" when it comes to political participation. In the case of *Täsä*, this group is strongly over-represented compared to the general public in Finland (+18 %, p < .01). In the case of the *Malmö Initiative*, in contrast, the share of *traditional ideal citizens* is representative for the general public in Scania (+1 %, p > .1). Hence, there is among these two cases a great variation in the tendency to mobilize the usual suspects; i.e., citizens that are more prone to be engaged in traditional forms of political participation as well.

The two cases are similar in the overrepresentation of *critical citizens*. In the Malmö Initiative almost 40 % of the participants fall into this category, compared to only 10 % of the general public in Skåne (+29 %, p < .01). About a third of the *Täsä* participants are *critical citizens*, compared to a fifth of the Finnish general public (+12 %, p < .05). Both e-participation processes investigated in this study show evidence of successfully bringing *critical citizens* back in, and thus form pathways for (semi-) institutionalized political participation that are attractive to this group of citizens, who are, in earlier studies, found to be more prone to protest politics.

5   Conclusion

The aim of this article was to investigate whether or not e-participation lives up to the goal ascribed to it to increase civic engagement in the representative democracy's institutions by way of mobilizing citizens to participate beyond the "usual suspects". Our analysis has been conducted through an analysis of two e-participation processes: the *Malmö Initiative*, an e-petitioning system implemented in the city of Malmö in Sweden, and *Täsä*, an innovative mobile participation process in the city of Turku, Finland. The study goes beyond the standard approach to investigating this research topic by way of analysing not only the socio-economic profiles of participants but also attitudinal predispositions creating a framework of citizen profiles with regards to interest in politics and satisfaction with democracy.

Earlier research has shown that citizens who are satisfied with democracy tend to engage in traditional, top-down initiated and institutionalized forms of participation such as voting and party engagement, while dissatisfied citizens tend to engage in bottom-up oriented protest politics. An important question is: Can e-participation processes, which position themselves between top-down institutionalized politics and bottom-up citizen originated forms of engagement, bring critical citizens back in to more institutionalized arenas for political participation and function as channels for critical voices to reach political institutions?

The results of our analysis indicate, in agreement with much earlier research, that participants in e-participation processes are not socio-economically representative of the general public. Specifically, citizens engaging in e-participation are often younger, in the case of *Täsä*, more often male, and, in the case of the *Malmö Initiative*, more educated than the general public.

Turning to the attitudinal predisposition, the analysis of the two e-participation cases indicates that e-participation can indeed bring critical citizens back in. Critical citizens who are interested in politics but dissatisfied with democracy are overrepresented in relation to the general public in both analysed cases. This result indicates that while e-participation has a long way to go to bridge the socio-economic gaps related to political engagement and influence, such processes can play a role in engaging critical citizens in constructive political processes. This is an important function in political systems that need to foster an understanding of critical perspectives on policies and democratic institutions.

References

1. Oscarsson, H., Holmberg, S.: Nya svenska väljare. Nordstedts Juridik (2013)
2. EVS: European Values Study 2008, 4th wave, Integrated Dataset. GESIS Data Archive, Cologne, Germany, ZA4800 Dataset Version 2.0.0, 30 November 2010. doi:10.4232/1. 10188
3. Dalton, R.J.: Citizen Politics: Public Opinion and Political Parties in Advanced Industrial Democracies. Cq Press, Beverly Hills (2004)
4. Schlozman, K.L., Verba, S., Brady, H.E.: The Unheavenly Chorus: Unequal Political Voice and the Broken Promise of American Democracy. Princeton University Press, Princeton (2012)
5. Norris, P.: Critical Citizens. Global Support for Democratic Governance. Oxford University Press, Oxford (1999)
6. Stoker, G.: Why Politics Matters: Making Democracy Work. Palgrave Macmillan, Basingstoke (2006)
7. Thomassen, J., Poguntke, T., Rossteutscher, S., Schmitt-Beck, R., Zmerli, S.: What's gone wrong with democracy, or with theories explaining why it has? In: Citizenship and Democracy in an Era of Crisis: Essays in Honour of Jan W. Van Deth, 34 (2015)
8. ESS Round 6: European Social Survey Round 6 Data. Data file edition 2.2. Norwegian Social Science Data Services, Norway – Data Archive and distributor of ESS data for ESS ERIC (2012)
9. Birch, S., Allen, N.: How honest do politicians need to be? Polit. Q. **81**(1), 49–56 (2010)
10. Mair, P.: Ruling the void: the hollowing of western democracy. New Left Rev. **42**, 25–51 (2006)
11. Hooghe, M., Marien, S.: A Comparative analysis of the relation between political trust and forms of participation in Europe. Eur. Soc. **15**(1), 131–152 (2013)
12. Christensen, H.: Power sharing and political dissatisfactions: a multilevel analysis of the impact of institutional power sharing on kinds of political dissatisfaction in 24 European democracies. Paper presented at ECPR Joint Sessions, 10–15 April 2014
13. Easton, D.: A Framework for Political Analysis, vol. 25. Prentice-Hall, Englewood Cliffs (1965)
14. Hibbing, J.R., Theiss-Morse, E.: Stealth Democracy: Americans' Beliefs about How Government Should Work. Cambridge University Press, Cambridge (2002)
15. Hay, C.: Why We Hate Politics. Polity Press, Cambridge (2007)
16. SOM-institutet. Riks-SOM 2011. Version 1.0. Svensk Nationell Datatjänst (2013). http://dx. doi.org/10.5878/002326
17. Anduiza, E., Gallego, A.G., Cantijoch, M.: Online political participation in Spain: the impact of traditional and internet resources. J. Inf. Technol. Polit. **7**(4), 356–368 (2010)
18. Carman, J.: Barriers are barriers: asymmetric participation in the Scottish public petitions system. Parliam. Aff. **67**(1), 151–171 (2014)
19. Åström, J., Jonsson, M., Karlsson, M.: Democratic innovations: reinforcing or changing perceptions of trust? Int. J. Public Adm. (2016, Forthcoming)
20. Inglehart, R., Welzel, C.: Modernization, Cultural Change, and Democracy: The Human Development Sequence, p. 262. Cambridge University Press, Cambridge (2005)

Open Governance in Authoritarian States: A Framework for Assessing Digital Participation in the Age of Mass Surveillance

Fadi Salem[✉]

University of Oxford, Oxford, UK
Fadi.Salem@sant.ox.ac.uk

Abstract. With the growing utilization of "smart" technologies, social media and "Internet of Things" applications, citizen-government interactions are rapidly changing. These changes have substantially transformed participatory models where governments apply e-participation measures not necessarily for participatory goals. As cosmetic e-participation applications and mass online surveillance increase in scope, there is a critical need to re-assess the applicability of dominant frameworks of analysing participatory practices. The paper aims to provide a nuanced understanding of the role of the internet in citizen-government interactions in authoritarian contexts based on a critical assessment of dominant participation models. It first maps key analytical typologies and models of public participation based on an extensive literature review. This is intended to help identify potential models that explain public participation—or lack thereof—in authoritarian contexts. The outcomes of this review are (1) revealing a scholarly gap of substantial policy relevance on e-participation in authoritarian contexts, and (2) assessing the applicability of dominant e-participation analytical models in such contexts. The findings indicate that, in the digital era, the transformations in citizen-government interactions lack contemporary understanding. Based on this comparative review, an analytical framework is proposed which extends and adapts Arnstein's ladder of participation to the digital era. The paper argues that the proposed model helps better understand emerging practices of citizen-government interaction, especially in authoritarian contexts, but also in some democratic contexts where e-participation measures are utilized for mass-surveillance or as political façade.

Keywords: e-Participation · Authoritarian states · Digital governance · Citizen engagement · Citizen-government interaction · Mass Surveillance

1 Introduction

Over the past two decades, studying the multifaceted impact of digital technologies on governance has become an essential part of multidisciplinary research and policy agendas. In policymaking today, it is widely accepted that "digital governance" has become central to contemporary governance [1, 2]. With almost 3.5 billion individuals online, a critical mass of the world's population is gaining access to a wide range of

© IFIP International Federation for Information Processing 2016
Published by Springer International Publishing Switzerland 2016. All Rights Reserved
E. Tambouris et al. (Eds.): ePart 2016, LNCS 9821, pp. 94–105, 2016.
DOI: 10.1007/978-3-319-45074-2_8

digital technologies, leading to increased social acceptance of technological means as interfaces between governments and citizens [3]. More recently, with 8 billion "things" connected to the internet, this growth has been coupled with disruptive advances in internet applications and innovative uses of social networking and "smart" technologies, which influenced further changes in the ways citizens participate in governance worldwide [4, 5].

These fast-paced changes in technological fields have increased the complexity of contemporary policymaking. For example, the adoption of social media by governments, and by society to interact with government, present numerous challenges to the centrality of government and its ability to remain the connecting node in the state. They challenge governments' organizational capacity, specifically, the adequacy of human resources and technology. They also challenge governments' authority, as the only legitimate and official power, with numerous other societal forces increasing their organizational capacity and societal influence through the use of such technologies. In addition to loss of *de jure* authority, governments are also faced with an important shift of *de facto* power away from public institutions [6–9]. In reaction, some governments were pushed to adapt, accommodating increased public participation in governance through technological means. In many cases, the outcome of this adaptation in democratic states meant widening public participation in governance. However, in some authoritarian states this lead to further enforcement of authoritarian rule with governments extending their controls to the digital sphere. In others this enabled substantive opportunities for public participation in governance for the first time. How are these authoritarian states adapting; and are they really becoming more open towards public participation in policymaking in the digital era?

This paper is both a critical review of related literature and a foundation for exploring this question. The objective is to explore the scholarly foundations of digital governance and citizen participation in key social science disciplines, and critically assess their applicability to these emerging changes in authoritarian contexts. The scope covers multidisciplinary scholarly literature, as well as influential policy reports produced by established international organizations.

The paper is ordered as follows: The first section provides a review of influential models of citizen participation and citizen-government interactions before and after the digital age. It then provides an overview of authoritarian uses of participatory measures in the digital age as discussed in the literature. Based on the comparative review, a framework is then proposed by extending and adapting Arnstein's ladder of participation for the digital era, with focus on authoritarian states.

2 Public Participation and the "Ladder of Participation"

Citizen participation in policymaking is an established cornerstone of democratic governance [10]. Over the past fifty years numerous models have been developed to analyse contemporary public participation in multiple aspects of governance [e.g. 11, 12, 13]. The "ladder of citizen participation" proposed by Arnstein, continues to be one of the most influential [11]. The eight stages of the "ladder" conceptualize the changes in balance of power between citizens and government in participatory engagements.

The model describes a redistribution of power in such interactions, in which citizens gain power as government loses it in the participation process. The eight rungs of the ladder are grouped into three stages:

(1) Non-participation stage. This stage includes the "manipulation" and "therapy" rungs of the ladder, where no public participation takes place, but a perception of participation may exist.
(2) Tokenism stage. This includes the "informing", "consultation" and "placation" rungs, in which "tokens" of participation are provided, in what can be described as cosmetic attempts by government.
(3) Citizen power stage. Including "partnership", "delegated power" and "citizen control" rungs, where meaningful levels of public participation are actually happening.

According to Arnstein, this eight-level typology of citizen participation—or lack of —starts from a stage where the government introduces what seems to be participatory means, with the aim of controlling or manipulating the public, with no citizen participation actually taking place. In contrast, the upper rung of the "ladder" then describes a stage where even "have-not citizens" gain a voice over government decisions.

Over the past four decades, Arnstein's ladder was extended to numerous disciplines in the aim of explaining public interactions with government [for example: 14, 15, 16]. However, as modes of public engagement developed, the model has been critiqued on several fronts. For example, the "ladder" design indicates evolution and progression and implies that the upper rungs on the ladder are "better" than lower ones. While this may be true in numerous cases, in others, "consultation" for example, may provide much better outcomes than full "citizen control" [13]. Moreover, the zero-sum power balance the ladder implies, where the government loses power as citizens gain it going up the ladder, is limited and one-dimensional. In reality there are cases where the process of public participation itself may lead to increasing social learning, knowledge sharing, social capital or trust generation [17]. In such cases, the participation process itself may lead to increasing both citizens' and governments' power, or at least does not undermine government's power. Overall, the common critiques of Arnstein's ladder can be summarized in (1) its sole focus on the power dimension between government and citizens, were the governments and citizens struggle for more share of power in decision-making, (2) its focus on the outcomes of the participation process, without considering the value of the process itself, and (3) its limited focus to citizen participation within democratic environments [13, 16, 17].

However, despite its criticism, a key contribution of Arnstein's ladder is its sophisticated view of the power relations in which citizen-government engagements take place. It recognizes the possibility of government manipulation of public engagements, compared to the overly optimistic view of citizen participation as an unequivocal good [13]. In authoritarian contexts, this is particularly useful where the "non-participation" and "tokenism" stages of the ladder are often prevalent.

3   Public Participation in the Digital Era

The impact of technology on citizen participation in governance has been addressed long before the internet emerged as an interface between the public and government. As early as 1977, Laudon proposed a typology of three ways that communication technologies are changing the interface between citizens and government, namely "data transformation", "managerial democracy" and "mass participation" [18]. A decade later, DeSario and Langton explored the role of technology and information in public policymaking and its impact on "technocratic" and "democratic" citizen participation. They argued that government decisions are increasingly affected by technology, and that citizen participation will be an outcome of the intrinsic characteristic of information as a resource that can be shared without being depleted [19]. In the digital era, numerous models have been further developed. For example, Chadwick and May used a three dimensional model to explain citizen-government interactions within digital governance contexts: (1) The "managerial" efficiency model, borrowed from Laudon, which focuses on the delivery of efficient public services, (2) the "consultative" model which aims to develop better policies through engaging different interests in society through digital technology, and (3) the "participatory" model which involves engagement in the democratic process. The authors argued that the focus on public service efficiency (or "managerial") model of digital governance is marginalizing its participatory and democratic potential [20]. Observations from authoritarian contexts suggest that the "managerial" view is a prevailing political agenda with regards to the role of digital governance [21].

More recently, with the growing influence of social technologies, Fung et al., proposed an explanatory model of citizen-government interactions, specifically in political participation. They argued that political interaction between government and citizens in the digital sphere is taking place in six distinct ways, but that the three most likely to occur are "truth-based" advocacy, crowd-sourced "social monitoring" and constituent mobilization [22]. The increased adoption of social media by governments expanded the citizen participation theme beyond merely the political level. The critical mass of users and growing sophistication of big data tools are reducing scepticism about the effectiveness of participatory digital governance, compared to a decade ago [22, 23]. An increasing number of frameworks and explanatory models are emerging to evaluate the impact of social media utilization in different aspects of civic engagement [for example: 24, 25, 26]. Today, governments' use of social technologies in co-design, co-production and co-delivery of public policy and services is common practice in numerous countries.

Beyond the citizenry, the use of the social media by governments to engage with international communities is also growing. For example, government engagement in "digital diplomacy" or "e-diplomacy" initiatives through social media is growing in sophistication. This ranges from diplomats and embassies reaching out to citizens in host countries for social and political objectives, to foreign affairs departments running international campaigns to push political agendas or analyse perceptions on a global scale. Social media is becoming institutionalized in foreign affairs departments and used by diplomats and politicians to affect international relations and generate "soft power" in the application of foreign policy [27, 28].

Today, participatory digital governance, or what is commonly referred to as "e-participation", is considered an important pillar of maintaining the "quality of government" by numerous governments, policy organizations and scholars [1, 4, 22, 29, 30].

4   e-Participation in Authoritarian States

This paper is primarily concerned with changes in public-government interactions in authoritarian states in the digital age. For the purpose of exploring the research question proposed, this paper utilizes a well-established conceptualization of authoritarianism as a point of reference. According to Linz, a democratic system is a political system that provides the public with a free space for political preferences to form by using basic freedoms of information, communication and association for the objective of enabling non-violent competition by political leaders to validate their claim to rule at set intervals. Accordingly, authoritarian systems are defined as political systems with limited political pluralism and a lack of extensive mobilization, in which a leader or a small group exercises power within ill-defined—but predictable—limits. As such, authoritarian states in this paper refer to countries in which the system of governance is characterized by, strong central power, limited political pluralism, minimal social mobilization, ill-defined legitimacy, vague executive power structure [31]. Today, there are at least 44 countries categorized as "authoritarian" [32]. These countries host a large percentage of the world's population. Many of them are increasingly utilizing participatory digital technologies in policymaking.

However, in a fast-evolving digital age, the powers that technological advancements, such as Internet of Things (IoT) applications and advanced big data analytics, hand to governments and societal powers alike, are blurring the line between how digital technology is used in authoritarian and democratic contexts [33, 34]. For example, in numerous cases, what looks like participatory digital governance applications are in reality, utilized in mass online surveillance, breach of privacy and other human rights supposedly protected by the rule of law in democratic contexts. These transformations are creating several similarities in the ways participatory digital technologies are implemented, regardless of the nature of the state [35, 36].

Generally, the literature on public administration and digital governance has viewed the impact of participatory technologies on citizen-government interactions from two key angles. First, in established democratic systems, main streams in the literature viewed the increased penetration of technology, and more recently the use of social media, as another channel or influencer of democratic participation and digital citizenship [for example: 22, 37, 38, 39, 40]. This thread led by political science and related disciplines, largely narrows "e-participation" to the political dimension, where technology facilitates or improves an existing democratic process. Second, in non-democratic contexts, where no formal channels of political or civic participation exist in the first place, the literature has largely dismissed online citizen participation as non-existent or irrelevant. Instead, it primarily focused on what can be referred to as the "collective action thesis", or the role of digital technologies in enabling collective action against authoritarian regimes through citizen empowerment, mobilization, organization and revolt [for example: 7, 9, 41, 42, 43, 44]. However, there is little discussion in this thread of the literature, beyond the collective action thesis, on the role participatory digital technologies are playing in citizen-government interactions in authoritarian states where civic applications actually exist. Both of these main threads in the literature have narrowed down the scope of e-participation's definition, over-looking the potential for participatory digital governance beyond the democratic political process or popular collective action.

In reality, digital technologies are being used by states in a wide scope of civic engagement activities. These include, for example, contributing to public administration activities, policymaking, government decision-making and service improvement, among many others. Several socioeconomically advanced authoritarian states are increasingly providing participatory governance initiatives to engage citizens in policymaking and government decision-making. In such contexts, unlike the case of democratic states, there is little room to use these technologies in democratic political processes, which are rare in the first place. Also, in many of these socioeconomically advanced authoritarian states, there is arguably little citizen demand for democratization, and little appetite to use these technologies for anti-government collective action, let alone revolt. This is unlike the case of brutal military dictatorships and classic autocracies. A more nuanced understanding of the emerging uses of participatory technologies in such authoritarian contexts is needed.

A critical examination of the few existing studies on this emerging phenomenon in authoritarian states indicates several shortcomings. First, much of the literature sub-scribes to a technology-deterministic view [45], following a prevailing trend in the wider digital governance literature. Second, it largely focuses on the supply of par-ticipatory technologies by states, regardless of the level of adoption by citizens of such technologies, the quality of use, or whether the uses are actually enabling participation. Third, a large number of these studies assume that "democracy"—in its western incarnations—is the intended and ultimate outcome of public participation through technology. The latter shortcoming may be due in part to the classic coupling of democracy with development in the western-dominated development literature, influenced by the "modernization theory" [46, 47]. This shortcoming also led to a prevailing confusion in terminology. The terms "e-participation" and "e-democracy" have been used interchangeably in the literature tackling citizen participation and digital gover-nance, whether in democratic or authoritarian states, without serious attempts to understand the distinction. These shortcomings suggest that there is room for nuanced studies of the roles participatory digital technologies play in authoritarian contexts.

5   Assessing Citizen Participation in the Digital Era

The "e-participation" area of research remains an emerging and relatively young field of study. It still suffers from disciplinary and geographic biases, lack of depth and theoretical clarity and wide inconsistency in definitions [48].

Analytical models assessing participatory digital governance have largely focused on "developed" and democratic countries [48]. Considering the limitations of existing "e-participation" research, especially with regards to authoritarian states, few models may be applicable when analysing citizen-government interactions in authoritarian contexts. Table 1 provides a comparison between three influential citizen participation typologies, which are not internet-specific. It lists the stages of participation proposed according to each of Arnstein's ladder, the OECD's three-stage citizen participation model and the International Association for Public Participation's "spectrum" of citizen participation [11, 30, 49]. This is followed by Table 2, which provides a summary of four internet-focused models of citizen participation which have also been influential [4, 39, 50, 51]. Clearly, all typologies and models share the basic pillars of citizen participation, with some variation in sophistication and scope.

Table 1. Citizen participation analytical typologies (non-internet specific)

Public participation frameworks	(Arnstein, 1969) [11]	(IAP2, 2014) [30]	(OECD, 2009) [49]
Stages	Manipulation		
	Therapy		
	Informing	Inform	Information
	Consultation	Consult	Consultation
	Placation	Involve	
	Partnership	Collaborate	Participation
	Delegated power	Empower	
	Citizen control		

Most of these typologies have either been designed with democratic processes in mind, or to be neutral towards the political processes. None has been designed to take into account a potential participatory process in an authoritarian context. If we are to design, or extend, a model for analysing technology-driven public participation in authoritarian states, it needs to accommodate the balance of power and all possible explanations for adopting participatory technologies in such contexts. Arnstein's ladder provides a suitable and inclusive starting point, given that the spectrum implied includes possible stages which are non-participatory. Considering the potential explanations for the adoption of participatory digital governance in authoritarian contexts, and the nature of some of these in the digital era (surveillance, control, etc.) as found in the literature, Arnstein's ladder provides a suitable starting point for developing a model to help understand participatory approaches in authoritarian states.

Table 2. Citizen "e-participation" analytical typologies (internet specific)

e-Participation frameworks	(Neuman et al. 2011) [39]	(Macintosh, 2004) [50]	(European commission, 2013) [51]	(UN DESA 2014) [4]
Stages			Information	e-Information
	Inclusion on platform	e-Enabling	Consultation	e-Consultation
	Capacity to influence agenda	e-Engaging	Cooperation	
	Platform's capacity to enable collective will formation	e-Empowering		e-Decision making
	Platform's equality attributes (participation not influenced by contributor's status, language)			
	Absence of external coercive constraints			
	Absence of systematic distractions from participatory deliberations			

Building on Arnstein's ladder, an extension is proposed here as a basis for an analytical model to assess participatory approaches in authoritarian states. The proposed ladder (Table 3) introduces new "rungs", namely "government control", "surveillance" and "façade". A few other rungs are renamed for more clarity ("selective participation" instead of "placation", and "empowerment" instead of "delegated power"). It is safe to assume that it will be highly unlikely that in authoritarian states, the "citizen control" rung of the ladder will be ever used. Indeed, this would be impossible *ex hypothesi*. For if citizen control occurs, the state is no longer authoritarian by definition. As such, that top rung of Arnstein's ladder is removed from the proposed extension.

Based on this discussion, there has been some residual dissatisfaction in all of these attempts with regards to applicability to authoritarian contexts. Adapting and developing the ladder of participation, to take into account the specificities of citizen

Table 3. A proposed extension of Arnstein's ladder of citizen participation for the digital era, considering authoritarian contexts

Participation level	Stage	Example
Non-participation	Government control	No participation process exists and the government practices firm control on policymaking
	Surveillance	Online public-government interaction processes and platforms may exist, but serve only as sources of information for government surveillance, monitoring and profiling, with no contribution to policymaking taking place

(*Continued*)

Table 3. (*Continued*)

Participation level	Stage	Example
	Façade	Public-government interaction platforms and initiatives are signalled to the public but they do not function or merely serve as a cosmetic layer
Tokenism	Informative	Some types of information and datasets are made open for the public to be able to make decisions (though not necessarily always updated or in useful formats)
	Consultative	Initiatives are put in place where the public are consulted and crowdsourced but government does not commit to include input in policymaking
	Selective participation	Selected members of the public are invited (not necessarily based on merit or expertise) to take part in closed online participation processes
Participation	Collaborative (partnership)	Functioning public initiatives and online platforms are established for public contribution to policymaking, where policymaking takes place interactively
	Empowerment	A transparent process (and platforms) exists where the government reports details and outcomes of the participatory process, including outcomes which do not fit government stated agendas

participation in authoritarian states in the digital era is a starting point towards a better model for analysing public participation in the digital era, within authoritarian contexts.

6 Conclusion

Studying the impact of participatory technologies on policymaking and government-decision making is critical to widen the understanding on how citizen-government relations are being transformed in the digital era. This is especially important in authoritarian states, where dominant literature has largely been defined by the collective action "thesis". This paper provided a critical review of dominant frameworks for assessing participatory digital implementations and citizen-government interactions in an ever changing digital world. The proposed framework here arguably provides a novel perspective to assess e-participation in authoritarian contexts. However, with the increased exploitation of participatory tools for non-participatory practices, such as mass surveillance, even in democratic contexts, the utility of this framework can be universal.

References

1. OECD: Recommendation of the Council on Digital Government Strategies. Public Governance and Territorial Development Directorate, Organisation for Economic Co-operation and Development (2014)
2. WEF: Future of Government Smart Toolbox. World Economic Forum (2014)
3. ITU: ICT Facts and Figures: The World in 2016. International Telecommunication Union (2016)
4. UNDESA: UN E-Government Survey 2014: E-Government for the Future We Want. United Nations Department of Economic and Social Affairs (2014)
5. ITU: Measuring the Information Society Report 2015. International Telecommunication Union (2015)
6. Hood, C., Margetts, H.: The Tools of Government in the Digital Age. Palgrave Macmillan, Basingstoke (2007)
7. Owen, T.: Disruptive Power: The Crisis of the State in the Digital Age. Oxford University Press, Oxford (2015)
8. Mickoleit, A.: Social Media Use by Governments: A Policy Primer to Discuss Trends, Identify Policy Opportunities and Guide Decision Makers. OECD, Paris (2014)
9. Lynch, M.: After Egypt: the limits and promise of online challenges to the authoritarian arab state. Perspect. Polit. **9**, 301–310 (2011)
10. Pateman, C.: Participation and Democratic Theory. Cambridge University Press, Cambridge (1970)
11. Arnstein, S.R.: A ladder of citizen participation. J. Am. Inst. Plan. **35**, 216–224 (1969)
12. Cooper, T.L., Bryer, T.A., Meek, J.W.: Citizen-centered collaborative public management. Public Adm. Rev. **66**, 76–88 (2006)
13. Fung, A.: Varieties of participation in complex governance. Public Adm. Rev. **66**, 66–75 (2006)
14. Wilcox, D.: The Guide to Effective Participation. Partnership, Brighton (1994)
15. Burns, D., Hambleton, R., Hoggett, P.: The Politics of Decentralisation: Revitalising Local Democracy. Macmillan, Holtzbrinck (1994)
16. Choguill, M.B.G.: A ladder of community participation for underdeveloped countries. Habitat Int. **20**, 431–444 (1996)
17. Tritter, J.Q., McCallum, A.: The snakes and ladders of user involvement: moving beyond Arnstein. Health Policy **76**, 156–168 (2006)
18. Laudon, K.: Communications Technology and Democratic Participation. Praeger Publishers Inc., Santa Barbara (1977)
19. DeSario, J., Langton, S.: Citizen Participation in Public Decision Making. Greenwood, New York (1987)
20. Chadwick, A., May, C.: Interaction between states and citizens in the age of the internet: "e-government" in the United States, Britain, and the European Union. Governance **16**, 271–300 (2003)
21. Ciborra, C., Navarra, D.D.: Good governance, development theory, and aid policy: risks and challenges of e-government in Jordan. Inf. Technol. Dev. **11**, 141–159 (2005)
22. Fung, A., Russon Gilman, H., Shkabatur, J.: Six models for the internet+politics. Int. Stud. Rev. **15**, 30–47 (2013)
23. Henman, P.: Government and the internet: evolving technologies, enduring research themes. In: Dutton, W. (ed.) The Oxford Handbook of Internet Studies. Oxford University Press, Oxford (2013)

24. Zavattaro, S.M., Sementelli, A.J.: A critical examination of social media adoption in government: introducing omnipresence. Gov. Inf. Q. **31**, 257–264 (2014)
25. Warren, A.M., Sulaiman, A., Jaafar, N.I.: Social media effects on fostering online civic engagement and building citizen trust and trust in institutions. Gov. Inf. Q. **31**, 291–301 (2014)
26. Mergel, I.: A framework for interpreting social media interactions in the public sector. Gov. Inf. Q. **30**, 327–334 (2013)
27. Nye, J.: Soft Power: The Means to Success in World Politics. PublicAffairs, New York (2004)
28. Ross, A.: Digital diplomacy and US foreign policy. Hague J. Dipl. **6**, 451–455 (2011)
29. WEF: The Global Information Technology Report 2016: Innovating in the Digital Economy. World Economic Forum (2016)
30. IAP2: Public Participation Spectrum. International Association for Public Participation (IAP2) (2014)
31. Linz, J.J.: Totalitarian and Authoritarian Regimes. Lynne Rienner Publishers, Boulder (2000)
32. Marshall, M.G., Cole, B.R.: Conflict, Governance, and State Fragility - Global Report 2014. Center for Systemic Peace, Vienna (2014)
33. Howard, P.: Pax Technica: How the Internet of Things May Set Us Free or Lock Us Up. Yale University Press, New Haven (2015)
34. Mayer-Schönberger, V., Cukier, K.: Big Data: A Revolution That Will Transform How We Live, Work, and Think. Eamon Dolan/Houghton Mifflin Harcourt, Boston (2013)
35. Kelly, S., Earp, M., Reed, L., Shahbaz, A., Truong, M.: Freedom on the Net 2015: Privatizing Censorship. Eroding Privacy, Freedom House (2015)
36. Lyon, D.: The Electronic Eye: The Rise of Surveillance Society-Computers and Social Control in Context. Wiley, Hoboken (1994)
37. Margetts, H.: The internet and democracy. In: Dutton, W. (ed.) The Oxford Handbook of Internet Studies. Oxford University Press, Oxford (2013)
38. Mossberger, K., Tolbert, C.J., McNeal, R.S.: Digital Citizenship: The Internet, Society, and Participation. MIT Press, Cambridge (2008)
39. Neuman, W.R., Bimber, B., Hindman, M.: The internet and four dimensions of citizenship. In: Shapiro, R.Y., Jacobs, L.R. (eds.) The Oxford Handbook of American Public Opinion and the Media, pp. 22–42. Oxford University Press, Oxford (2011)
40. Gibson, R., Cantijoch, M.: Conceptualizing and measuring participation in the age of the internet: is online political engagement really different to offline? J. Polit. **75**, 701–716 (2013)
41. Hussain, M.M., Howard, P.N.: What best explains successful protest cascades? ICTs and the fuzzy causes of the arab spring. Int. Stud. Rev. **15**, 48–66 (2013)
42. Howard, P., Hussain, M.: Democracy's Fourth Wave? Digital Media and the Arab Spring. Oxford University Press, Oxford (2013)
43. Bennett, W.L., Segerberg, A.: The logic of connective action. Inf. Commun. Soc. **15**, 739–768 (2012)
44. Castells, M.: Networks of Outrage and Hope: Social Movements in the Internet Age. Wiley, Hoboken (2013)
45. Medaglia, R.: eParticipation research: moving characterization forward (2006–2011). Gov. Inf. Q. **29**, 346–360 (2012)
46. Przeworski, A.: Democracy and Development: Political Institutions and Well-Being in the World, 1950–1990. Cambridge University Press, Cambridge (2000)
47. Diamond, L.: The Spirit of Democracy: The Struggle to Build Free Societies Throughout the World. Macmillan, Holtzbrinck (2008)

48. Susha, I., Grönlund, Å.: eParticipation research: systematizing the field. Gov. Inf. Q. **29**, 373–382 (2012)
49. OECD: Focus on Citizens: Public Engagement for Better Policy and Services. Organisation for Economic Co-operation and Development (2009)
50. Macintosh, A.: Characterizing e-participation in policy-making. In: Proceedings of the 37th Annual Hawaii International Conference on System Sciences, p. 10. IEEE (2004)
51. European Commission: eCitizen II - Towards citizen-centered eGovernment in European cities and regions. The Baltic Institute of Finland (2013)

Implementations

Russian e-Petitions Portal: Exploring Regional Variance in Use

Andrei V. Chugunov[1], Yury Kabanov[2(✉)], and Ksenia Zenchenkova[1]

[1] ITMO University, Saint-Petersburg, Russia
chugunov@egov-center.ru, rabota.ks@mail.ru
[2] National Research University Higher School of Economics,
Saint-Petersburg, Russia
ykabanov@hse.ru

Abstract. The paper presents the results of research on factors explaining the level of e-petitioning in Russian regions. The main goal is to reveal socio-economic, technological and institutional problems the regions face, and hence to embed the Russian case into the broad research agenda on online engagement. We concentrate on the federal e-petitions portal – Russian Public Initiative – and use the automated monitoring system to analyse subnational dynamics of online petitions submissions and voting on the aggregate level. The data are used to quantitatively assess the drivers and obstacles for e-participation. Our findings suggest that more active e-petition portal usage in regions is associated with higher socio-economic and technological development, as well as with demo-cratic institutions and better e-government policy. One of the main obstacles to active use of the portal is its institutional design that at the moment provides regions with different opportunities and reinforces participation divides. Future steps, implications for automated monitoring system and some policy recom-mendations are also discussed.

Keywords: e-Petitions · e-Participation · e-Government · Russian public initiative · Resource model · Digital divide · Institutions · Russian regions · Automated monitoring system

1 Introduction

Electronic petition systems are considered an important field of inquiry within multi-disciplinary e-participation research [26, 33]. They are usually characterized as "[o]ne of the most prominent and widely used e-democracy tools," [39: 453] being "at the forefront of official, fully operational e-democracy activities of governments and par-liaments" [24: 1]. As more countries are entering the era of e-participation, more opportunities for e-participation students have arisen to test existing theories with empirical data and provide tools for new projects' assessment. Russia is not an exception. In 2012 a campaign pledge of Vladimir Putin to make the Internet work for "direct referendum democracy"[1] turned into the Russian Public Initiative portal

---

[1] Putin, V.V.: Democracy and Quality of Government [in Russian]. Kommersant, 6.02.2012, http://www.kommersant.ru/doc/1866753.

© IFIP International Federation for Information Processing 2016
Published by Springer International Publishing Switzerland 2016. All Rights Reserved
E. Tambouris et al. (Eds.): ePart 2016, LNCS 9821, pp. 109–122, 2016.
DOI: 10.1007/978-3-319-45074-2_9

(www.roi.ru, RPI), a national e-petition portal launched in April 2013.[2] Despite the fact that few petitions really gain the required number of votes and achieve any practical results, the dynamic of e-petitioning seems more complicated, especially on the regional level. While some regions are relatively active in submitting and voting for petitions, many others remain reluctant to new take advantage of opportunities for participation. Exploring and understanding these disproportions seems quite topical and relevant, both for testing existing theories and better policy-making.

This paper seeks to explore patterns, dynamics and factors of RPI usage variance by Russian regions. Using aggregate level data on RPI petitions and vote counts from the automated monitoring system developed by the eGovernance Center at ITMO University, as well as drawing on existing theories on public engagement, we run quantitative analysis to answer the following research question: *What factors can explain the regional differences in e-petitioning (submitting and voting for e-petitions)?* Although being a part of a broader online-engagement concept, RPI usage seems a valid and measurable proxy to study the Russian case and contribute to the comparative studies of e-petitions initiatives around the globe.

The paper is structured as follows. First we give an overview of the automated monitoring system developed by the eGovernance Center and used for analysing RPI dynamics. Secondly, using this tool, we describe the retrospective and current state of RPI usage. Thirdly we review existing relevant theories on online engagement, e-petitioning and e-participation. Finally, we present the results of the analysis to find predictors of e-petitioning in Russia, and define future steps of research.

2 The Dynamics of e-Petitioning in Russia: Application of Automated Monitoring Approach

2.1 Automated Monitoring Tool for RPI Analysis

Since the opening of the RPI portal in 2013, the eGovernance Center of ITMO University has launched an automated monitoring system for it.[3] To aggregate data from the portal we use the official Application Programming Interface that provides information about all initiatives and their status: name, description, votes for and against, status, progress and dates of voting. The system allows monitoring dynamics of voting for petitions at a minimum interval of one hour, overall number of votes a day, total voting in the country and regions. It also gathers data of all petitions and has several filters: (1) level of an initiative (federal, regional, and municipal); (2) region; (3) status; (4) categories (topics); (5) votes for and against, etc. In short the system allows for getting any data that is presented in the portal and is valuable for research, in a format ready for analysis. The key research topics it is tuned to address include: (1) positive feedback on the initiative; (2) negative feedback analysis; (3) issue salience

---

[2] Decree of President of the Russian Federation № 601 On General Directions of Public Government System Development [in Russian], 7.05.2012, http://rg.ru/2012/05/09/gosupravlenie-dok.html.

[3] http://analytics.prior.nw.ru/.

in certain regions and on the federal level; (4) dynamics of citizens' interest in e-petitioning facilities; (5) petition submitting and voting patterns.

Exploring data retrieved from e-participation portals has proven to make valuable contributions to understanding civic engagement, especially when it comes to the analysis of voting behavior and petitions' success and failure. Here we can mention studies of punctuated equilibrium formation in the case of the US portal *We the People* [7], voting dynamics, e-petition success factors and strategies, and media effects in the UK [12, 40], correlations of social media use and e-participation in Russia [3]. All cases show the advantages of automated monitoring of usage in several respects. First, unlike surveys, it allows work with a larger sample, if not a general population. Secondly, it helps to see detailed dynamics of petitioning and voting behaviour in short time intervals. Thirdly, the monitoring is run online to instantly access the effectiveness of e-participation that could be valuable both for citizens and decision-makers. Generally it facilitates building and testing hypotheses on citizens' behavior and issues' salience. However there are some limitations. The major one is that data cannot be analysed at the individual level of a petitioner or a voter. Hence to reveal factors of e-participation we need to use aggregate level data.

2.2   RPI and e-Petitioning in Russia: National and Subnational Dynamics

This section addresses the dynamics and state-of-the-art in RPI usage that can be revealed via the system described above. As figures show, neither is public interest in RPI stable, nor are citizens overactive in placing their ideas on the portal. In terms of e-petition submission (Fig. 1), the number of initiatives submitted declined rapidly in two months after RPI had been launched, apparently with the loss of media attention to this platform. In August 2015 a rise in activity can be seen, since several salient issues were put into the form of e-petitions, like those connected to the Ukrainian crisis (e.g. to ban destruction of foodstuffs under sanctions). However, at the moment the number of submissions is decreasing and is far from its initial rates. It should be noted that of all the e-petitions about 88 % are federal ones, meaning that citizens tend to influence the national government to establish a federal legal framework rather than to persuade regional or municipal authorities, although these levels seem to be closer to people and easier to get to. The overall voting dynamics (Fig. 2) is to a large extent preconditioned by topics' salience and media attention. The majority of votes are given to popular initiatives, while the rest gain few votes to go any further.

Although the national dynamics is as described, the picture is much more complicated when we consider a regional dimension of RPI usage. Eighty five regions of Russia demonstrate different patterns of submission and voting, as well as a repertoire of topics. About 40 % of all petitions are submitted by three regions: Moscow, the Moscow Region and St. Petersburg, while others on average constitute from 0.5 to 2.5 %. In the case of regional petitions, the abovementioned 3 regions' share is nearly 60 %. Moscow and the Moscow region are also active on the municipal level, jointly forming 26 % of e-petitions, while other regions' share varies from 0 to 5.5 % (the Nizhegorod Region). It means, first, that against the background of the decline in public interest, we have as many as 85 different dynamics of e-petitioning and voting.

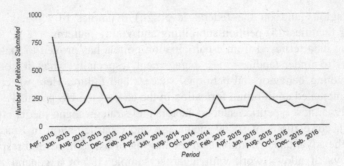

Fig. 1. The number of petitions submitted via RPI portal. (**Source**: Automated E-Petition Portals Monitoring System by eGovernance Center).

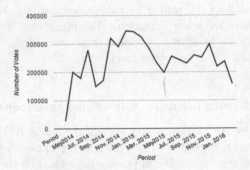

Fig. 2. The number of votes submitted via RPI portal. (**Source**: Automated e-Petition Portals Monitoring System by eGovernance Center).

Secondly, despite the democratic and mobilisation promise of RPI, there are severe disproportions of regional representation, interest to e-petition and opportunities to participate. This problem needs to be addressed in order to determine the factors affecting RPI usage and improve decision-making.

3   Exploring Divides in e-Petitioning: RPI and Russian Regions

3.1   Factors of Online Engagement: A Review and the Russian Context

To approach the question of regional disproportions in e-petitioning we employ several major theoretical perspectives and concentrate on the overlapping ideas that political participation can be shaped by social and economic characteristics, costs and incentives to participate, as well as institutional context. These theories seem quite applicable to the analysis of a broad range of participation practices and tools, both online and offline, and are frequently used by scholars.

Plenty of works emphasise that political participation is practiced by wealthier and more educated citizens, i.e. it is the socio-economic status that matters. But the causal mechanisms that unite education, occupation and income are different. A popular concept is the *Resource Model*, which includes time, money and civic skills as necessary resources to participate, and which appear to be unequally distributed and possessed by people of higher socio-economic status [6]. The rise of the Internet has provoked a debate on whether e-participation will have a mobilisation or reinforcement effect, and whether the digital divide will add to the political one [28]. Empirical literature mainly supports the reinforcement effect, although the structure of divides has been in some respects altered. The fact that those participating and petitioning online are usually men with a higher level of education and income, but usually younger than traditional offline participants, has been found in cases of the United States [4], Germany, Scotland and Norway [8, 23, 24, 32]. The patterns of inequalities are not the same everywhere. For instance, online petitions in Australia, as argued by Sheppard, can help to overcome traditional barriers like income or gender [35]. In the case of Taiwan, the research by Lee et al. shows that e-petitions may mobilise those Internet-users that will not otherwise participate offline [22]. As shown by Vicente and Novo, e-participation may alter gaps surprisingly: while in Spain a gender gap remains, unemployed people are more engaged online due to the lower costs [36]. Despite traditional resources, new Internet-skills are becoming important [27].

Another explanation of the importance of socio-economic status derives from the *Theory of Social Capital*. It seems that it can also be a meaningful driver of online participation [10], as well as its key components - high level of general and institutional trust [21], although some studies have found an inverse relationship [11]. One more theory is proposed by Inglehart, who argues that modernisation leads to culture and value shifts. Political actions, like petitions, correlate strongly and positively with the rise of postmaterialist values [14: 210–230]. So, be it due to resources, social capital or values, socio-economic characteristics may seriously affect e-petitioning.

Another perspective points out the significance of incentives and motivations, starting from Olson's theory pointing out the necessity of selective incentives or coercion for collective actions [29: 2] Although some scholars argue the Internet has altered the way collective actions work [5, 25], Olson's logic remains relevant to e-petition portals like RPI, where the activities remain voluntary and anonymous. One way to solve the free-riders problem are collective incentives, generated by social media and deliberation [37]. Another factor is political efficacy, as in the perception of ability to influence politics, or of government responsiveness [9]. Some studies have shown a strong positive relationship between e-participation and political efficacy [19, 20], meaning that citizens' intent to participate is based not only on rational calculation, but some personal perceptions of this decision.

Incentives and efficacy always operate within a certain institutional environment and are shaped by public policy. Institutions shape behavior, provide information and incentives, minimize costs and provide collective actions [13]. There are plenty of institutions that affect online participation. We can start from a political regime that may restrict free flows of information and build e-participation for the sake of legitimacy only [17, 18]. The policy towards e-government and open government also matters [36]. Finally, we should consider the institutional design of e-participation portals as well as the procedures of e-petition processing [38]. Government policy can support the mobilisation effect or reinforce existing inequalities, provide incentives or impose costs. Several works successfully combine social and institutional perspectives and reveal that resources, incentives and institutions are interrelated in shaping the level of online engagement [15, 31].

What are the implications of the theories to the Russian case? It seems that e-petitioning in the country can be explained by all of them. Public opinion polls indicate low interest in traditional petitions: just 4 % of the population in 2013 participated in such an activity, and the level of political efficacy is low. There are no signs that the Internet has changed anything.[4] While institutional trust is high towards the President (80 %), the addressees of petitions – the national Parliament, regional and municipal authorities – are trusted much less (40, 38 and 32 % accordingly).[5] It may explain why the lower the level of government is, the fewer petitions are submitted. Public participation in Russia is also highly disproportionate in social and economic terms [34]. The situation is more complicated on the regional level, while regions differ drastically in terms of economic, social and political development.

On the other hand, institutional development of e-government and e-participation in Russia should be considered. The first feature is a variety of subnational political regimes [30] and problems with democracy on the national level, which creates costs to public participation. Russia is not an exception to use e-services as legitimacy - building tool rather than to encourage online engagement [1, 2], but regions demonstrate different approaches to e-government and participation policy [16].

Another feature is the institutional design of RPI.[6] To submit or vote for a petition one must register via the Unified System of Identification and Authentication (USIA), which is also used to get e-services. Registration requires time-consuming official procedures and hence creates additional costs. To be considered by authorities a federal petition should get 100 000 votes in favor, regional or municipal petitions require 5 % of the population of the respective regions or municipalities to vote (if the population of a region is over 2 million, 100 000 votes are needed). The problem is that although the number of citizens registered in the USIA has increased since 2013, the USIA population varies drastically within the regions. To illustrate how it works we have developed a simple index of the USIA effect for federal and regional petitions (Table 1). We divide the USIA population by a number a votes needed for a petition to be considered by authorities. The higher the index rate, the higher is the probability of petition success at this stage. We see that while citizens of Moscow can cast the necessary votes nearly 28 times it is impossible for Ingushetia to make their petition successful at any level. For the majority of regions about half of users should be mobilised, which is nearly impossible.

One more institutional feature that might hinder collective incentives is the absence of deliberation opportunity on the RPI portal. It is impossible to launch a discussion or

---

[4] Policy of Non-Interference [in Russian], WCIOM, 10.04.2013, http://wciom.ru/index.php?id=236& uid=113870 .

[5] Institutional Trust [in Russian], Levada – Center, 07.10.2015, http://www.levada.ru/old/07-10-2015/ institutsionalnoe-doverie .

[6] Decree of President of the Russian Federation № 183 On Consideration of Public Initiatives Submitted by Citizens of the Russian Federation with the Usage of Internet – Resource "Russian Public Initiative" [in Russian], 4.03.2013, http://base.garant.ru/70326884/#ixzz44ErQGaGk .

information campaign within the portal, unless a petitioner has resources to attract media support from the outside. Another problem of the institutional design is that there is a special commission that decides whether a petition goes any further. It has rejected several popular initiatives and insults that such a system lacks legitimacy and trust, and in fact lowers the potential efficacy of participants and increases costs of engagement, despite the promise to change the existing institutions.[7]

Table 1. Indices of the USIA effect on regional and federal e-petitions

(**Source:** Authors calculations based on data by the Russian Ministry of Communication and Russian Statistics Service)[a]

Region	Accounts in the USIA, 2015	Votes needed for regional petition	Index of the regional USIA effect	Index of the federal USIA effect
Moscow	2 793 113	100 000	27.93	27.93
St. Petersburg	1 415 858.4	100 000	14.16	14.16
Murmansk Region	201 381.4	38 300	5.26	2.01
Novgorod Region	62 457.1	30 950	2.02	0.624
Republic of Ingushetia	19 998.4	23 200	0.862	0.2

[a]Indices are calculated as follows: we divide the USIA population by a number a votes needed for petition to be considered by authorities. The higher the index rate, the higher is the probability of petition success at this stage.

In sum, it seems relevant to apply these theories to the Russian case. *We hypothesise that higher levels of submission and voting for petitions are associated with:* a higher socio-economic performance of the region, in terms of education (1), income (2), Internet use (3) and social well-being (4); more favorable institutional and policy environment, i.e. a more democratic political regime (5), effective e-government (6) and open government (7) policies; institutional design of RPI itself (i.e. lower USIA effect (8), i.e. opportunities for e-petitioning are structured by the rules of registration.

3.2   Research Design

To test hypotheses formulated in Sect. 3.1 we use quantitative methods of correlation and regression analysis: while the former helps to see whether any relationship exists, the latter allows understanding causal mechanisms and relative weight of possible e-participation predictors. Our analysis is run on the aggregate level; we analyse the activity of the region in RPI usage rather than a particular individual's attitude. It helps

---

[7] The Paranormal on RPI, or Something Must Have Gone Wrong [in Russian], 28.11.2014, https://navalny.com/p/3976/ .

to attract aggregate data on significant characteristics of the region. There are 83 cases in our sample out of 85 Russian regions.

We use two dependent variables: the number of all e-petitions submitted by a region on federal, regional and municipal levels via RPI (RPI_PET) and the number of votes for all petitions cast in a region (RPI_VOTE). The data for variables is retrieved by means of the automated monitoring system described above. In order to solve the problem of data skewness for analysis we calculate a mean for the period of 2013–2015 and then use natural logarithm of RPI_VOTE and a square root of RPI_PET.

To measure independent variables we use data from the Russian Statistics Service, the Ministry of Communication of the Russian Federation, and indices provided by several Russian analytical centers. To overcome some problems with regional statistics we employ a mean of variables taken for the available period within 2007–2015. All variables are divided into two groups. The first one describes the key socio-economic characteristics of the region: the level of higher education (EDU), natural logarithm of middle income (INCOME), unemployment rate (UNEMP) the share of urban and rural population in the region (URBAN and RURAL), and the Internet use (INTERNET). The second group includes variables that depict institutional and policy features of a certain region: regional political regime in 2012 (REGIME) [30], e-government policy performance (eGOV),[8] information openness of regional executive authorities' websites (OPEN)[9] and the index of the USIA factor presented in the previous section, for federal and regional e-petitions (USIA_REG and USIA_FED).

3.3   Analysis, Results and Discussion

The results of correlation analysis are presented in Table 2. First, we can see a strong and positive correlation between two dependent variables, which means that some regions are overall active in petitioning and voting, others might show no signs of both types of activities. Secondly, the analysis indicates that practically all chosen variables have strong and significant associations.

The socio-economic portrait of a region active in submitting and voting for e-petitions looks as follows. First, its citizens tend to be more educated and wealthy, and a region should have less unemployment, which speaks well for resource models and the reinforcement effect of online participation. Secondly, there are clear urban/rural and digital divides among regions that affect their opportunities to participate: more urbanised and Internet-connected regions are more active in RPI use. These factors seem relatively less important for voting (especially income), which might suggest that these two forms of activities require different resources to mobilise.

Institutional settings matters no less than socio-economic characteristics. First, active e-petitioning and voting is positively correlated with a more democratic sub-national political regime (REGIME) that apparently allows more in terms of free opinion sharing, media freedom and public policy openness. Secondly, the need for

---

[8] Index of Russian Regions E-Readiness (http://eregion.ru/en/information-inequality-regions), 2007 - 2014.

[9] The "Infometer" Research Project (http://www.infometer.org/), 2013–2015.

e-government development, which is also strongly associated with e-petitioning, might be interpreted in several ways. On the one hand, it can be a technical factor: as better e-government facilities increase their importance and convenience for citizens, more people register into the USIA, which in turn means that they can submit or vote for petitions. On the other hand, we can speak about institutional learning, when authorities and citizens tend to trust and become more accustomed to new technologies as a means of political communication. On the contrary, regional government openness appears insignificant and even negative. This confirms that regional authorities are not the key point of reference for citizens. Thirdly, the analysis shows that the institutional design of RPI is crucial, particularly in the case of petition submission.

Table 2. Results of Pearson's correlation analysis (**Source**: Authors' calculations)[a]

Region	RPI_PET	RPI_VOTE
RPI_PET	1	.607**
RPI_VOTE	.607**	1
EDU	.692**	.426**
INCOME	.427**	.273*
UNEMP	−.383**	−.419**
URBAN	.563**	.504**
RURAL	−.563**	−.504**
INTERNET	.391**	.347**
REGIME	.408**	.322**
eGOV	.597**	.402**
OPEN	−.158	−.097
USIA_REG	.845**	.497**
USIA_FED	.887**	.548**

[a]Correlation is significant at the 0.01 level, * - Correlation is significant at the 0.05 level (2-tailed).

Correlation analysis cannot grasp the interrelationship of factors and tells nothing about causality, hence the second step we have taken is a multiple linear regression analysis (ordinary least squares). Our task was to look at how independent variables interact with each other and the dependent one.

The results presented in Table 3 seem confusing: while many factors have shown strong correlation, few remain significant in regression models. Models 1 and 2 take RPI_PET as a dependent variable, and show that e-petitions submission can be explained by level of education and regional e-government performance. These factors lose their significance when controlling for the USIA effect. Models 3 and 4 that use RPI_Vote as a dependent variable show almost the same situation: no factors seem significant except the USIA effect. Of course a further model specification is needed to address the problem of predictors' correlations. However the analysis shows compli-cated dynamics of e-petitioning in Russian regions, bearing in mind that the USIA effect correlates strongly with all other factors (e.g., 693** with the level of education, 532** with e-government development and, 451** with rural population). Both the explanatory force of the USIA effect and its relationship to socio-economic and institutional factors should be interpreted.

First, we assume that inequalities in the USIA registration reinforce socio-economic disparities and regional institutional context. On the one hand, since the USIA is used primarily to get public services online, we may suppose that people with higher education, income and well-being are more likely to have accounts in the system, because they tend to apply for e-services more often.[10] Rural areas and low Internet penetration, e.g. in the regions of Caucasus, are also obstacles to successful diffusion of e-services, while citizens of urbanised and Internet-developed regions, like Moscow and St. Petersburg, have much more motivation and opportunities to use them. On the other hand, regional policies matter as well. Some regions are active in promoting the USIA (Primorsky Krai, Khabarovsky Krai), some show progress in open government (Rostov and Tula regions) and e-government (Tatarstan). The citizens of such regions are hence more informed and motivated to use USIA and e-services in general. The connection of the USIA to RPI may hence divide participation among people in one region, and exacerbate the gap between regions with different levels of socio-economic and policy development. Secondly, taken broadly, the institutional design of RPI presents a range of obstacles for active e-petitioning: time costs for registration via the USIA, absence of deliberation mechanisms and need for extra media attention, as well as high number of initiatives rejected. These factors negatively affect political efficacy and collective action. But again, the importance of such problems may vary across the regions due to differences in subnational political regimes, social capital, government transparency,

Table 3. Results of regression analysis, dependent variables: RPI_PET and RPI_VOTE (**Source**: Authors' calculations)

Models	Std. Beta – Coefficients			
Variables	Model 1	Model 2	Model 3	Model 4
EDU	.435**	.083	.118	−.126
INCOME	−.041	-	-	-
UNEMP	−.023	–	−.120	−.148
RURAL	−.183	–	−.251	−.220
INTERNET	−.135	–	.020	−.004
REGIME	.082	–	.042	.040
eGOV	.385**	.161*	.098	.034
USIA_FED	-	.745**	-	.473**
Adjusted R – square	.578	.809	.188	.290
Std. error	1.77211	1.36486	1.68089	1.57207

---

[10] For instance, the most popular e-services in Russia are payments of fines for road laws violations, tax payments and applications for travel documents, which seem more topical for people with high income and education in the Russian context.

media freedom, as well as the penetration of alternative online platforms to promote initiatives (e.g. social networks).

The findings need to be further examined by more elaborate research models. Overall we conclude that though regional e-petitioning dynamics depends on political, digital and socio-economic divides, as well policy context, the institutional design of RPI strongly and negatively affects this causal relationship.

4 Conclusion, Recommendations and Future Steps

Institutionalisation of e-petitioning in Russia in a form of the official governmental portal is a new topic that requires constant attention, as changes affecting online participation patterns are constantly emerging. It is the key rationale to apply automated monitoring systems, which unlike surveys are more precise in fixing the dynamics of submitting and voting for petitions. The data retrieved from the system, as we have shown, can be applicable to a range of research tasks, and helps to understand the complexity of regional variance in use of RPI and test theories on empirical data.

In this paper we have explored some patterns of regions' inclusion in e-petitioning, and have confirmed the necessity for further research here. On the one hand, the results are well in line with the resource model and previous case studies (Germany, the USA, etc.) showing that e-petitioning replicates existing socio-economic and digital divides, as well as those works that emphasise the importance of favorable institutional environment and effective government policy for incentives, efficacy and collective actions. On the other hand, the institutional design of the petition portal seems to play a meaningful role as an obstacle to equity in regional representation.

To provide more robust results several techniques should be further applied. First, we are planning to use panel data and see the dynamics of change in factors' significance (as the USIA share is changing rapidly at the moment), as well as to use other dependent variables (like the salience of issues in a region) and more elaborate research models. Secondly, new hypotheses should be tested, for example, the role of media effects that can be done via the automated monitoring system as well. Thirdly, the analysis can be well accompanied by case studies to understand details.

The analysis shows the necessity for policy changes as well. First, extra effort should be given to provide equal representation of the regions in the USIA. For the transition period it might be better to change the procedure of petition consideration, and calculate the necessary percent of votes from the share of the USIA population in the region. Secondly, anonymity and lack of deliberation facilities should be addressed, to provide incentives for better collective actions. Thirdly, regarding the opportunities for automated monitoring, the provision of generalised data on social and demographic characteristics (age, gender and residency) could enhance the monitoring process and help to understand the existing divides to properly address them.

References

1. Åström, J., Karlsson, M., Linde, J., Pirannejad, A.: Understanding the rise of e-participation in non-democracies: domestic and international factors. Gov. Inf. Q. **29**, 142–150 (2012). doi:10.1016/j.giq.2011.09.008
2. Bershadskaya, L., Chugunov, A., Trutnev, D.: e-Government in Russia: is or seems? In: Proceedings of the 6th International Conference on Theory and Practice of Electronic Governance, 22–25 October 2012, pp. 79–82. ACM, New York (2012). doi:10.1145/2463728.2463747
3. Bershadskaya, L., Chugunov, A., Trutnev, D.: Evaluation of e-participation in social networks: Russian e-petitions portal. In.: Janssen, M., Bannister, F., Glassey, O., Scholl, H.J., Tambouris, E., Maria A. Wimmer, M.A., Macintosh, A. (eds.) Innovation and the Public Sector. IFIP EGOV 2014 and EPart 2014, vol. 21, pp. 76–83. IOS, Amsterdam (2014). doi:10.3233/978-1-61499-429-9-76
4. Best, S.J., Krueger, B.S.: Analyzing the representativeness of internet political participation. Polit. Behav. **27**, 183–216 (2005). doi:10.1007/s11109-005-3242-y
5. Bimber, B., Flanagin, A.J., Stohl, C.: Reconceptualizing collective action in the contemporary media environment. Commun. Theor. **15**, 365–388 (2005). doi:10.1111/j.1468-2885.2005.tb00340.x
6. Brady, H.E., Verba, S., Schlozman, L.: Beyond SES: a resource model of political participation. Am. Polit. Sci. Rev. **89**(2), 271–294 (1995). doi:10.2307/2082425
7. Dumas, C.L., LaManna, D., Harrison, T.M., Ravi, S.S., Kotfila, C., Gervais, N., Hagen, L., Chen, F.: Examining political mobilization of online communities through e-petitioning behavior in we the People. Big Data Soc. **2**, 1–20 (2015). doi:10.1177/2053951715598170
8. Escher, T., Riehm U.: Petitioning the German Bundestag: Political Equality and the Role of the Internet. Parliamentary Affairs. doi:10.1093/pa/gsw009. Accessed 10 Mar 2016
9. Finkel, S.E.: Reciprocal effects of participation and political efficacy: a panel analysis. Am. J. Polit. Sci. **29**, 891–913 (1985). doi:10.2307/2111186
10. de Zúñiga, H.G., Jung, N., Valenzuela, S.: Social media use for news and individuals' social capital, civic engagement and political participation. J. Comput.-Mediat. Commun. **17**, 319–336 (2012). doi:10.1111/j.1083-6101.2012.01574.x
11. Goldfinch, S., Gauld, R., Herbison, P.: The participation divide? Political participation, trust in government, and e-government in Australia and New Zealand. Aust. J. Public Adm. **68**, 333–350 (2009). doi:10.1111/j.1467-8500.2009.00643.x
12. Hale, S., Margetts, H., Yasseri, T.: Understanding the dynamics of internet-based collective action using big data: analysing the growth rates of internet-based petitions. Paper presented at the Annual Conference of the UK Political Studies Association, Cardiff, Wales, 25–27 March 2013. https://www.psa.ac.uk/sites/default/files/1050_571_0.pdf
13. Hall, P.A., Taylor, R.C.R.: Political science and the three new institutionalisms. Polit. Stud. **44**, 936–957 (1996). doi:10.1111/j.1467-9248.1996.tb00343.x
14. Inglehart, R., Welzel, C.: Modernization, Cultural Change, and Democracy: the Human Development Sequence. Cambridge University Press, New York (2005)
15. Jho, W., Song, K.J.: Institutional and technological determinants of civil e-participation: solo or duet? Gov. Inf. Q. **32**, 488–495 (2015)
16. Kabanov, Y., Sungurov, A.: Regional e-governments in Russia: institutional and resource constraints. In: State and Citizens in Electronic Environment: Theories and Technologies of Research, pp. 61–72. ITMO University, St. Petersburg (2015). [in Russian]
17. Karlsson, M.: Carrots and sticks: internet governance in non–democratic regimes. Int. J. Electron. Gov. **6**, 179–186 (2013). doi:10.1504/IJEG.2013.058405

18. Katchanovski, I., La Porte, T.: Cyberdemocracy or Potemkin e-villages? Electronic governments in OECD and post-communist countries. Int. J. Public Adm. **28**, 665–681 (2005). doi:10.1081/PAD-200064228

19. Kenski, K., Stroud, N.J.: Connections between internet use and political efficacy, knowledge, and participation. J. Broadcast. Electron. Media **50**, 173–192 (2006). doi:10. 1207/s15506878jobem5002_1

20. Kim, B.J.: Political efficacy, community collective efficacy, trust and extroversion in the information society: differences between online and offline civic/political activities. Gov. Inf. Q. **32**, 43–51 (2015). doi:10.1016/j.giq.2014.09.006

21. Kim, S., Lee, J.: E-participation, transparency, and trust in local government. Public Adm. Rev. **72**, 819–828 (2012). doi:10.1111/j.1540-6210.2012.02593.x

22. Lee, C., Chen, D., Huang, T.: The interplay between digital and political divides: the case of e-petitioning in Taiwan. Soc. Sci. Comput. Rev. **32**, 37–55 (2014). doi:10.1177/0894439 313497470

23. Lindner, R., Riehm, U.: Broadening participation through e-petitions? An empirical study of petitions to the German parliament. Policy Internet **3**, 1–23 (2011). doi:10.2202/1944-2866. 1083

24. Lindner, R., Riehm, U.: Electronic petitions and institutional modernization. international parliamentary e-petition systems in comparative perspective. JeDEM **1**, 1–11 (2009)

25. Lupia, A., Sin, G.: Which public goods are endangered? How evolving communication technologies affect the logic of collective action. Public Choice **117**, 315–331 (2003). doi:10.1023/B:PUCH.0000003735.07840.c7

26. Medaglia, R.: eParticipation research: moving characterization forward (2006–2011). Gov. Inf. Q. **29**, 346–360 (2012). doi:10.1016/j.giq.2012.02.010

27. Min, S.J.: From the digital divide to the democratic divide: internet skills, political interest, and the second-level digital divide in political internet use. J. Inf. Technol. Polit. **7**, 22–35 (2010). doi:10.1080/19331680903109402

28. Norris, P.: Digital Divide: Civic Engagement, Information Poverty and the Internet Worldwide. Cambridge University Press, New York (2001)

29. Olson, M.: The Logic of Collective Action: Public Goods and the Theory of Groups. Harvard University Press, Cambridge (1971)

30. Petrov, N., Titkov, A.: Rating of Democracy by Moscow Carnegie Center: 10 Years in Service. Moscow Carnegie Center, Moscow (2013). [in Russian]

31. Phang, C.W., Kankanhalli, A., Huang, L.: Drivers of quantity and quality of participation in online policy deliberation forums. J. Manag. Inf. Syst. **31**, 172–212 (2014). doi:10.1080/ 07421222.2014.995549

32. Saglie, J., Vabo, S.I.: Size and e-democracy: online participation in Norwegian local politics. Scand. Polit. Stud. **32**, 382–401 (2009). doi:10.1111/j.1467-9477.2009.00235.x

33. Sanford, C., Rose, J.: Characterizing eparticipation. Int. J. Inf. Manag. **27**, 406–421 (2007). doi:10.1016/j.ijinfomgt.2007.08.002

34. Sedova, N.N.: The formats, factors, and social base of civic activism in today's Russia. Sociol. Res. **54**, 284–306 (2015). doi:10.1080/10610154.2015.1123531

35. Sheppard, J.: Online petitions in Australia: information, opportunity and gender. Aust. J. Polit. Sci. **50**, 480–495 (2015). doi:10.1080/10361146.2015.1049512

36. Vicente, M.R., Novo, A.: An empirical analysis of e-participation. The role of social networks and e-government over citizens' online engagement. Gov. Inf. Q. **31**, 379–387 (2014). doi:10.1016/j.giq.2013.12.006

37. Warren, A.M., Sulaiman, A., Jaafar, N.I.: Social media effects on fostering online civic engagement and building citizen trust and trust in institutions. Gov. Inf. Q. **31**, 291–301 (2014). doi:10.1016/j.giq.2013.11.007

38. Wright, S., Street, J.: Democracy, deliberation and design: the case of online discussion forums. New Media Soc. **9**, 849–869 (2007). doi:10.1177/1461444807081230
39. Wright, S.: Assessing (e-)democratic innovations: "Democratic Goods" and downing street e-petitions. J. Inf. Technol. Polit. **9**, 453–470 (2012). doi:10.1080/19331681.2012.712820
40. Wright, S.: Populism and downing street e-petitions: connective action, hybridity, and the changing nature of organizing. Polit. Commun. **32**, 414–433 (2015). doi:10.1080/10

Efforts at the Boundaries: Social Media Use in Swedish Municipalities

Livia Norström[1](✉) and Monika Hattinger[2]

[1] Department of Business and IT, University West, Trollhättan, Sweden
livia.norstrom@hv.se
[2] Department of Engineering Science, University West, Trollhättan, Sweden
monika.hattinger@hv.se

Abstract. Social media is used by the majority of Swedish municipalities. However, the highly interactive features of social media are often not taken advantage of. The study aims to get a better understanding of why social media is not used to its full potential in the municipality. Findings from an interview study with communicators in three Swedish municipalities reveal that the motivation for using social media is often difficult to turn into action. Tensions emerging in the use of social media result in hesitation, uncertainty and a slowing down of work practice. The processes of managing the tensions are characterized by boundary crossing between different communities, such as municipal communicators, elected officials and citizens, with social media itself as an equally important actor. The processes of boundary crossing by the municipal communicators are discussed in terms of learning processes and new emerging competences that might redefine the role of the municipal communicator and hence perhaps the public servant in general.

Keywords: Social media · Municipalities · Communicators · Public servants · E-participation · Boundary crossing · New competence

1 Introduction

Social media in government has been extensively studied because of its believed potential to support the work of reaching out with information to old and new audiences, and because of its two-way communication characteristics, making available more direct communication with the target audience [1]. Social media is assumed to have potential to stimulate new opportunities for governments to share information, create dialogue, co-create content and network [2]. It generates a new and unique source of information for both governments and citizens, created in interaction with each other [3]. Beyond the possibilities of providing information and making communication available, social media enables increased transparency, which is important for building trust. Easy access and trust are necessary conditions for an increased engagement and participation [1]. Social media is also a place where many people spend their time and live their lives [4–8]. Even though different social media services come and go, the citizens' adoption of Internet and social media is still increasing. In 2015, 93 % of the Swedish population had Internet connection, while 70 % of these

E. Tambouris et al. (Eds.): ePart 2016, LNCS 9821, pp. 123–137, 2016.
DOI: 10.1007/978-3-319-45074-2_10

Internet users used Facebook (the most common social media service) now and then, and 50 % used it every day [7].

Thus, social media is an interesting possibility for e-government to explore to improve activities and services, and to strengthen democracy with increased e-participation [9]. E-government in this study is used as a term for processes related to digitalization of government with the aim to create a better, i.e., more open, transparent and accessible government [10]. E-participation is used as a subcategory of e-government and a concept that specifically addresses and problematizes the relationship between government and citizens [11–13]. E-participation tackles the transformation of power, work and activity in government, by means of Information Technology (IT) [14]. In this piece of research it is studied through the use of social media.

Municipalities represent the governmental body with the closest relationship to citizens and with activities directly linked to citizens' everyday life such as work opportunities, education and infrastructure [15]. The physical nearness and relevance of activities motivate citizens' engagement with the municipality [16]. This, in combination with the speed and directness of social media, has made social media a popular approach among municipalities for reaching out to citizens. From a Swedish municipality context, Facebook is the most commonly used social media site. In 2014, 67 % of Swedish municipalities had a general Facebook page [17].

The explosion of social media use in municipalities has generated a huge quantitative, as well as qualitative variety of use, and questions still prevail as to whether and how social media can support a transparent, participatory government [18, 19]. According to Khan et al. [1] and Dixon [20] there is little evidence in current research showing that social media use by government leads to increased citizen engagement and involvement. Even if governments do see the potential with IT for better government, most efforts have been focused on e-service and e-administration, rather than on activities more dedicated to democracy, such as increased citizen influence and improved governance [21]. From a citizen perspective, e-government is not experienced either as an activity that stimulates engagement in democratic processes [22].

Several studies suggest that governments are lagging behind in the adoption of social media compared to adoption by private people and several scholars argue that social media is not used to its full democratic potential [18, 19, 23]. Instead governments tend to use social media in a top-down manner. Information is mainly pushed out to citizens and the governments have problems keeping up with the quantity and speed of information [22]. The capabilities of social media as a generator of *user* content [24] is not taken advantage of. Rather social media is conceptualized as equivalent to traditional media and is used mainly for broadcasting, marketing and advertising [23].

In sum, interaction between government and citizens seems to be going on with tools that have potential to give citizens more power over the agenda for the interaction, but still the service is mainly one-way, top-down directed without much space for citizen influence. Hence, e-government might make everyday life more convenient to citizens with accessible information and good service, but it is critical whether it contributes to democratic decision-making for societal change.

To understand the reason for this the different relationships within e-government need to be problematized. Recent research show how democratic processes are primarily taking place between elected officials and citizens, while the relationship between the public servants and citizens are mainly characterized by service i.e. providing information [4, 21, 25]. When social media is used by public servants this service-relationship to citizens is challenged. Societal dialogues become part of the public servants' everyday work, as well as considerations of how to reach out, to what groups of citizens, with what kind of information etc. - in order to get feedback and be responsive. Public servants become important actors, not only as providers of information, but also as facilitators of democratic logics. The question is though if the public servants have the competence required for this new task and if they understand and agree on the potential of social media as a tool for increased democracy? According to Charalabidis and Loukis [26], success with social media for participation and democracy needs new organizational units with experts in the new channels, who can analyse and act on the quantitative and qualitative data generated in social media.

The current study is motivated by the curiosity to gain deeper understanding of why participatory and democratic aspects of social media are not always applied by municipalities. It aims to give a contribution to the understanding of challenges of social media use in the municipality, with a special focus on public servant communicators' (further referred to as 'communicators') interaction with the citizens on the general municipal Facebook page. The communicators are of special interest for the study since they serve as facilitators for how social media is used in the municipality and their work is constituted by a mediating role at the boundaries between the main municipal stakeholder groups: public servants, citizens and elected officials [4, 27].

Hence, the study seeks to detect and understand how communicators in the municipality handle emerging tensions and dynamics in their daily work at the boundaries between public servants, citizens and elected officials and how new work tasks emerge and challenge the professional identity. The research question is: *How is social media use challenging the work and identity of communicators in the municipality?*

2   Social Media in the Municipality

There has always been a mutual dependence between government and citizens [28]. Citizens depend on government for infrastructure and service in their everyday life and government needs citizens' trust and feedback for future work. However, with social media use in government this relationship is challenged in a variety of ways related to the foundation of social media technology.

Firstly, social media use is characterized by three different affordances: editability, persistence and spreadability [29]. 'Editability' enables the user to change the posts before sharing, 'persistence' of text, image and sound allows posts to be stored and used for later purposes, while 'spreadability' relates to functions that enable the user to directly spread the post to a large and unidentified audience [30]. All three features are of importance for the practice of social media since people must, to some extent, accept that their actions are public [29].

Secondly, social media can be understood as a technology and a philosophy based on 'user-generated content' [24] which changes the conception of online communication from a top-down, linear sender-receiver, push view, to a network perspective [31, 32]. User-generated content can be seen as a product of 'procrastinated bindings' which means the design of social media, i.e., the information filling it and the rules set up for use, is decentralized and distributed in ecosystems and platforms [33]. It is no longer the service provider (e.g. Facebook) and the organization (e.g. government) implementing the system that drives the creative process of defining functions and purpose of use. Rather, the service provider enables a space for activity, where the user of the service creates meaning in the actual use. In the case of social media in the municipality, meaning is created in the interaction between communicators, elected officials, citizens, and the service provider (in this case Facebook). The challenged relationship between e-government and citizens can thus be partly related to the social media use of these different actors.

Consequently, social media affords new arenas for citizens to engage in municipal issues, where they get fast response and avoid bureaucracy. Today most societal discussions take place away from the governmental arenas on external social media platforms [34]. The user-generated content approach means that government is no longer only informing and serving citizens. Transparency is taken to a higher level by making conversations between government and citizens potentially visible to everyone. The openness of the conversations in social media gives opportunities for learning for both municipal workers and citizens. It provides essential data to the municipality which is necessary to make better decisions and be more relevant in the information to citizens about decisions made. It also helps citizens to understand why and how decisions are being processed [23]. Responsiveness from the government's side means being transparent, accessible and relevant, which has proven to increase citizens' trust in government [35] and hence, increased trust motivates engagement [2, 23].

Three different strategies for social media use in an organization are detected in the literature: push, pull and networking strategy [36]. A push strategy means providing information while a pull strategy relates to the initiatives to direct the audience to the intended communication channels. Push and pull strategies are effective for information sharing purposes. In a government context that could be e.g. news about weather, construction work, traffic jams, and natural disasters. A networking strategy implies using social media to stimulate the audience to participate in decision-making processes by commenting, giving feedback and discussing [1]. In the context of the government organization 'in short the push and pull strategies are content-driven and only facilitate one-way communication, while the networking strategy is action-driven and promotes two-way social interactions between the government and citizens' [1, p. 100].

A 'Facebook page' is an example of a social media service that is commonly used by governments in the interaction with citizens. It is an open online page visible to everyone on the Internet and can be set up by public profiles, businesses and organizations who wish to have a professional presence on Facebook. Anyone can connect with a Facebook page by 'liking' the page and thereby become a follower of the page [37]. However, to increase the possibilities of getting the news flow of a Facebook page in the private news flow, the follower not only needs to click 'like' at the page, s/he must also interact with the page, such as like, share and comment on posts on the page [38].

3 Boundary Objects and Boundary Crossing

With help of theories of boundary crossing and boundary objects [39, 40] the study seeks to detect and understand how communicators in the municipality handle emerging tensions and dynamics in their daily work at the boundaries between public servants, citizens and elected officials and how work and professional identity of the communicators are negotiated in the social media practice.

According to Akkerman and Bakker [39], boundaries exist within all workplaces between diverse communities such as groups with different expertise and working tasks and different sociocultural background. However, boundaries can only be conceptualized *between* different communities. The goal can be the same for the different communities but when they work together contradictions and negotiations might arise. By studying the boundaries between the communities, sociocultural differences might be apparent. It is also on the boundaries where collaboration can potentially be developed and where processes of change in practice can take place and new practices develop without consensus between the different actors [39].

Individuals working at the boundaries can be understood as 'boundary crossers'. These people build bridges between the different communities but they are also representing both communities. It can be hard work being a boundary crosser but they often gain credibility in the long run for changing the work practice. 'Boundaries' both connect and disconnect different communities. They also define no man's land. That implies that boundary crossers represent all different groups of people and practices involved in the interaction but also practices beyond the ones already existing. Boundary crossers both uphold agreed boundaries and define new. In that sense boundaries are blurred and ambiguous. 'Boundary objects' have different meanings for different sociocultural communities but they have a structure that makes them recognizable and that, to some extent, unites people using them. The objects become boundary objects and get meaning in the interaction between the different communities. Boundary objects are also flexible in the sense that they sometimes have a boundary function and sometimes not. Boundary objects tend to be invisible but if we unpack them learning occasions might be visible [39].

3.1 Learning Mechanisms at the Boundaries

Akkerman and Bakker [39] use the concept of learning in a broad sense as a process of gaining new understanding, creating new practices and developing the institution. They have identified four different learning mechanisms occurring at the boundaries: 'Identification', 'Coordination', 'Reflection' and 'Transformation'. Two of the learning mechanisms - Identification and Coordination – are used in this paper to understand the boundary practice of the communicators on the municipal general Facebook page.

'Identification' relates to the learning potential of identifying related and competing practices, as well as new and competing practices. Two different identification processes are ongoing in the meeting at boundaries: 'Othering' and 'Legitimating co-existence'. Othering is a process of reshaping boundaries. When different practices meet tensions arise related to whom to identify oneself with. People tend to compare practices, and what was thought of as different practices might be more similar than expected. Overlapping practices can be perceived as a threat and consequently lead to questioning one's own identity. In the process of othering boundaries between different practices are constantly redefined and shaped in order to protect one's own identity in relation to competing practices. In the process of 'legitimating co-existence' on the other hand, a profession can change its identity to continue to exist and be accepted to co-exist with the new competitors. Acceptance or legitimization of different identities can be hard, sometimes political and often sensitive.

Learning at the boundaries is also about 'coordination' of work when consensus among participants does not exist. The learning potential in the process of coordination is not about reshaping boundaries, as in the case of identification. Coordination is rather about overcoming the boundaries to get continuity in the work flow. Four necessary resources are highlighted for coordination work: 'Communicative connections', 'Efforts of translation', 'Enhanced boundary permeability' and 'Routinization'. 'Communicative connections' are vital for coordination. These connections serve as common objects where information is passed through, but the meaning of it can come out differently for different communities. Communicative connections can be established with help of boundary objects that are shared by many. 'Efforts of translation' are processes of trying to translate the information into meaningful communication for different communities. Efforts of translation can increases the possibility of common agreement. Boundary objects can help in the process of translation. 'Enhanced boundary permeability' means that interactions on the boundaries run smoothly with no effort and no problematic discontinuities. 'Boundary permeability' can be enhanced when boundaries are repeatedly crossed. 'Routinization' refers to the process of finding regular ways of acting, i.e., to automate the practice.

Social media practice as defined above is used in this paper in order to move away from the two extreme but common scholarly conceptualizations of social media as either (1) a bare technology determining the activity and change of users and organizations or (2) something (undefined) that is socially constructed in the organization [41, 42]. Instead, in this study, communicators, citizens and social media, together and in interaction, are conceptualized as equally important actors constituted in the boundary practice.

4   Method

The paper reports on findings from a study of social media use in three Swedish municipalities. It explores work conditions for communicators at the municipal department of communication. The study focuses on the communicators' social media interactions with citizens on Facebook. Strategic and/or hands-on work related to social media was included in the work tasks for all of the communicators and that has been the criteria for the selection of respondents for the study.

4.1   Data Collection

Eight communicators at the three respective city hall communication departments were interviewed; two in one municipality, and three in each of the other two municipalities.

The eight respondents had, to some extent, different functions and tasks. Five of them were either managers or communicators responsible for the overall internal and external communication including general responsibility for social media activities. That means representing the whole municipality in central and official social media channels and to support, organize, and to some extent, control the social media work in other administrative departments. Out of the additional three respondents, one had a specialization in consumer counselling, one was a coordinator of democracy issues, and finally one was an IT manager responsible for IT infrastructure.

Social media was part of the communication strategy in all three municipalities and was supposed to complement other communication channels for external communication with citizens and organizations such as websites, online forms, telephone, e-mail, e-services and physical meetings. The respondents had all been using social media, and Facebook specifically, professionally for about two to four years but considered the municipality as being in the start-up phase of their social media use.

The interviews took between 40 and 90 min each and were transcribed verbatim and continually analysed. The interviews were followed up by a participant-observation in a reflection workshop with communicators and communication managers from seven different municipalities in the same region. A total of 16 people participated in the workshop. Three of the interviewees were also participants in the workshop. The workshop was audio recorded and afterwards listened to while notes were taken.

The data collection was guided by a general, open-minded curiosity about finding out why municipalities were not using social media to its full potential, as related research told us. The data collection was therefore inductively conducted with open-ended interviews and workshop questions [43] about the start-up of social media in the municipality, its use today and thoughts about the future (Table 1). The aim was to grasp what the respondents themselves found were important aspects of social media use.

Table 1. Main themes and the researchers' purposes of the themes from the interviews and workshop.

Question themes	Aim/purpose
Start-up process and present organisation of social media	Get an overview of how use of social media was initiated in the municipality and how it is organized today, i.e., how diffused social media is in the organization and who is responsible for which channels
Present social media use	Gain a deeper understanding of how social media is used in the municipality in general and at the management level in particular, with focus on how strategies and policies, potential opportunities and challenges are understood and acted on
Future social media use	Get insight into perceived trends, upcoming cooperation with other organizations, future opportunities and challenges – related to social media in the municipality

4.2 Data Analyses

To get an overview of the collected data material, text documents from interview transcripts and workshop notes were read through multiple times. Content analyses [44] was conducted and resulted in two main categories, described in the next section. The theoretical lens of boundary object, boundary crossing and learning mechanisms at the boundaries did not guide the categorization but instead emerged as a possible tool for interpretation and explanation of the empirical findings later on during the analyses.

5 Findings

Based on the content analysis two main categories were identified: one category mapping the motives for social media use, and one category describing the perceived tensions emerging in the social media practice.

5.1 Motives for Social Media Use

Provide Civic Information. All communicators suggested that the main motivation for using social media was to provide the citizens with fast and easily accessible civic information, which was said to be part of a transparent and open approach. Civic information could be news about upcoming events and meetings in the city council or practical information about e.g. road closures, reconstruction work or weather information.

Increase Democracy. The communicators also emphasized the importance of social media as a forum for increased democracy where citizens could ventilate opinions and feelings about their municipality. The role of the communicators was not to govern but rather to bring up relevant issues that the citizens can react to in their own forums: *'Sometimes the discussion continues by itself on social media and citizens reply to each other [...] It's a nice feeling when the citizens support us. Then we feel we are doing the right thing'*. The response they get from citizens was said to be important for their own future work: *'Social media is a way of taking the temperature of the municipality's work and to see how the citizens react on information and activities'*.

Promote the Municipality. Promoting the municipality was an additional important strategy. To promote the municipality meant to shed light on positive news, make the citizens feel proud of their region and make outsiders want to work and live in the municipality: *'It's about showing the municipality from its best side to make citizens feel proud [...] It's about external communication and a little bit of marketing'*.

Network and Manage Emergency Response. Some participants emphasized the importance of social media for building an extensive network: *'In case of an emergency it is important to be able to instantly reach out to as many citizens as possible'*. It was a common view that it is difficult to get response from citizens on social media, which is crucial to keeping the citizens in their networks. Therefore networking was about stimulating interaction, and not so much about pushing out information: '*It is less important what is posted but from the perspective of preparing for an emergency it is important to have a well-used trail and make it as much used as possible. It's about building network. To pat the users [citizens] a bit so that we get a response when it's needed*'.

The motives mentioned above were not always easy to turn into action. The following section describes the tensions emerging in the actual social media practice.

5.2   Emerging Tensions in Social Media Practice

Increased and Reduced Control. A feeling of lack of control over how the posts will be understood and responded to by citizens was expressed to be always present: '*I do a great deal of writing on the website and that's never any problem, but when I am about to write a Facebook post I always get nervous [...] what you are scared of is that the posts reach so many people and that it spreads so fast*'. The worry was related to the lack of control over what citizens' reactions would be: '*We never know what the responses will be. A post that we find positive might as well turn out to be a negative posting according to the citizens*'.

However, the feeling of reduced control was mixed with a feeling of increased control. The openness and immediacy of Facebook gives the communicator a chance to control the communication: '*The negative dialogue will always be there. That it's taking place in social media is just good because then it's visible. And we can respond to it immediately*'. In that sense, the dialogue as such was valuable, no matter whether it is driven by citizens' satisfaction or displeasure. Thus, the potential fast and vast spread was perceived as scary and uncontrollable, but also contributed to valuable opinions that could easily be followed up before it went viral, which instead increased the control over the communication.

Personal and Authoritative Content and Tone. Another cluster of challenges were related to the struggle to balance a personal content and tone with a more formal and neutral approach. Because communicators are public servants and not politicians not all topics were considered suitable in social media: '*Topics related to unemployment, housing shortage and refugee issues are better published on the website with a link to our official e-mail address in order to avoid generating racist and bitter discussions [...] the negative spreads very fast in social media so sometimes it's better to choose channels that you can more easily control*'. At the same time as they struggled to be neutral and avoid political topics they were also strongly driven by the potential of social media for openness, transparency and a democratic approach. All of the communicators emphasized the importance of letting the citizens decide what topics were important or not. Here we see a tension between the communicators' motives to be democratic and let everyone speak about anything, at the same time as they feel they need to be neutral and keep control of political discussions.

Neutrality was also about not being too personal: *'The citizens should feel that it is the public employee that is the voice of the municipality and that there is a thought behind the posting that is neutral'*. The problem with neutral postings such as civic information was that they got very little response on Facebook: *'When I post an announcement about an upcoming meeting in the city council I get no response at all'*. Instead postings with a more personal content and tone that reveals the person behind the post tended to get attention: *'They [the citizens] like when they see that we are also humans, eating lunch like anyone' [...] 'Most "liked" are posts with a good picture from the new plantings in the city, a check-in and a photo from the lunch restaurant or a man sweeping the streets from gravel after the snowy winter'*.

In the next section the findings are discussed with the aim to understand how perceived tensions and motives are challenging the work and identity of the communicators at different boundaries.

6 Discussion

The communicators are *boundary crossers* in the sense that they operate in, between and beyond different communities. The three main communities are public servants, elected officials and citizens. The communities are connected with a *boundary object*, in this case the municipal Facebook page. The Facebook page is open in its character and admits anyone in any of the communities to participate in the dialogue. The open approach allows for multiple communicative connections. One can argue that the communicators are actively participating in a boundary practice where their activities at the boundaries are challenging, but of vital importance.

The communicators' main motives for social media use are to reach out to citizens, enable forums and issues for discussion, get feedback and build networks. To do so they need to be both accountable and neutral as well as responsive and personal. This is not always easy and tensions between increased and decreased control and personal and authoritative approach on Facebook are a fact.

The discussion section continues with the argumentation that the sometimes difficult work of the communicators as boundary crossers has a lot of learning potential. The tensions occurring in the social media practice trigger processes of negotiation of both the communicators' professional identity as well as their coordination of work.

6.1 Negotiation of Identity

To be professional in social media means to balance an authoritative approach with a more personal attitude. Neutrality is important for the municipal communicators when they define their own identity and try to make it clearly separate from that of citizens, elected officials and from the private domain. The process of keeping a distance to the citizens is a process of *othering*, and involves showing good knowledge of the organization by notifying about news and events and being informative, correct and politically independent. In the process of othering the relationship between the communicators and citizens can be understood as a boundary that becomes important to control and uphold. A process of othering can also be seen between the communicators and the elected officials. Here too, the boundary is to be maintained and controlled. It is not included in the role of the municipal communicator to defend political decisions or debate sensitive issues. Therefore posts are kept neutral both in content and tone. Issues regarding sensitive concerns, such as refugees, unemployment etc. are avoided because of the lack of control of the speed and spread of potential citizens' comments. Thus, to keep a distance is at the same time to preserve a boundary.

However, the boundaries are not only controlled and upheld, they are also crossed. A main motive for social media use in the municipality is to increase democracy by involving the citizens in the municipality's activities and to receive feedback on existing work. To do so the communicators need to reach out and make citizens engaged in what they are saying and doing. They strive, to some extent, to achieve a *legitimatized co-existence* with the citizens. This includes attempts to get feedback from the citizens so they know if their work is interesting enough, and to make citizens share and co-create what they are posting. Such work means changing the social media strategy from push of content to pull of feedback as well as adopting a more persuasive networking approach [36]. The social media activity needs to enable the citizens to develop an interest in municipal activities, discuss and make sense of the activities and spread it to their own social media channels and in the physical world. For this to happen content and tone needs to be relevant, personal and clearly directed to citizens. The communicators need to cross the boundary between the citizens and the public servants, and keep one foot in the citizens' world, in order to be one of them. This is difficult since upholding the boundary and the communicator's professional identity are equally important.

The upholding and crossing of boundaries between the different communities show how the communicators negotiate their professional identity both in processes of *othering* and processes of *legitimating co-existence*. In the process of othering they try to bring out the character of a public servant and make that identity visible in the social media practice. The boundary between public servants and citizens is defined and defended. In the process of legitimating co-existence the communicators step over the boundary and become one of the citizens. This process means a practice where content and tone speak directly to the citizens. The tone is personal and the content related to citizens' everyday life.

In this sense the communicators' social media practice means working at the boundary between two or more diverse groups with one foot on each site and with the aim to build bridges. But it is also about not having a foot on any site. The lack of a home on any site is mirrored in the fact that the communicators cannot act as public servants are supposed to, because then they will not reach out. But at the same time it is not always considered professional behavior to act as a civic person because that will not give a cohesive impression of the communicator and the municipality.

6.2   Coordination of Work

Work at boundaries between diverse groups can also be understood as processes of coordination in order to maintain the work flow. Coordination requires *communicative connections, efforts of translation, enhanced boundary permeability* and *routinization*

[39]. What is posted in social media can be understood as a 'boundary object' giving rise to *communicative connection* between different actors. The municipal general Facebook page, in this case, is one place where citizens meet the municipality. Since Facebook, as used in the municipality, is open in its character and admits anyone to join the conversation, it connects not only the main target group (citizens), but also other potential actors such as e.g. private friends, family, colleagues etc. And moreover, the target group (citizens) is diverse as such since it represents the whole population. The boundary object is in this perspective connecting a potential diversity of actors, which makes it difficult for the municipal communicators to anticipate how posts are going to be understood and replied to. This uncertainty, related to tensions between strategies and what is appropriate to do as a public servant, tends to slow down the workflow. Moreover, the multiple sites and communicative connections tend to flatten the social media presence. When the audience is everyone content and tone are made neutral, and even if posts are informative and correct, they do not reach out.

To view the social media practice as an *effort of translation* can be useful in order to understand the importance of adjusting the posts to their different target groups. Efforts of translation can, in this context, be related to the efforts of making the municipal activities translated into a content and tone that is understandable, but also stimulating and engaging. Such translation of posts on Facebook have the potential to stimulate reaction from the citizens and consequently be spread. Today only one single translation of the municipal activities in social media is done. To view effort of translation as a learning process can help communicators to work with more nuanced strategies for reaching out, e.g. working more strategically with channel choice and target groups could limit the number of potential communicative connections, which might reduce the hesitation and hence improve the workflow.

All communicators in the study describe variously how they are in the start-up phase of social media use in the municipality. Even the citizens are not very experienced in how to communicate with the government in social media since social media has so far mainly been used for private communication purposes [24]. That can explain why social media practice in the municipality is to some extent still missing *enhanced boundary permeability* and processes of *routinization*, i.e., why interactions at the boundaries are demanding and the discontinuities experienced as troublesome rather than developing. However, the study shows how the communicators are repeatedly crossing boundaries to reach out and develop the municipality towards a more participatory government. And in those processes roles and identities of the communicators are constantly negotiated and developed towards what seems to be a new emerging practice within e-government.

7 Implications and Conclusion

Social media with its new technological features and user-generated content, in combination with a public audience that has long adopted social media for private use, creates new challenges for the municipality. E-participation is no longer a matter relevant only on the agenda of elected officials, but public servants, like the communicators in this study, also need to act as representatives for the democratic ideals in the municipality. Municipal service not only means serving standard formatted information to the citizens in a top-down, one-way direction. Rather, with social media as a driving force, a more participatory approach is starting to emerge, in which the citizens, together with the public servants define the agendas, arenas and activities.

However, this new way of enabling service to the citizens challenges both the identity of the communicators as well as the organization of their work. Social media constantly strains what is legitimate to do as a public servant and what ought to be done in order to improve e-participation. The different processes of negotiations outlined in this paper can be understood as learning processes towards a new role of the municipal communicator, and perhaps public servants in general. The new role means being a mediator between the elected officials and the citizens and it means a different kind of nearness to citizens. The reason for why the learning processes are sometimes hard could be explained by lack of necessary social media and e-participation skills. The communicators are trained to serve the citizens but not necessarily to enact democracy logics, i.e., problematize democratic ideals and put them into action.

The constant negotiation of identity and coordination of work, as we show in this study, can then be understood as a learning process towards improved competence for public servants where democratic logics and social media skills seem to be crucial ingredients and where boundary-crossing activities are an embedded part of the expertise.

8 Further Research

Future research could further explore the cooperation between public servants and elected officials. How explicit is this cooperation to the actors today? How could the cooperation be developed for even better e-participation? And how generalizable are the findings in this study for public servants in general? Furthermore, social media and e-participation activities are challenging not only those boundaries brought up in this article. To get a more complete understanding of the new role of the communicator, additional boundaries and boundary crossing activities need to be explored. Two examples of a boundaries that are not mentioned in this study are those between workplace and home and between different workplaces. How is the professional role of public servant communicators affected by the fact that social media blurs both spatial and temporal aspects of work, e.g. municipal Facebook feed is checked on free time and colleagues are 'friends' on private Facebook accounts? And how is social media use and e-participation negotiated in online forums such as e.g. national Facebook groups for social media in public sector?

References

1. Kahn, G.F., Yoon, H.Y., Kim, J., Park, H.W.: From e-government to social government: Twitter use by Korea's central government. Online Inf. Rev. **38**(1), 95–113 (2012)
2. Bertot, C.J., Jaeger, P.T., Grimes, J.M.: Using ICTs to create a culture of transparency: e-government and social media as openness and anti-corruption tools for societies. Gov. Inf. Q. **27**(3), 264–271 (2010)

3. Golbeck, J., Grimes, J.M., Rogers, A.: Twitter use by the US congress. J. Am. Soc. Inf. Sci. Technol. **61**(8), 1612–1621 (2010)
4. Bernhard, I.: E-government and e-governance: local implementation of e-government policies in Sweden. Doctoral thesis, The Royal Institute of Technology, Stockholm, Sweden (2014). http://www.diva-portal.org/smash/get/diva2:750658/FULLTEXT02.pdf
5. Briggs, X.S.: Democracy as Problem Solving: Civic Capacity in Communities Across the Globe. MIT Press, Cambridge (2008)
6. Richard, H., Rohm, A., Crittenden, V.: We're all connected: the power of the social media ecosystem. Bus. Horiz. **54**(3), 256–273 (2011)
7. Findahl, O., Davidsson, P.: Svenskarna och Internet 2015. En årlig studie av svenska folkets internetvanor. [The Swedes and the Internet 2015], 1st edn. iis.se (2015). www.soi2015.se. Extracted 17 Feb 2016
8. Kavanaugh, A.L., Fox, E.A., Sheetz, S.D., Yang, S., Li, L.T., Shoemaker, D.J., Xie, L.: Social media use by government: from the routine to the critical. Gov. Inf. Q. **29**(4), 480–491 (2012)
9. Jansson, G.: En legitim (elektronisk) förvaltning? Om IT-utveckling i kommunal förvaltning. Doctoral thesis, Linköping University, Linköping (2013)
10. OECD: Public sector innovations and e-Government in OECD, Government at a Glance 2013 (2013). http://www.oecd.org/gov/public-innovation/. Accessed 1 Mar 2014
11. Mossberger, K., Yonghong, W., Crawford, J.: Connecting citizens and local governments? Social media and interactivity in major US cities. Gov. Inf. Q. **30**(4), 351–358 (2013)
13. Coursey, D., Norris, D.F.: Models of e-government: are they correct? An empirical assessment. Public Adm. Rev. **68**(3), 523–536 (2008)
14. Øystein, S., Rose, J., Skiftenes Flak, L.: The shape of eParticipation: characterizing an emerging research area. Gov. Inf. Q. **25**(3), 400–428 (2008)
15. Oakerson, R.J.: Governing Local Public Economies: Creating the Civic Metropolis. ICS Press, Richmond (1999)
16. Taylor-Smith, E., Lindner, R.: Social networking tools supporting constructive involvement throughout the policy-cycle. In: Proceedings of 2010 4th International Conference on Electronic Democracy, Centre for E-Government (2010)
17. SALAR: E-tjänster och appar – hur är läget i kommunerna? E-Förvaltning och E-Tjänster i Kommunerna 2014. Sveriges kommuner och landsting [The Swedish Association of Municipalities and Regions], Stockholm (2014)
18. Bonsón, E., Torres, L., Royo, S., Flores, F.: Local e-government 2.0: social media and corporate transparency in municipalities. Gov. Inf. Q. **29**, 123–132 (2012)
19. Larsson, A.O.: Bringing it all back home? Social media practices by Swedish municipalities. Eur. J. Commun. **28**(6), 681–695 (2014)
20. Dixon, B.E.: Towards e-government 2.0: an assessment of where e-government 2.0 is and where it is headed. Public Adm. Manag. **15**(2), 418 (2010)
21. Giritli Nygren, K., Wiklund, H.G.: En IT-styrd förvaltning – en fjärde förvaltningsdoktrin? In: Lindblad-Gidlund, K., Ekelin, A., Eriksén, S., Ranerup, A. (eds) Förvaltning och medborgarskap i förändring (in English: Ongoing changes in public administration and citizenship – established practice and critical perspectives), pp. 215–227. Studentlitteratur, Lund (2010)
22. Kolsaker, A., Lee-Kelley, L.: Citizens' attitudes towards e-government and e-governance: a UK study. Int. J. Public Sect. Manag. **21**(7), 723–738 (2008)
23. Ellison, N., Hardey, M.: Developing political conversations? Social media and English local authorities. Inf. Commun. Soc. **16**(6), 878–898 (2013)
24. Kaplan, A.M., Haenlein, M.: Users of the world, unite! The challenges and opportunities of Social Media. Bus. Horiz. **53**(1), 59–68 (2010)

25. Grönlund, A.: What's in a field – exploring the eGovernment domain. Soc. Sci. Comput. Rev. **21**(1), 55–72 (2005)
26. Charalabidis, Y., Loukis, E.: Transforming government agencies' approach to eParticipation through efficient exploitation of social media. In: ECIS (2011)
27. Johannessen, M.R., Flak, L.S., Sæbø, Ø.: Choosing the right medium for municipal eParticipation based on stakeholder expectations. In: Tambouris, E., Macintosh, A., Sæbø, Ø. (eds.) ePart 2012. LNCS, vol. 7444, pp. 25–36. Springer, Heidelberg (2012)
28. Feldman, M., Hadjimichael, T., Lanahan, L., Kemeny, T.: The logic of economic development: a definition and model for investment. Environ. Plann. C Gov. Policy **34**, 5–21 (2015). 0263774X15614653
29. Leonardi, P.M.: Materiality, sociomateriality, and socio-technical systems: what do these terms mean? How are they different? Do we need them? In: Leonardi, P.M., Nardi, B.A., Kallinikos, J. (eds.) Materiality and Organizing: Social Interaction in a Technological World, pp. 25–48. Oxford University Press on Demand, Oxford (2012)
30. Scott, S.V., Orlikowski, W.J.: Great expectations: the materiality of commensurability in social media. In: Leonardi, P.M., Nardi, B.A., Kallinikos, J. (eds.) Materiality and Organizing: Social Interaction in a Technological World, pp. 113–133. Oxford University Press on Demand, London (2012)
31. Bertot, C.J., Jaeger, P.T., Grimes, J.M.: Promoting transparency and accountability through ICTs, social media, and collaborative e-government. Transform. Gov. People Process Policy **6**(1), 78–91 (2012)
32. Rainie, L., Wellman, B.: Networked: The New Operating System. MIT Press, Cambridge (2012)
33. Yoo, Y., Boland Jr., R.J., Lyytinen, K., Majchrzak, A.: Organizing for innovation in the digitized world. Organ. Sci. **23**(5), 1398–1408 (2012)
34. Sæbø, Ø., Rose, J., Nyvang, T.: The role of social networking services in eParticipation. In: Macintosh, A., Tambouris, E. (eds.) ePart 2009. LNCS, vol. 5694, pp. 46–55. Springer, Heidelberg (2009)
35. Tolbert, C.J., Mossberger, K.: The effects of e-government on trust and confidence in government. Public Adm. Rev. **66**(3), 354–369 (2006)
36. Mergel, I.: Social media adoption and resulting tactics in the US federal government. Gov. Inf. Q. **30**(2), 123–130 (2013)
37. Facebook: Facebook Help Center, Pages Basics (2010). https://www.facebook.com/help/281592001947683/. Accessed 31 Mar 2016
38. Facebook: Facebook for Business, Organic Reach on Facebook: Your Questions Answered (2014). https://www.facebook.com/business/news/Organic-Reach-on-Facebook. Accessed 31 Mar 2016
39. Akkerman, S.F., Bakker, A.: Boundary crossing and boundary objects. Rev. Educ. Res. **81**(2), 132–169 (2011)
40. Star, S.L.: This is not a boundary object: reflections on the origin of a concept. Sci. Technol. Hum. Values **35**(5), 601–617 (2010)
41. Cecez-Kecmanovic, D., Galliers, R.D., Henfridsson, O., Newell, S., Vidgen, R.: The sociomateriality of information systems: current status, future directions. MIS Q. **38**(3), 809–830 (2014)
42. Treem, J.W., Leonardi, P.M.: Social media use in organizations: exploring the affordances of visibility, editability, persistence, and association. Commun. Yearb. **36**, 143–189 (2012)
43. Kvale, S., Brinkmann, S.: Interviews: Learning the Craft of Qualitative Research Interviewing. Sage, London (2009)
44. Bryman, A.: Social Research Methods. Oxford University Press, Oxford (2015)

Motivations to Use a Mobile Participation Application

Titiana Petra Ertiö[1(✉)], Sampo Ruoppila[1], and Sarah-Kristin Thiel[2]

[1] Department of Social Research, University of Turku, Turku, Finland
{titiana.ertio,sampo.ruoppila}@utu.fi
[2] AIT Austrian Institute of Technology, Vienna, Austria
sarah-kristin.thiel@ait.ac.at

Abstract. This paper reports results on presumably the first city-wide mobile participation trial (Living Lab) examining citizen participation in urban planning, conducted in Turku, Finland, in 2015. The questions examined are the socio-economic characteristics of the application users, as well as their motivations to participate. The inclusion of online participation has been discussed widely in literature on e-participation and the digital divide, arguing for a great influence of socio-economic factors, interest in the topic, and users' online skills. The results reveal that this application, too, was used predominantly by young adults and middle-aged, highly educated, and technology savvy citizens, who were already interested in urban planning. Their use of the application was motivated primarily by the opportunity to bring their own ideas and issues to the city authorities' attention, rather than participating in missions given by the municipality or discussing planning issues with fellow citizens, indicating a rather individualistic usage interest. The location-based features and ease of use of a mobile application were valued highly. Those who idled reported predominantly technical challenges with the app.

Keywords: Mobile application · Citizen participation · Urban planning · Digital divide

1 Introduction

Digital inclusion is a key question for governance, since many public engagement opportunities and services have moved online. One area of interest has been urban planning, in which variations of Public Participation Geographic Information Systems (PPGIS) have become widely used for collecting citizens' viewpoints. Recently, the increasing usage of smartphones and tablets has created new possibilities for mobile participation [1–6]. A plethora of so-called reporting apps have emerged, enabling citizens to send maintenance requests to the local authorities. Another type of participation app employs the so-called citizen sensing approach, where built-in sensors in citizens' mobile devices collect the data and submit it to a back-end database [7]. These applications tie

© IFIP International Federation for Information Processing 2016
Published by Springer International Publishing Switzerland 2016. All Rights Reserved
E. Tambouris et al. (Eds.): ePart 2016, LNCS 9821, pp. 138–150, 2016.
DOI: 10.1007/978-3-319-45074-2_11

"the problem to be solved" to a place, thereby situating engagement [1]. In fact, situated (in-situ) engagement is one of the biggest promises of mobile participation: it enables citizens to discuss topics of interest at the particular location where they occur [4]. However, little is known about which citizens would be interested in using mobile participation apps for civic engagement and why. Neither have the questions of digital inclusion yet been investigated in the realm of mobile participation.

This paper is based on - to the best of our knowledge - the first city-wide trial of mobile participation in urban planning carried out in the world to date. The mobile application Täsä ("here" in Turku dialect), developed in the research project "Building Pervasive Participation" (b-Part; www.b-part.eu), was tested in a Living Lab run in cooperation with the City of Turku (Finland) between June and October 2015. The app enabled citizens to add and discuss georeferenced urban development ideas (referred to as contributions in the app) visible to all users. Any contribution could be enhanced by adding a title, short description, photo, feeling, location, and tags (e.g. green areas, transportation, culture) (see Fig. 1). Most of the features were implicitly recognisable to users familiar with social media. Contributions could be commented and voted upon, forming the bi-directional communication between city officials and citizens, as well as among citizens. Users could further choose to participate in so-called missions, which were in-app tasks given by the municipality to solicit feedback on certain topics. In fact, both city officials and citizens could create missions, but in practice only the officials did. For example, one mission invited citizens to vote and comment on the question of whether to build a new light-traffic bridge in a particular place in Turku.

The Täsä application was built on the participatory sourcing approach, meaning that users were encouraged to contribute their own ideas and voice concerns (bottom up), which were then processed by authorities to eventually inform decisions. Täsä extended this approach by putting a main focus on the communication between citizens and city authorities. In this respect, city officials and urban planners responded to citizens' input, but also asked for input on specific topics (missions) themselves (top down). During the Living Lab, Täsä was formally one official participation channel of the municipality.

Täsä was available for Android, iOS, and Windows phones free of charge. 780 users downloaded Täsä, of which one third (32 %) produced content (contributions, comments, votes, or likes) within the app. The Täsä website was visited by more than 1 700 unique users. Täsä was marketed through social media (predominantly Facebook) by the municipality, as well as by the research team, using flyers, mailing lists, and electronic newsletters. It was also featured in several stories published in local newspapers and on radio. Information was also disseminated via speaking engagements and events organised for neighbourhood associations. Täsä had its own website with video tutorials on how to download the app and how to use it. In addition, users could contact the research team and ask for instructions, if needed.

Fig. 1. Screenshots of the Täsä application used in Turku. Map view (left) and contribution list (right)

Drawing on the results of the Täsä user surveys, this paper discusses what added value mobile applications can bring to citizen participation. More precisely, we will discuss who chose to participate in Turku's urban planning through the Täsä application, and why. The study contributes to the growing literature on digital inclusion in terms of the motivations for adopting new technologies, the factors encouraging their usage, barriers to adoption, and benefits of implementation.

2   Inclusive E-Participation and Motives for Adopting New Technologies

The inclusion of self-selected participants online has been discussed widely in literature on e-participation and - more broadly, including adopting new technologies - on the digital divide, arguing for a great influence of socio-economic factors, interest in the topic, and users' online skills.

2.1   Inclusive E-Participation

Perhaps the greatest promise of e-participation is its potential to broaden the pool of participants. Compared to traditional (off-line) forms of participation, e-participation can involve almost a limitless number of participants. Meanwhile, the greatest challenge remains the inclusion of disengaged citizens and also giving less articulated groups a voice in the political arena.

The popularity of e-participation channels has been on the rise. For example, in Germany, online petitions have been increasing in number, as have registered users of official participation portals [8]. Compared to face-to-face participation, e-participation has a number of other advantages. For instance, [9] enumerates the anonymity of participants, as well as the speed and reach of ideas posted online. The adoption of new technologies has been boosted with the shift towards Web 2.0, which has emphasised the role of citizens as active knowledge producers [10]. These new skills that citizens have learned have proven to be transferable to many fields of activity, including participatory urban planning [11].

The empirical results of various e-participation platforms, however, have given little support for enhancing inclusive participation, in terms of representativeness at least. The "usual suspects" in online participation are well-educated men, already active in other areas of political life [8,12]. While they may propose useful arguments and various relevant viewpoints, the challenge remains that this may also reinforce previously existing power imbalances [13]. Conversely, the characteristics of non-participants (feminine gender, low social-economic status, age, ethnic background, disability) have significant consequences for the process and the outcomes [14]. The empirical studies on e-participation indicate that interest in it reflects interest in political participation in general. Interests in politics, time, money, and (civic) skills are the most important predictors of political participation [15]. The specific novel technology, however, may require the effort of learning new skills, which might raise the participation barrier [16]. On the other hand, new technologies may also be a tempting factor. For instance, some studies indicate that citizens would prefer to use social media tools to engage with planning [17,18].

Despite benefits and pitfalls, scholars and pundits alike agree that e-participation tools have gained momentum and interest [8] especially because they support deliberative processes among participants, and between citizens and public officials [19]. The lack of statistical representativeness "does not necessarily mean a poverty of views, information, and arguments and low quality deliberation" [19, p. 2].

2.2   The Digital Divide in the Mobile Internet Era

The exclusion caused by the adoption of new technologies has been discussed in the literature on the digital divide. The traditional topic of this discussion has been access to the Internet and, more recently, differentiation in its usage. The discussion is useful in examining the gradual diffusion of Internet-related participation technologies. It has been asserted that socio-economic background factors (notably education, income, age) are associated with Internet access [20,21]. As access to the Internet became more common, the focus of the discussion shifted to differences in what the Internet is used for, mediated by online skills (and indirectly education), a phenomenon known as the second-level digital divide [22,23]. The current debate is focused on differences in digital skills and the consequent differentiation between types of users [21,24–26]. [27] summarizes how the variety of activities online is a critical indicator of digital inequalities. Far from being dismissed, socio-economic factors influence usage far beyond skills; more affluent people engage in more competence-enhancing activities compared with lower income people, whose usage concentrates on entertainment [24,25,28]. Consequently, the benefits are spread unequally; "those who are already in more privileged positions are more likely to use the medium for activities from which they may benefit" [28, p. 615]. Considerable effort has been put into investigating the users of online technologies and the disadvantages of low or non-usage [29,30].

Nonetheless, overall Internet access continues to improve, and consequently basic digital skills are becoming increasingly common sense. Moreover, the mobile Internet offers an access breakthrough for lower socio-economic groups worldwide [31]. If users' skills are limited or the technology is modest, disadvantaged groups might not be able to exploit the potential of mobile phones to the fullest, which can lead to consecutive exclusions online [32]. The mobile Internet might reduce the access divide but widen the usage gap [33]. Digital skills are directly associated with online participation, including expressing an opinion, or participating in consultation or petitioning [34].

In addition to material access, skills, and usage, motivation continues to be the most important factor mediating digital inclusion [20]. Hence, there is a constant concern that if users do not see value in using the Internet for a particular purpose, they leave it unused despite having access and skills [20]. [35] identify an emotional (technophobia) and a rational factor (no need for a specific technology) in such a lack of usage motivation. Further, they found that the relation between access quality and skills fully mediates motivation in content-related skills [35].

The perceived usefulness of a technology affects users' motivation to try it, leading to its use or not. [36] extended the Technology Acceptance Model (TAM) and applied it to Internet use and non-use. [30] found that non-users have negative attitudes towards online technologies and feel uncomfortable using them. Such attitudes have been attributed to lower perceived skills in handling technologies (indirectly mediated by education), coupled with a lack of confidence [37]. [30] also found that education is the strongest predictor when differentiating between broad and narrow uses. Another study showed that positive attitudes towards online technologies were significant predictors for differentiating between low-users and non-users [29].

The rapidly increased use of the mobile Internet, coupled with increased social media usage, has also opened new avenues for electronic participation. Through the myriad of social media applications, citizens learn new mobile usage skills. Social media, including the likes of Facebook and Twitter, are already ranked third as the preferred interaction channels between citizens and a municipality, after email and municipal websites [38]. [39] found that social media use explains more variance than socio-economic factors in the political participation of young people. In part, this finding is explained by the ease of engagement: liking, sharing, and retweeting entail less effort than commenting on a post [40]. Attaching a photo as well as posting about public services (transportation, urban planning) also elicits a high level of engagement [40]. The effects of attaching a location to a post are unknown. Especially on mobile phones, attaching a location to a social media post is easy and quick, thanks to the GPS embedded in the phone. The skills and mobile communication practices that citizens appropriate through social media are easily transferable to other contexts, including participatory urban planning.

3   Research Questions and Data

The research question leading this inquiry is what characterised the citizens who adopted the new mobile participation tool, and what were their motivations for using it? Specifically, we are interested in

RQ1. Who signed up for the Täsä application trial?

RQ2. What was their initial motivation to download the app?

RQ3. What factors encouraged usage of the app?

RQ4. What factors discouraged usage of the app?

The first two questions are answered based on the data of a pre-survey of registered users of the Täsä application. After downloading the app and registering, a pop-up window appeared on their device containing the survey, with questions regarding their social background (gender, age, educational achievement), experience with mobile devices, and attitudes towards urban planning and politics. During the trial, reminders were sent to complete the survey. 185 people, out of 780 who downloaded the app, answered the pre-survey.

Answers to the last two questions are based on the data of a post-survey, which was sent out to all registered users at the end of the trial. In the post-survey, respondents were asked about their experiences in using the application, including motivating factors, evaluations of the app and mobile participation, and improvement ideas. This survey was answered by 97 users. The overlap of those who answered both the pre- and post-survey was rather small (39 users). In addition, to address the last question more profoundly, we conducted, during a period late in the trial, 12 telephone interviews with passive users, meaning those who had downloaded the app and created user accounts but had not produced any content in the app. These people consisted of onlookers, who used the app just for observing other people's input, and those who quickly abandoned usage altogether. Passive users were sampled randomly and approached by e-mail initially. Interviews were conducted until data saturation was achieved. Interviews were recorded after the participants were informed and had consented. Participants were asked about their impression of the app, factors that hampered their participation, and features that would make the application more appealing.

4   Findings

4.1   Täsä Application Users

The self-selected users of the mobile participation application were mostly young adults and middle-aged people with a high level of education - like a number of previous e-participation trials. Men outnumbered women, but not greatly. Compared with the inhabitants of Turku (Fig. 2), for Täsä the 21–40 age group was considerably over-represented (72 %), but Täsä lacked participants younger than 21 and especially senior citizens. The average education level of participants was high: more than half had an academic degree - another considerable difference compared to the city population overall. Most respondents reported good to excellent perceived skills in using mobile phones (89 %), which also presumably differentiates them from the average.

Although the trial was intended for all smartphone users (more than 70 % of the Finnish population by the time of the trial), the users needed to own a device with a rather recent operating system for the application to work well, which favoured the participation of people of active working age, with a good socio-economic status, and good mobile phone usage skills (and/or requirements for their phones), which is a classic restricting access factor of the digital divide.

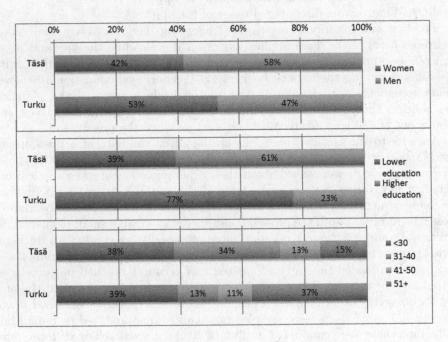

Fig. 2. Täsä users compared with the Turku population: gender, education, and age. Source: Pre-survey of registered users of the application (N = 185) and the City of Turku population statistics.

4.2   Motivation to Download the App

The results indicate the two most important reasons to download and start using the application. First, almost half of the respondents were initially motivated fairly or very much by curiosity to test the mobile participation application (Fig. 3). Citizens also rated highly their desire to be informed about ongoing discussions about Turku's urban planning. Interestingly, taking action by using the

Täsä app to communicate a specific idea of something in need of change to the City of Turku, or getting engaged in dialogue on planning issues with fellow citizens, was reported as less important. Secondly, when we asked about respondents' general interest in Turku's urban planning, almost all of them were very (64 %) or fairly interested (30 %), which indicates that they did not download the app solely because of their curiosity in testing the app.

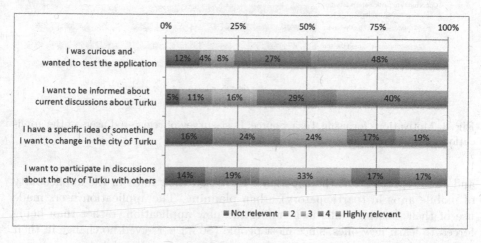

Fig. 3. Initial motivation to download the Täsä application. Source: Pre-survey of registered users of the application (N = 185)

4.3   Factors Encouraging Usage

If one of the main reasons to download the application was curiosity to test a new tool, at the end of the trial, we inquired what factors actually motivated its usage (Fig. 4). In hindsight, the greatest motivator was the opportunity to bring one's own idea to the attention of city authorities, which 45 % of respondents reported as influencing their participation very much. On the other hand, receiving feedback from the authorities motivated people much less than anticipated [2]. In addition, participating in missions (tasks) given by the city administration in the app and communicating with peers were not rated highly. In fact, people stated a will to use (and also used) the app largely as a reporting tool, making little use of its many interactive features, which functioned akin to social media. This finding indicates a more individualistic usage mode than expected.

Affordances specific to the mobile participation tool were also given great importance, which is a promising result regarding further development. The ability to give in-situ feedback, as well as ease of mobile participation usage, motivated the participants highly.

When asked, as many as 46 % of post-survey respondents reported they had learned fairly or very much about how a mobile app could assist urban planning,

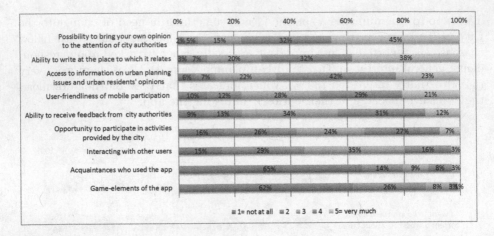

Fig. 4. Motivations for using Täsä. Source: Post-survey of registered users of the application (N = 97).

and 71 % reported that the experience increased their faith in the applicability of mobile apps in (participatory) urban planning. The application users made use of their existing skills in handling the new application, rather than being forced to learn new ones, since most people (86 %) perceived no change in their general mobile device using skills after participating in the trial.

4.4   Factors Discouraging Usage

In order to understand which factors discouraged the use of the application, interviews were conducted with passive users, meaning those who had created user accounts, but had not produced any content in the app. The interviews confirmed that these people were partly onlookers and partly those who had quickly abandoned usage altogether. Unsurprisingly, the main reason for abandoning usage was technical challenges in their many forms. Some had trouble downloading and registering, some complained about the bugs in the app, while others would have preferred to participate through a webpage using a personal computer rather than a mobile phone. Even when active participation was not the case, interviews revealed that users still read and followed up on content posted in Täsä because they were interested in accessing topical information regarding Turku's urban planning. When we asked interviewees what it would take for them to use the app, the theme of the webpage - mobile optimized webpage - surfaced again. Another feature that would enhance participation would be a better structure for the content.

5   Conclusions and Discussion

The rapid development of mobile technologies has raised interest in broadening the realm of e-participation towards mobile participation [3]. However, applying new technologies to societal matters, such as participatory urban planning, comes with concerns regarding the "digital divide", meaning limiting factors influencing their usage.

This paper has reported results on the socio-economic characteristics of participants and their motivations to participate, analysed through surveys conducted when they registered as users and after the large mobile participation trial (Living Lab) conducted in Turku, Finland, in 2015.

The self-selected users of our mobile participation application were mostly young adults and middle-aged people with a high level of education, and a great interest in urban planning topics. As in a number of other previous e-participation initiatives, Täsä users insufficiently represented Turku's inhabitants. However, while Täsä might have given a voice to people in advantageous positions, it certainly gave it to those who have been notoriously absent from traditional face-to-face participation. For those young adults and middle-age people, perhaps at the busiest stages of their lives, juggling job and family responsibilities, mobile participation proved its potential for civic engagement. Mobile participation's affordances, such as ubiquity and simplicity, appealed to this particular group, to bring their issues to the municipality's attention. Hence, the results suggest that mobile participation can have a complementary role in developing tools for citizen engagement.

Aiming for inclusive participation, the easiest step forward would be to introduce a mobile-optimised web-based participation platform alongside the mobile application. Websites are well-suited to involve those with older phones or those who take time to ponder by the keyboard. This idea surfaced in the feedback received during the trial, the interviews, and open questions in the post-survey. Our results are in line with recommendations that in-situ engagement should be complemented with ex-situ engagement [1]. Unsurprisingly, we found that the technical challenges quickly displaced the initial motivation to try a new application, and led to passive usage or giving up use of the app altogether. Thus user-friendliness, ease of use, and technical reliability are certainly drivers of loyalty.

The self-selection process of the users was driven by curiosity towards the new application, confirming the "novelty effect" [41] as one motivator. Courtois and Verdegem regard confidence in one's own skills to be indirectly supported by motivation [35]. In a similar manner, most of our users reported excellent mobile usage skills from the beginning. We can only estimate how much the "second-order digital divide" [22] played a role among our young adults and middle-aged user groups, and how much their skills and their trust in them affected their self-selection. Nonetheless, the same users reported learning a lot about how a mobile application can contribute to developing participatory urban planning. This result indicates that early adopters of a technology expand their knowledge-base, which in turn helps them to better navigate future participation opportunities.

Participation in the Täsä trial happened mainly out of an interest in the city's urban planning. The results indicate that most citizens were motivated to use the mobile participation opportunity primarily as a tool to bring their own ideas to the attention of the city authorities. Despite the fact that the app had many features affording interaction among citizens, as well as between citizens and city officials, the respondents were much less interested in receiving feedback from the municipality, participating in missions (tasks) given by the municipality, or discussing planning ideas with fellow citizens. These findings on the motivation to use the app primarily independently are slightly surprising. Moreover, they also conflict with previous studies, which have found that citizens are eager to engage with planners using social media tools [17,18]. Living labs are highly context specific and their rollouts might have unexpected turns [42]. Perhaps the technical difficulties confronted by many users might explain why the application did not develop into a more socially active platform. On the other hand, as many as half of the post-survey respondents (52 %) were so-called passive users, who might have reflected upon an intention rather than the actual experience of using the app. Providing further insights into the relation between intentions and actual usage (based on saved back-end data) is beyond the scope of this paper, but will be addressed in a future analysis. Nevertheless, the large number of passive users who responded to the post-survey, giving constructive critique and encouraging comments, indicates a broad interest in an improved app. Such findings are consistent with the Technology Acceptance Model (TAM) and suggest a positive future usage intention, after realising the potential of mobile apps as participatory tools in urban planning.

Acknowledgements. The research project Building Pervasive Participation was funded by JPI Urban Europe. The authors would like to thank the two anonymous reviewers for their constructive comments.

References

1. Korn, M.: Situating engagement: ubiquitous infrastructures for in situ civic engagement. Doctoral dissertation. Aarhus University (2013)
2. Ertiö, T., Ruoppila, S.: Supporting "Participation" in mobile participation. In: Janssen, M., et al. (ed.) Electronic Government and Electronic Participation. Innovation and the Public Sector, vol. 21, pp. 3–12. IOS Press, Amsterdam (2014)
3. Kleinhans, R., Van Ham, M., Evans-Cowley, J.: Using social media and mobile technologies to foster engagement and self-organization in participatory urban planning and neighbourhood governance. Plann. Pract. Res. **30**(3), 237–247 (2015)
4. Ertiö, T.: Participatory apps for urban planning - space for improvement. Plann. Pract. Res. **30**(3), 303–321 (2015)
5. Desouza, K., Bhagwatwar, A.: Citizen apps to solve complex urban problems. J. Urban Technol. **19**(3), 107–136 (2012)
6. Evans-Cowley, J.: There's an app for that. Int. J. E-Plann. Res. **1**(2), 79–87 (2012)
7. Höffken, S., Streich, B.: Mobile participation: citizen engagement in urban planning via smartphones. In: Citizen E-Participation in Urban Governance: Crowdsourcing and Collaborative Creativity, pp. 199–225. Information Science Reference, Hershey (2013)

8. Lindner, R., Riehm, U.: Broadening participation through e-petitions? An empirical study of petitions to the German parliament. Policy Internet 3(1), 1–23 (2011). Article 4

9. Brabham, D.C.: Crowdsourcing the public participation process for planning projects. Plann. Theory 8(3), 242–262 (2009)

10. Kubicek, H.: The potential of e-participation in urban planning: a European perspective. In: Handbook of Research on E-Planning: ICTs for Urban Development and Monitoring, Hershey, PA (2010)

11. Saad-Sulonen, J.: Combining participations. Expanding the locus of participatory e-planning by combining participatory approaches in the design of digital technology and in urban planning. Doctoral Dissertation. Aalto University (2014)

12. Jonsson, M.E.: Democratic innovations in deliberative systems – the case of the Estonian citizens' assembly process. J. Public Deliberation 11(1) (2015). Article 7. Available: http://www.publicdeliberation.net/jpd/vol11/iss1/art7. Accessed 14 Mar 2016

13. Carman, C.J.: Barriers are barriers: asymmetric participation in the scottish public petitions system. Parliamentary Aff. 67, 151–171 (2014)

14. Aitken, M.: E-planning and public participation: addressing or aggravating the challenges of public participation in planning? Int. J. E-Plann. Res. 3(2), 38–53 (2014)

15. Brady, H.E., Verba, S., Schlozman, K.L.: Beyond SES- a resource model of political participation. Am. Polit. Sci. Rev. 89(2), 271–294 (1995)

16. Steinmann, R., Krek, A., Blaschke, T.: Analysis of online public participatory GIS applications with respect to the differences between the US and Europe. In: Proceedings of the Urban Data Management Symposium, Chioggia, Italy (2004)

17. Evans-Cowley, J., Hollander, J.: The new generation of public participation: internet-based participation tools. Plann. Pract. Res. 25(3), 397–408 (2010)

18. Williamson, W., Parolin, B.: Web 2.0 and social media growth in planning practice: a longitudinal study. Plann. Pract. Res. 28(5), 544–562 (2013)

19. Aitamurto, T., Landemore, H.: Crowdsourced deliberation: the case of the law on off-road traffic in Finland. Policy Internet (2016). (early view)

20. Van Dijk, J.: The Deepening Divide Inequality in the Information Society. SAGE, London (2005)

21. Deursen, A., van Dijk, J., Peters, O.: Rethinking internet skills: the contribution of gender, age, education, internet experience, and hours online to medium- and content-related internet skills. Poetics 39, 125–144 (2011)

22. Hargittai, E.: Second-level digital divide: differences in people's online skills. First Monday 7 (2002). http://firstmonday.org/article/view/942/864

23. Deursen, J., van Dijk, J.: The digital divide shifts to differences in usage. New Media Soc. 16(3), 507–526 (2013)

24. Deursen, A., Courtois, C., van Dijk, J.: Internet skills, sources of support, and benefiting from internet use. Int. J. Hum.-Comput. Interact. 30(4), 278–290 (2014)

25. Van Dijk, J., Deursen, A.: Digital Skills: Unlocking the Information Society. Palgrave Macmillan, New York (2014)

26. Zillien, N., Hargittai, E.: Digital distinction: status-specific types of internet usage. Soc. Sci. Q. 90, 274–291 (2009)

27. Wei, L.: Numbers matters: the multimodality of internet use as an indicator of the digital inequalities. J. Comput.-Mediated Commun. 17, 303–318 (2012)

28. Hargittai, E., Hinnant, A.: Digital inequality. Differences in young adults' use of the internet. Commun. Res. 35, 602–621 (2008)

29. Reisdorf, B.: Non-adoption of the internet in Great Britain and Sweden: a cross-national comparison. Inf. Commun. Soc. **14**(3), 400–420 (2011)
30. Reisdorf, B., Groselj, D.: Internet (non-)use types and motivational access: implications for digital inequalities research. New Media Soc. Online First (2015). doi:10.1177/1461444815621539
31. Pearce, K.E., Rice, R.E.: Digital divides from access to activities: comparing mobile and personal computer internet users. J. Commun. **63**, 721–744 (2013)
32. Hargittai, E., Kim, S.J.: The Prevalence of Smartphone Use Among a Wired Group of Young Adults. Institute for Policy Research Northwestern University, Working Paper Series (2010). www.ipr.northwestern.edu/publications/docs/workingpapers/2011/IPR-WP-11-01.pdf. Accessed 14 Mar 2016
33. Mascheroni, G., Ólafsson, K.: The mobile internet: access, use, opportunities and divides among European children. New Media Soc. **17**, 1–23 (2015)
34. Vicente, M.R., Novo, A.: An empirical analysis of e-participation. The role of social networks and e-government over citizens' online engagement. Gov. Inf. Q. **31**(3), 379–387 (2014)
35. Courtois, C., Verdegem, P.: With a little help from my friends: an analysis of the role of social support in digital inequalities. New Media Soc. 1–20 (2014). doi:10.1177/1461444814562162
36. Porter, C.E., Donthu, N.: Using the technology acceptance model to explain how attitudes determine internet usage: the role of perceived access barriers and demographics. J. Bus. Res. **59**(9), 999–1007 (2006)
37. Helsper, E.J.: The Emergence of a Digital Underclass. Digital Policies in the UK and Evidence for Inclusion. LSE Media Policy Project Brief 3 (2011). http://www.lse.ac.uk/media%40lse/documents/MPP/LSEMPPBrief3.pdf. Accessed 14 Mar 2016
38. Johannessen, M.R., Flak, L.S., Sæbø, Ø.: Choosing the right medium for municipal eParticipation based on stakeholder expectations. In: Tambouris, E., Macintosh, A., Sæbø, Ø. (eds.) ePart 2012. LNCS, vol. 7444, pp. 25–36. Springer, Heidelberg (2012)
39. Xenos, M., Vromen, A., Loader, B.D.: The great equalizer? Patterns of social media use and youth political engagement in three advanced democracies. Inf. Commun. Soc. **17**(2), 151–167 (2014)
40. Bonsón, E., Royo, S., Ratkai, M.: Citizens' engagement on local governments' Facebook sites. An empirical analysis: the impact of different media and content types in Western Europe. Gov. Inf. Q. **32**(1), 52–62 (2015)
41. Kormi-Nouri, R., Nilsson, L., Ohta, N.: The novelty effect: support for the novelty-encoding hypothesis. Scand. J. Psychol. **46**(2), 133–143 (2005)
42. Åström, J., Ruoppila, S., Ertiö, T., Karlsson, M., Thiel, S.: Potentials and challenges of a living lab approach in research on mobile participation. In: Adjunct Proceedings of the 2015 ACM International Joint Conference on Pervasive and Ubiquitous Computing and Proceedings of the 2015 ACM International Symposium on Wearable Computers, pp. 795–800. ACM, New York (2015)

Policy Formulation and Modelling

A Web-Based Information Market to Support Policy Decision Making

Niki Nikolakakou, Efthimios Bothos[✉], and Gregoris Mentzas

Institute of Communications and Computer Systems,
National Technical University of Athens, Athens, Greece
{nikolaka, mpthim, gmentzas}@mail.ntua.gr

Abstract. Reliable and timely information about current economic and environmental conditions is crucial for policy makers to take decisions and for steering agents' expectations formation about the state of the economy. While the usefulness of monitoring expectations, opinions and sentiments of economic agents is undoubted, one can argue that existing indices are based on a selected number of surveys and a low monitoring frequency resulting in a partial view of more complex dynamics. In this paper we present a web based tool based on the concept of Information Markets that can be used to aggregate expectations on policy indices and provide accurate and timely information to policy makers and policy modellers.

Keywords: Policy modelling · Information markets · Predictions of policy indices

1 Introduction

Reliable and timely information about current economic and environmental conditions is crucial for policy makers to take decisions and for steering agents' expectations formation about the state of the economy [1]. Nowadays several institutions in industrialized countries collect data regarding expectations on the outcome of future events and periodically (monthly, quarterly etc.) release aggregated indices. Many policy makers and modellers take recourse to survey evidence to measure current conditions in the economy; policy related reports frequently point to survey evidence when describing the current macroeconomic situation. For example, the Survey of Professional Forecasters (SPF) and the Purchasing Manager Indices (PMI) have gained great attention as they are regularly mentioned in monetary policy communications [2]. Other approaches rely on data of higher frequencies, including financial series and monthly data on real economic activity. The first category is often labelled as 'soft' data, while the latter as 'hard' indicators of real activity that measure certain components directly (e.g. industrial production as evidence of the GDP). Soft data are available promptly, while real activity data are published with a significant delay. On the other hand, the hard data contain more precise signals for indices [2]. Related work (see e.g. [3]) shows that these indices closely follow the economic situation as described by variables, like GDP, inflation or interest rates, and even anticipate turning points in the economic cycle.

Published by Springer International Publishing Switzerland 2016. All Rights Reserved
E. Tambouris et al. (Eds.): ePart 2016, LNCS 9821, pp. 153–161, 2016.
DOI: 10.1007/978-3-319-45074-2_12

While the usefulness of monitoring expectations, opinions and sentiments of economic agents is undoubted, one can argue that existing indices are based on a selected number of surveys and a low monitoring frequency resulting in a partial view of more complex dynamics. For example, the first (advance) data release of GDP growth for the current quarter is released about six weeks after the end of the quarter [4]. In order to gauge the continuously evolving state of the real economy alternative sources of information need to be employed. Moreover, survey based methodologies are often not incentive compatible and therefore can be of low precision in revealing the 'real' preferences and expectations of experts and the population at large [5].

In this paper we present a web based tool based on the concept of Information Markets that can be used to aggregate expectations on policy indices and provide accurate and timely information to policy makers and policy modellers. The paper proceeds as follows. Section 2 provides an overview of Information Markets, Sect. 3 describes the design elements of our tool while Sect. 4 presents a walkthrough usage scenario. In Sect. 5 we provide insights on the current status of our work and we conclude Sect. 6 with our final remarks and next steps.

2 Overview of Information Markets

Information Markets (IMs) rest on the concept of bringing a group of participants together via the Internet and allowing them to trade shares of virtual contracts which yield payments based on the outcome of unknown future events [6]. Contract prices provide a reasonable estimate of what the participants (traders) in aggregate believe to be the probability of the future events, and as such, markets are able to generate forecasts. IMs are designed and run for the primary purpose of mining and aggregating scattered among traders information and subsequently use of this information in market values in order to make predictions about specific future events [7].

There are various theories supporting the information and expectations' aggregation efficiency of IMs and markets in general. According to the subjective theory of probability [8], probability is a rate at which an individual is willing to bet on the occurrence of an event. As it is natural for humans to consider probabilities and bets, an Information Market can provide a space where participants can reveal their probabilities of future events by thinking in terms of wagering their money to alternate future states of the world. Moreover, the efficient markets' hypothesis states that when a market reaches equilibrium, it reflects all available information about future events into market prices [9]. The efficient market hypothesis requires that participants have rational expectations, that on average the population is correct (even if no single participant is) and whenever new relevant information appears, the participants update their expectations appropriately. An implication of the efficient market hypothesis is that share prices reflect their true expected value, therefore markets provide accurate forecasts of their underlying commodities and securities. Last but not least, recent research shows the connections between cost function based IMs and online learning [10].

IMs are considered an example of collective intelligence and they are characterized by their accuracy, easy deployment, and ability to dynamically incorporate new information available to traders by continuously adjusting an event's price [11]. However despite the benefits expected, the public sector seems rather reluctant to introduce IMs in order to improve public decision making. In [12] information markets are proposed as a new tool that will revolutionize governance, while in [13] a framework and the main characteristics an information market should fulfil in order to perform well in situations relevant for policy decision making are described. Recently, the use of information markets has been suggested as a tool which can foster the participation of citizens in European public policy [14] or support macro-economic forecasts for governments [15].

3   The PolicyOracle Information Market

PolicyOracle is an Information Market which provides the mechanisms to aggregate participants' expectations and provide forecasts of economic, environmental and energy indicators in order to support policy making. It relies on play money as the resource for buying or selling contracts, which means that participants receive a number of points that can be used for trading upon their registration. This design was adopted as previous research has shown that the accuracy of play money Information Markets is similar to those that use real money, while the use of real money even for research purposes has to consider legal issues. Furthermore, PolicyOracle resembles a virtual stock market which means that a number of market design elements were considered, including: the market mechanism which affects how transactions are processed, the type of contracts that determine what expectations are aggregated and the participants who perform transactions and set the market prices.

3.1   Market Mechanism

The market mechanism determines how the buy and sell orders that participants place are cleared. Similarly to the first version of the Information Market tool, PolicyOracle uses a mechanism based on an Automated Market Maker (AMM). This means that all transactions are processed by the AMM which is practically a function that determines the cost or gain of buy and sell transactions respectively. In more details, when a participant places a buy or sell order for a particular contract, the system validates the order and it is always ready to process it, acting as an "always there" buyer and seller. The AMM price function in PolicyOracle follows the work of [16] and simulates real life supply and demand conditions. If we let s_i be the net amount of shares a given contract that has been sold, then the price of contract i is given by formula (1) where b represents a scaling factor that controls the market's depth and determines the rate of price changes when traders buy or sell shares from the AMM (low values of b cause greater price fluctuations and higher volatility) and c represents the maximum price of an outcome.

$$P_i = \frac{ce^{s_i/b}}{\sum_k e^{s_k/b}} \tag{1}$$

$$b = \frac{-K}{c \log \frac{N\left(1-\frac{P_{upper}}{c}\right)}{N-1}} \tag{2}$$

In order to facilitate trading and make users feel comfortable with contract prices, we selected a span of prices between 0 and 100. So, we set $c = 100$ and the P_i prices sum to 100. Another aspect that needs to be considered before running a market refers to the value of the constant b. As mentioned above, the elasticity constant b controls how much prices change after a transaction. Setting b requires special attention as a low value can lead to great price fluctuations after a transaction while a high value can cause low price movements which will not reflect the aggregate opinions of the participants adequately. We follow the approach described in [17] and calculate a variable price of b, based on the total amount of money K which is available in the market and the desired target upper price P_{upper} of a contract which is given if all of the money is invested in that contract. The value of b is given by formula (2) where N represents the possible mutually exclusive contracts in the market and we set $P_{upper} = 99$. In order to keep the market elasticity constant, we adjust and re-calculate the b value each time a new trader registers in our platform (at this time new money is introduced into the market as the trader receives an initial amount of 20000 points) as well as when a question is resolved and contracts are rewarded (when a contract is rewarded new money is introduced into the market as winners receive money).

3.2   Contracts

Contracts represent the mutually exclusive possible outcomes of policy questions and are the tradable assets of the market. For example the question "Will the inflation in Europe rise in 2016" may have two answers, "YES" or "NO" and thus two contracts. Contracts expire when the event they refer to is realized and provide a payoff value. We follow the "winner-takes-all" payoff rule which means that a contract is worth 100 points if the outcome of the event the contract represents is realized, and 0 points otherwise.

In order to be able to aggregate information on a variety of policy indices, we have designed three types of questions: binary, multiple choice and multiple interval. Binary questions have two contracts one referring to a positive answer, the YES contract, and another referring to the negative answer, the NO contract. Market participants invest on the YES answer (contract) of the question if they believe that the GDP will be higher than 13.920B euros, else on the NO answer (contract). This kind of questions are suitable for aggregating expectations on the trends of policy variables.

Multiple choice and multiple interval questions can have two or more answers and consequently two or more contracts. An indicative example of such a questions is "What will the official quarterly GDP growth rate for Q1 2015 in Spain be?". The possible answers depend on the values the policy maker or modeller wishes to set and receive feedback. In our example there can be 10 answers each corresponding to certain range as follows: '<−0.9 %', '−0.9−−0.5 %', '−0.4−0.1 %', '0.0−0.4 %', '0.5−0.9 %', '1.0−1.4 %', '1.5−1.9 %', '2.0−2.4 %', '2.5−2.9 %', '>2.9 %'.

In all cases described above, contract prices range between 0 and 100 and reflect the likelihood of the event, that the answer which the contract represents, to be realized.

3.3   Participants

Participants access the system through a web interface and we have defined three user roles who have access to different functionalities: administrators, traders and visitors. Administrators set up the questions and the answers. They are the policy makers and policy modellers who want to have the aggregated expectations of experts and interested stakeholders. Traders express their expectations by signing up and selecting the contracts which they want to trade. Visitors monitor the likelihood of the events defined in the market. The following table summarizes how different stakeholder groups can use PolicyOracle (Table 1).

Table 1. Stakeholder groups and use of PolicyOracle

Stakeholder group	Use of PolicyOracle
Policy makers (Politicians, European Central Bank, Bank of England)	They are the key actors who take the actual decisions PolicyOracle supports them by offering access to experts' aggregated expectations
Policy advisors (e.g. Global Climate Forum, German Watch, National Central Banks of the Eurozone)	They are the actors who support policy makers in their decisions. They may engage stakeholders (e.g. industry representatives) in discussions on the impact of alternative policy options. PolicyOracle supports them by offering access to experts' aggregated expectations
Industry (Large Enterprises (e.g. Siemens, RWE, Allianz etc.)	They are actors who influence the opinion of policy advisors and policy makers PolicyOracle allows them to express expectations on policy variables or monitor the results
Civil society (Environmental NGOs (e.g. WWF), civil society actors like unions (e.g. IG BAU))	They are institutions and organizations that manifest interests and will of citizens PolicyOracle allows them to express expectations on policy variables or monitor the results
Citizens (SME owners, Public servants, Young generation, Employees)	PolicyOracle allows them to express expectations on policy variables or monitor the results
Academia (Universities and research organizations)	PolicyOracle allows them to express expectations on policy variables or monitor the results

4 A Walkthrough Scenario

In this section we show the main functionalities of PolicyOracle and how these can be used for the aggregation of expectations on macroeconomic and environmental policy indices.

Assume that a policy expert named John logs into the system. He is provided with a list of available questions as illustrated in Fig. 1-A. By clicking on the question he is interested in, the user is directed to the trading screen where he can provide a prediction by investing his play money. By default, he sees the simple view of the trading screen (Fig. 1-B). In this view, he can provide an estimate about a possible outcome using a likert-scale like interface. The available options span from "likely" to "almost sure" depending on his belief in a 5 point interval. John is more experienced with markets

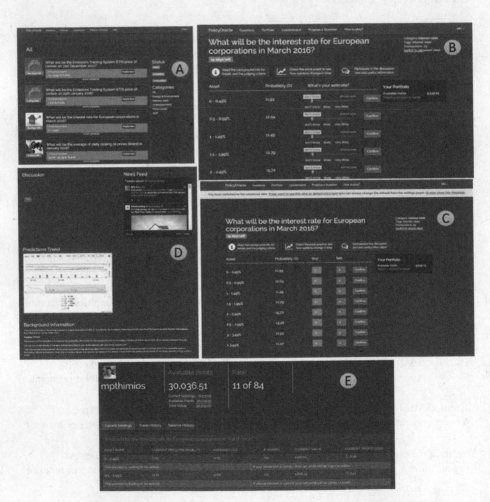

Fig. 1. Overview of the PolicyOracle main screens and functionalities.

and trading interfaces and chooses the advanced view (Fig. 1-C). This view resembles a stock exchange where John can set the exact amount of shares she would like to buy or sell.

The quantity of the shares is entered in the relevant boxes of each contract (i.e. the answers to the questions). Selling without owning an amount of shares is not permitted by the system. Before confirming a transaction, the system provides information related to the costs or gains of the transaction and the new contract prices. If John agrees, he confirms the transaction and his portfolio is updated. The trading screen provides additional information regarding the selected question. John can see how many days left while the question is open. Furthermore, there is information regarding the category of the question, relevant tags as well as the number of transactions.

John has a portfolio consisting of contracts and play money. As shown in Fig. 1-D, John can see the total value of his account, including the current value of his holdings and the available points. Moreover, the user can view his rank in comparison to other users. The market is a form of a prediction contest in order to foster participation. Other information includes a list of the contracts s/he currently owns is presented, together with the current profit/loss, the quantity of holding shares as well as the average cost of his transactions. The "sell" button is provided beneath each holding, so John has the option to sell his stake in case he changes his opinion.

In Fig. 1-E, the tool provides social functionalities that enable discussions and posts on twitter. He can provide comments and participate in discussions, enabling information and opinion exchange. A Twitter News Feed based on keywords related to the question is displayed in order to provide frequently updated social media information. Moreover, price charts show fluctuations in the prices of contracts as well as the trading volume over time. Finally, a section with background information provides a detailed description of the question as well as links to external information sources.

5   Current Status and First Results

Our tool is online at the http://experts.policyoracle.org url and is currently being used by stakeholders in the context of the SYMPHONY project (http://projectsymphony.eu/). We have already defined a number of indices in collaboration with policy modellers who participate in the aforementioned project, which have been introduced as questions in our Information Market. The indices are related to macroeconomic and energy variables, and are the following:

Gross Domestic Product (GDP): this is an aggregate measure of production equal to the sum of the gross values added of all resident, institutional units engaged in production. GDP estimates are commonly used to measure the economic performance of a whole country or region and can affect several economic policies, e.g. related to public investments and taxes.
Consumer Price Index (CPI): this index measures changes in the price level of a market basket of consumer goods and services purchased by households. CPI determines the real value of wages, salaries and pensions for regulating policies related to prices and deflating monetary magnitudes to show changes in real values.

Inflation Rate which shows the change of general price level of goods and services in an economy over a period of time. To ensure stability, current economic policies target for a steady and low inflation. Inflation forecasts determine how economic authorities (e.g. central banks) design and implement their monetary policies by setting interest rates, open market operations, and banking reserve requirements.

Unemployment Rate: this is a measure of the prevalence of unemployment and it is calculated as a percentage by dividing the number of unemployed individuals by all individuals currently in the labour force. Knowledge of unemployment tendencies can determine the monetary and fiscal policies for reducing unemployment caused by recessions (also termed as demand side policies).

Interest Rate: this is a measure of the cost-of-borrowing indicator for new loans to corporations.

Oil Prices: This refers to crude oil prices, the fluctuations of which affect monetary policies.

Electricity Prices: This index shows the changes of prices in the wholesale electricity market. Electricity is a very special commodity as it is economically non-storable, and power system stability requires a constant balance between production and consumption. At the same time, electricity demand depends on weather and the intensity of business and everyday activities. Low electricity prices improve industrial competitiveness and consumer's welfare, thus accurate forecasts can help policy makers to devise policies which will keep prices at low levels.

The questions on macroeconomic indices have been implemented for Spain, Italy, Germany, Greece and the EU as a whole. The energy related questions have been implemented for the EU as whole. Currently 84 users have registered and are performing transactions; we expect to have an analysis of the first results in the coming months.

6   Conclusions and Future Work

In this paper we presented a tool based on the concept of Information Markets in order to aggregate expectations on policy indices. We have presented its design elements, including the market mechanism, the contracts which represent answers to questions on the future value of policy indices and the type of participants including the benefits they can acquire from such a tool. A walkthrough scenario showed how our tool can be used to aggregate information related to the policy indices in the form of transactions in the Information Market. Last, we have selected a first set of macroeconomic and energy related indices which are relevant for policy decision making. The tools is already online and we plan to evaluate its usefulness to policy modelling and its prediction accuracy. To this direction we have already planned a series of focus group sessions with policy modellers where are going to showcase the tool and the results of the expectation aggregation process, in order to gather their feedback. Moreover as the real values of the policy indices are announced we plan to evaluate the tool's accuracy in predicting these values.

Acknowledgements. Research reported in this paper is partially funded by the European Commission project SYMPHONY (FP7 grant agreement no.: 611875).

References

1. D'Agostino, A., Schnatz, B.: Survey-based nowcasting of US growth: a real-time forecast comparison over more than 40 years. ECB Working Paper, n. 1455 (2012)
2. Bańbura, M., Rünstler, G.: A look into the factor model black box: publication lags and the role of hard and soft data in forecasting GDP. Int. J. Forecast. **27**(2), 333–346 (2011)
3. Manski, C.F.: Measuring expectations. Econometrica **72**(5), 1329–1376 (2004)
4. Giacomini, R.: Economic theory and forecasting: lessons from the literature. Econometrics J. **18**(2), 22–41 (2015)
5. Kranz, T., Teschner, F., Weinhardt, C.: Combining prediction markets and surveys: an experimental study. In: Proceedings of the 22nd European Conference on Information Systems (2014)
6. Spann, M., Skiera, B.: Internet-based virtual stock markets for business forecasting. Manag. Sci. **49**(10), 1310–1326 (2003)
7. Berg, J.E., Rietz, T.A.: Prediction markets as decision support systems. Inf. Syst. Front. **5**(1), 79–93 (2003)
8. De Finetti, B.: Logical foundations and measurement of subjective probability. Acta Psychol. **34**, 129–145 (1970)
9. Malkiel, B.G., Fama, E.F.: Efficient capital markets: a review of theory and empirical work. J. Finan. **25**(2), 383–417 (1970)
10. Abernethy, J., Chen, Y., Vaughan, J.W.: Efficient market making via convex optimization, and a connection to online learning. ACM Trans. Econ. Comput. **1**(2), 12 (2013)
11. Snowberg, E., Wolfers, J., Zitzewitz, E.: Prediction markets for economic forecasting (No. w18222). National Bureau of Economic Research (2012)
12. Hanson, R.: Decision markets for policy advice. In: Patashnik, E., Gerber, A. (eds.) Promoting the General Welfare. Brookings Institution Press, Washington, D.C. (2006)
13. Ledyard, J.: Design of information markets for policy analysis. In: Hahn, R.W., Tecklock, P.C. (eds.) Information Markets: A New Way of Making Decisions. The American Enterprise Institute Press, Washington, DC (2006)
14. Millard, J., Nielsen, M.M., Warren, R., Smith, S., Macintosh, A., Tarabanis, K., Tambouris, E., Panopoulou, E., Efpraxia, D., Parisopoulos, K.: European eParticipation Report (2009)
15. Teschner, F., Stathel, S., Weinhardt, C.: A prediction market for macro-economic variables. In: 2011 44th Hawaii International Conference on System Sciences (HICSS), pp. 1–9 (2011)
16. Hanson, R.: Logarithmic market scoring rules for modular combinatorial information aggregation. J. Prediction Markets **1**(1), 3–15 (2007)
17. Berg, H., Proebsting, T.A.: Hanson's automated market maker. J. Prediction Markets **3**(1), 45–59 (2009)

Passive Expert-Sourcing for Policy Making in the European Union

Aggeliki Androutsopoulou[1]([⊠]), Francesco Mureddu[2],
Euripidis Loukis[1], and Yannis Charalabidis[1]

[1] Department of Information and Communication Systems Engineering,
University of the Aegean, Samos, Greece
{ag.andr,eloukis,yannisx}@aegean.gr
[2] Information and Communication Science Department,
Universitat Oberta de Catalunya, Barcelona, Spain
fmureddu@uoc.edu

Abstract. The public sector gradually starts exploiting the crowdsourcing ideas initially developed in the private sector. However, there is much less knowledge on efficient and effective methods and practices for public sector citizen-sourcing in comparison with private sector crowd-sourcing, so extensive research is required in this area. This paper contributes to filling this research gap, by presenting an ICT-based method for 'passive expert-sourcing', with the latter term denoting the collection of policy relevant information, knowledge and ideas from experts, which aims at supporting policy making by the European Union (EU) by leveraging its large policy community. Its theoretical foundation is previous theoretical work on the relationships between democracy and technocracy, and also on policy networks. The main technological pillars of the proposed method are: EU policy experts' profiling and reputation management, relevant documents' opinion mining and relevance rating, and finally advanced visualized presentation of them. Finally, a first evaluation of the proposed method is presented, leading to encouraging results.

Keywords: Crowd-sourcing · Citizen-sourcing · Public policy · Technocracy · Policy network · Reputation management · Opinion mining

1 Introduction

Crowd-sourcing has been initially developed in the private sector, in order to exploit external information, knowledge and ideas possessed by 'crowds' of individuals for problem solving or for the development of innovations [4–6, 17, 18]. It is defined as 'a new web-based business model that harnesses the creative solutions of a distributed network of individuals, in order to exploit 'collective wisdom' and mine fresh ideas from large numbers of individuals' [4]. There has been extensive research and practice in this area, which has led to the development of efficient and effective crowd-sourcing methods and practices, and also to gaining a deeper understanding of them, their value, advantages a disadvantages, and also the specific contexts and kinds of problems for

© IFIP International Federation for Information Processing 2016
Published by Springer International Publishing Switzerland 2016. All Rights Reserved
E. Tambouris et al. (Eds.): ePart 2016, LNCS 9821, pp. 162–175, 2016.
DOI: 10.1007/978-3-319-45074-2_13

which each of them is more appropriate for; comprehensive reviews of this research are provided by Rouse [36], Hetmank [15], Tarrell et al. [41], Pedersen et al. [29] and Rechenberger et al. [35].

The public sector, motivated by the multiple 'success stories' of this new knowledge sourcing and innovation paradigm, and also by the increasing complexity of social problems and needs, has started making some first steps in this direction, by introducing forms of 'citizen-sourcing' in their policy making processes (see Sect. 2.1 for a brief review of relevant literature). However, there is much less knowledge on efficient and effective methods and practices for public sector citizen-sourcing in comparison with private sector crowd-sourcing. It is therefore necessary to conduct extensive research in this area, in order to develop highly efficient ICT-based methods for this purpose, which enable the effective collection of policy relevant information, knowledge and ideas from citizens, and then the advanced processing of them in order to calculate useful policy analytics, which can provide substantial support for public policy making, and addressing its specific needs. In general, it is important in the area of public sector citizen-sourcing to reach a level of knowledge, efficiency, effectiveness and maturity, comparable to those of the private sector crowd-sourcing.

This paper contributes to filling this research gap, by presenting an ICT-based method for 'passive expert-sourcing', with the latter term denoting the collection of policy relevant information, knowledge and ideas from experts, in order to support policy making by the European Union by leveraging its large policy community. The first evaluations of citizen-sourcing initiatives [1, 12, 23] have shown that they can provide valuable insights into the perceptions of the general public concerning important social problems and government activities for addressing them, and also existing and proposed public policies for addressing them. However, it is recommended that in order to collect information and knowledge of higher quality, it is necessary to target more knowledgeable communities having strong interest and good expertise on the particular topic/policy under discussion. On this question there has been extensive political sciences research, which has revealed the importance of both democracy (i.e. political consultation with all stakeholder groups) and technocracy (i.e. specialized knowledge of experts) for the development of effective public policies for addressing the complex problems of modern societies [7, 13, 14]. At the same time this research highlights the need of a relationship and balance between them (see Sect. 2.2 for more details on 'Democracy vs Technocracy in Public Policy Making'). Furthermore, another stream of political sciences research has examined the emergence of policy networks, as a result of the increasing complexity of social problems, in which participate various both governmental actors and non-governmental actors (such as associations of various businesses, professions, labor unions and other interest groups), and their increasing importance for the design and implementation of public policies; each of these actors has developed valuable expertise, usually focused on its particular perspectives and concerns, which can be quite useful for public policy making [33, 34, 40] (see Sect. 2.3 for more details on 'Public Policy Networks'). So, our research has as theoretical foundation this abovementioned previous work on the relationships between democracy and technocracy, and also on the public policy networks.

The research presented in this paper has been conducted as part of the European research project 'EU-Community' (project.eucommunity.eu/), partially funded by the

'ICT for Governance and Policy Modelling' research programme of the EU. This paper is structured in six sections. In the following Sect. 2 the background of our research is outlined (on public sector citizen-sourcing, democracy vs technocracy in public policy making, and also public policy networks). Then in Sect. 3 is presented the methodology we adopted for the design of the proposed method and then for a first evaluation of it. In Sect. 4 the proposed ICT-based method of passive expert-sourcing is described, followed by the results of a first evaluation of it in Sect. 5. Finally, in Sect. 6 conclusions are summarized and directions for further research are proposed.

2 Background

2.1 Public Sector Citizen-Sourcing

As mentioned previously in the Introduction, for public sector citizen-sourcing there is a lack of research similar to the one that has been conducted for private sector crowd-sourcing, having similar levels of breadth and depth, probably because the former is a more recent phenomenon than the latter. Limited research has been conducted concerning the application of crowd-sourcing ideas in the public sector, the development of efficient and effective methods and practices for this purpose, and the evaluation of them from various perspectives [12, 16, 22, 24, 27, 28, 37, 39].

Most of the existing literature on ICT-based methods for citizen-sourcing by government agencies is focusing on 'active citizen-sourcing', which aim at the use of government agencies' web-sites or social media accounts, in order to pose a particular social problem or public policy direction, and solicit relevant information, knowledge, opinions and ideas from citizens. In this direction Mergel and Desouza [27] describe and analyze the Challenge.gov initiative the U.S. Office of Management and Budget, which aimed at applying private sector crowdsourcing ideas in the public sector, in order to source from citizens ideas, knowledge, and solutions for specific challenges that government faces. This initiative was based on an ICT platform allowing U.S. federal agencies to launch contests, and at the same time citizens to find appropriate contests and participate in them providing solutions, or reviewing and evaluating solutions provided by others, voting on solutions, and even getting involved in the implementation of solutions and subsequent evaluation of them. Charalabidis and Loukis [8] and Ferro et al. [12] propose a method for the systematic, intensive and centralized exploitation of web 2.0 social media by government agencies on public policies (existing or under development). This method is based is on a central ICT platform, which (a) publishes automatically various types of policy-related content (e.g., short text long text, images, video) in multiple social media accounts of a government agency, using the application programming interfaces (API) of these social media, soliciting citizens' feedback on them; and (b) similarly collects automatically from them data on citizens' interactions with this content (e.g., views, comments, ratings, votes, etc.), and makes advanced processing of them. However, more recently, there has been some interest in 'passive citizen-sourcing', which aims to exploit political content that has been developed by citizens freely, without any direct stimulation or direction by government, in various external (= not belonging to government agencies) web-sites or social media, such as political fora, news web-sites, political blogs, Facebook, Twitter, etc. accounts [3, 9, 44].

Therefore, extensive further research is required in the area of public sector citizen-sourcing, in order to develop a considerable knowledge base on it, and through it a level of efficiency and effectiveness, comparable to those of the private sector crowd-sourcing area. Our research makes a contribution in this direction, by developing an ICT-based method of passive expert-sourcing.

2.2 Democracy vs Technocracy in Public Policy Making

The increasing complexity of the problems of modern societies, the globalization of the economy and the development of technology have increased the need for and importance of knowledge and expertise for the design and implementation of public policies [7, 13, 14, 21, 30, 31]. This has led to the establishment of various expert bodies (in government agencies competent for the formulation of public policies, and also the other public policy stakeholders, such as associations of professions, labor unions, businesses and other interest groups), which can have various forms, from committees to separate organizations (e.g. economic institutes). These expert bodies have become today highly important for and influential on the formulation of public policies, and this is termed as 'technocracy' [13, 21]. So today it is widely recognized that the two fundamental bases of public policy making are democracy (i.e. political consultation with stakeholder groups) and technocracy (i.e. knowledge of experts).

However, political sciences research in this area has highlighted the need of a relationship and balance between them, as each of them needs inputs from the other. In particular, participants in the democratic processes (various stakeholder groups, and even active citizens) need relevant knowledge and expertise, and the lack of them can have quite negative impacts [42]. At the same time the experts dealing with a particular social problem/public policy also need inputs from the political process, concerning diverse values and concerns of different stakeholder groups, and also their diverse perspectives, approaches and ideologies. For the above reasons Brown [7] argues that democracy and technocracy are not in conflict, and their combination is a necessity in todays' realities of highly complex social problems and needs, and globalization; they generate different kinds of knowledge, which are both necessary for public policy making. The ICT can be very useful for the required exchange of knowledge between democracy and technocracy. Our research contributes in this direction, developing an ICT-based method for transfer of knowledge from the latter to the former.

2.3 Public Policy Networks

The increased complexity of social problems and needs also led governments to realize that their 'classical' unilateral modes of governance are insufficient, and they need knowledge resources and cooperation of non-state actors (initially economic actors and later other social actors as well) in order to design and implement effective policies, and this resulted in the development of public policy networks [33, 34, 40]. They are defined as sets of formal and informal institutional linkages between various both governmental actors and non-government actors (such as associations of businesses, professions, labor unions and other interest groups) structured around shared interests in public policy-making and implementation. In public policy networks the non-state actors provide to the state actors on one hand information, knowledge and expertise, and on the other hand support for the design and implementation of public policies, and legitimization of them; in return the former have the opportunity to influence the public policies (e.g. legislation, allocation of government financial resources) towards directions that are beneficial to them [2, 19, 25, 43].

A critical characteristic of a network is the density of interactions among its participants; according to [25] higher density of interactions has positive impact on the timewise stability of the network, the development of shared values and beliefs concerning desirable policy objectives and instruments, and finally the effectiveness and outcomes of the network. Therefore, ICT can be very useful for increasing this critical characteristic at a low cost, and supporting the exchange of diverse expertise and knowledge among participants. Our research makes a contribution in this direction, developing an ICT-based method that supports the exchange of expertise and knowledge between the actors participating in a policy network.

3 Design and Evaluation Methodology

In order to design this ICT-based method of expert-sourcing and its supporting ICT platform thirteen workshops have been organized, with the first five of them aiming to gain a better understanding of the structure of the EU policy community, and then the next eight aiming to collect the requirements of potential users of our method and ICT platform, as part of the preparation and the implementation of the abovementioned EU-Community project. The EurActiv.Com (a leading EU policy online media network (www.euractiv.com), which participates as partner in the EU-Community project, and the Fondation EurActiv Politech (a public service foundation (www.euractiv.com/fondation) having as main mission 'to bring together individuals and organizations seeking to shape European Union policies', participating also as partner in this project, were the organizers of these workshops. The participants were representatives of important EU policy stakeholders (such as industry federations), members of the advisory boards of EurActiv.Com and Fondation EurActiv Politech, thematic experts in various EU policies, policy analysts, registered users of EurActiv.Com portals, and also permanent staff of various hierarchical levels from the European Commission.

In order to conduct an initial evaluation of the proposed method and its supporting ICT platform an evaluation session was organized with the participation of similar potential users. During this session the proposed method was introduced to the audience, together with the supporting ICT platform, and some first applications with their results. Then the participants had the opportunity to interact with the ICT platform by executing a set of predefined usage scenarios, under the observation of the organizers who supported them, and recorded any comments or difficulties, and as well feedback on possible improvements. Finally, we collected evaluation data from the participants in this session using mainly quantitative techniques, as they enable condensing and summarizing a large quantity of evidence in a few numbers that enable the easier drawing of conclusions [26, 32]. We developed our evaluation framework based on the models developed in previous technology acceptance research [10, 20, 38], which has concluded that the intention to use a new technology, is determined mainly by two factors: its perceived 'ease of use' (= the degree to which potential users believe that using it would require minimal effort) and its perceived 'usefulness' (= the degree to which potential users believe that using it will enhance their job performance) [11]. So our evaluation framework has been based on these three factors, which have been elaborated and analyzed into several detailed questions, taking into account the particular objectives and specificities of the proposed method. This elaboration has been made separately for each the two main components that the users of the ICT platform can access: the Euractory (which enables users' registration and reputation calculation, rating other users and also searching for experts on a topic) and the PolicyLine (which provides a visualization of document search results). Based on the above evaluation framework a questionnaire was designed to be filled by the session participants; the questions of the framework were converted to positive statements, and the respondents were asked to provide the degree of their agreement/disagreement with each of them in a five-levels scale (1 = totally disagree, 2 = disagree, 3 = neutral, 4 = agree, 5 = totally agree). The questionnaire is shown in Table 1. The data collected through the questionnaire were processed using Excel. Furthermore, after filling this questionnaire a qualitative discussion was conducted with the participants on the same questions, in order to get a deeper insight of their perceptions.

4 A Passive Expert-Sourcing Method

4.1 Description

From the interviews we conducted (see first paragraph of Sect. 3) it was concluded that the main need of EU policy stakeholders is to be better informed on the most knowledgeable and credible experts on a policy related topic they are interested in, and also the most relevant documents on such a topic; it will also be useful if these documents are associated with the various stages of the E.U. policy processes. Since experts usually do not have time to generate new content on a topic (social problem or public policy – existing or under development) they are interesting in, the use of 'active citizen-sourcing' would not be possible. Therefore, a 'passive citizen-sourcing' approach should be adopted, based on the retrieval, processing and exploitation of already existing experts' generated content. So, the proposed method is based on retrieving automatically information from various sources about experts on policy related topics, and then collecting the knowledge and opinions they share online through texts and postings in multiple web-sites and social media they are using. This can be achieved by crawling at regular time intervals the most relevant external sources of knowledgeable and credible experts on EU policies, and also of relevant documents of various types, and update automatically the corresponding databases of a supporting ICT platform. The practical application of this method will lead to the collection of a large amount of information concerning policy experts and content generated by them.

So, it is important to apply automated state-of-the-art techniques for processing and classifying this content, in order to extract interesting insights and knowledge from it concerning social problems and public policies. This textual content of documents, articles and social media posts will be processed using opinion mining and sentiment classification methods, in order to identify subjective information, extract opinions, identify the polarity of their orientation (positive, negative or neutral) and assess the relevance of them with relation to a topic (see [10] for more details). Furthermore, for the experts it is necessary to apply digital reputation techniques for assessing their reputation/credibility and provide a ranking of them per topic of interest. By storing the above data in a common database, and enabling search of it by the users and visual presentation of the results, public policy stakeholders will be able to find useful expert knowledge on complex policy debates, e.g. the most reputable/credible experts or the most relevant documents on a specific topic. An overview of the proposed method is shown in Fig. 1.

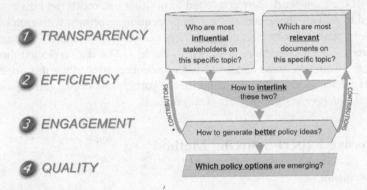

Fig. 1. An overview of the proposed method of passive expert-sourcing

The proposed method aims to foster collaboration and knowledge sharing among the different policy stakeholders on E.U. policy topics. For this purpose, in order to enable focus on a particular policy topic of interest, our method uses the concept of 'policy process', under which all relevant information on experts and documents is collected and clustered. In particular, as a policy process can be modelled any ongoing or completed EU legislative procedure, or political debate in general, on a topic, while each topic can be associated with one or more policy processes. Policy processes can be initiated by any policy stakeholder in order to enable the interconnection and presentation of all relevant information and aspects of policy consultations in a structured way.

4.2   ICT Platform

An ICT platform has been designed for supporting the implementation of the above method. It consists of two main components accessible by the users, called 'EurActory' and 'PolicyLine', with each of them including several sub-components, and also an additional component called 'CurActory', which is not directly accessible by the users, and includes the database storing the above information and the functionality for updating it by crawling pre-defined external sources at regular time intervals.

The EurActory component collects and maintains a directory of profiles of people with high levels of knowledge, expertise and credibility in one or more topics related with EU policies, usually having an active role in policy making processes at European level. According to their role they are categorized into the three types, which have been identified though our workshops: influencers, analysts and institutional decision makers. These people are included in the people database of the system in the Cur-Actory component automatically by the crawlers sub-component, or manually by using the self-registration capabilities provided by the EurActory component. The crawlers component crawls at regular time intervals various external sources, which can be pre-defined websites (e.g. Euractiv.com, EUR-Lex, Europa Whoiswho directory, RSS Feeds, blogs and news sites) or social media accounts (e.g. LinkedIn, Twitter), updating the CurActory database, which makes the relevant discovered information available through the EurActory or the PolicyLine.

Furthermore, this EurActory component provides rankings of the expert profiles according to their expertise on a set of topics of interest, through the 'reputation score' calculated by the Reputation Management sub-component for each expert per topic, based on the following criteria:

- Self-evaluation: direct input from the user on his/her own area of expertise.
- Peer-assessment: based on endorsements from other users made through EurActory
- Business Card Reputation: based on the reputation ranking of the organization and the user's position in the organization's hierarchy
- Document Assessment: results of authored documents' assessment by their readers
- Network Value: level of influence as the sum of network connections
- Proximity trust: level of connection in social media
- Past Measurements: taking into account reputation in previous months (its stability means credibility).
- Offline Reputation: manually added for persons with no online presence

Also, the EurActory provides the following capabilities to registered users:

- Search for an expert profile, by name, EU policy or topic, which returns experts found in descending reputation score order (i.e. the most reputable first).
- View an expert profile; the profile pages can also be shared on social media.
- Create own profile and curate personal information, connect social media accounts, claim expertise topics.
- Activation of an expert profile that has been already created by the system administrators, after the discovery of it by the crawlers, and also update of profile details.

The 'PolicyLine' component provides state-of-the-art visualization of policy rele-vant documents, which are structured according to policy processes, aiming to provide to the user a better understanding of the multi-actor processes related with the EU decision making procedures and policy debates. Therefore, in the core of PolicyLine functionality is the concept of 'policy process' (described previously in Sect. 4.1). We can have documents manually attached by users of the ICT Platform, to the specific 'policy process', as well as automatically discovered ones by the abovementioned crawlers sub-component, which searches on regular basis multiple web-sites and social media accounts in order to find significant documents published online (media articles, reports, tweets, policy proposals, legislative documents), authored by the experts' categories mentioned above.

In particular, PolicyLine provides statistical information for each policy process selected by the user, such as the total number of relevant documents and the number of visits of users on the specific policy process page. For a more detailed view, PolicyLine offers a timeline visualization (see Fig. 2), which structures the main documents (based on relevance as well as author's reputation) associated with this policy process in a temporal order, and clusters them under a set of user defined stages of the particular policy process. It also provides information with respect to their authorship (colors are used for this purpose to reflect different authors' categories and sub-categories), and also shapes (such as rectangles and circles) to reflect different types of documents (e.g. rectangles reflect the proposal documents, while general documents are represented by circles). Documents sub-categories are defined concerning the type of organization from which each document is originated (e.g. European Institution, National/Local Governance, Academic Institution, Civil Society Organization, Media, etc.). The sizes

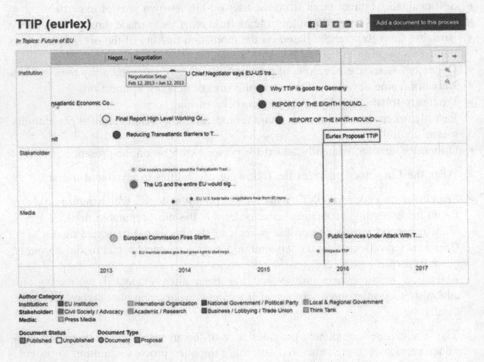

Fig. 2. PolicyLine timeline visualization

of the shapes representing these documents reflect their relevance and author's reputation (so more relevant documents written by more reputable authors are shown bigger).

Moreover, a user can select a particular document in order to view more details about it, including the results from the sentiment classification provided by the opinion mining sub-component (a linguistic analysis of the textual content of a document leads to an estimation of the polarity of the underlying text – see [10] for more details) and the relevant input provided by other platform users. In particular, PolicyLine for each document provides an interface where users can rate its accuracy, value, relevance and timeliness, and also enter comments on the document, so that an informal discussion on it can be stimulated.

5 Evaluation Results

In Table 1 are shown the results of the processing of the data collected through the evaluation questionnaire (average ratings for all questions) for the two main components that can be accessed by the users, EurActory and PolicyLine.

We can see that the respondents find the ease of use of the EurActory component high (the average rating of relevant questions is 3.9), and for the PolicyLine component moderate to high, but closer to the latter (the average rating of the relevant questions is 3.67). Slightly lower are their perceptions with respect to usefulness, which it is perceived as moderate to high for the EurActory component (average rating of relevant questions 3.5), and moderate to high, but closer to the former, for the PolicyLine

Table 1. Evaluation results

EurActory	Ease of use perspective	
	EurActory can be easily used without assistance	3.46
	Creating a profile is easy	4.08
	It is easy to access topic listings	4.15
	It is easy to rate peers	3.75
	Using EurActory has been a positive experience	4.08
	Usefulness	
	EurActory puts together information not found or collected under one roof elsewhere	3.15
		3.38
	EurActory allows me to be more productive	3.46
	EurActory improves the quality of my work	3.85
	EurActory assists me in identifying relevant experts	3.54
	EurActory provides me with all the needed information on relevant experts	3.54
	EurActory enables me to reinforce my expert positioning	
	Intention to use	
	I expect to use EurActory on a regular basis in the future	3.85
	I will advise colleagues to use EurActory	3.62

(*Continued*)

Table 1. (*Continued*)

PolicyLine	*Ease of use perspective*	
	PolicyLine can be easily used without assistance	3.64
	I can easily create a 'policy process'	3.69
	I can easily add a document in the 'policy process'	3.79
	I can easily rate/comment a document	3.5
	I can easily get an overview of the process	3.73
	Using PolicyLine has been a positive experience	3.71
	Usefulness	
	PolicyLine puts together information not found or collected under one roof elsewhere	3.29
	PolicyLine allows me to be more productive	3.29
	PolicyLine improves the quality of my work	3.43
	Intention to use	
	I expect to use PolicyLine on a regular basis in the future	4.14
	I will advise colleagues to use PolicyLine	3.71

component (average rating of relevant questions 3.3). Finally, high is the intention to use again the PolicyLine component again (average rating of relevant questions 3.9), and slightly lower for the EurActory component (average rating of relevant questions 3.75).

In the qualitative discussion with the participants of the evaluation session the latter agreed that this ICT platform, and the whole method behind it, constitute an easy to use tool for finding quickly high quality information and opinions on important policy related topics and policy formulation processes, authored by knowledgeable experts, and also debate over them with other users. Furthermore, it enables and promotes communication and exchange of knowledge among EU policy stakeholders. It also allows awareness of and also debate and criticism on policy initiatives carried out by the European Institutions. The usefulness of the EurActory component was assessed a bit higher than the PolicyLine; this probably reflects that the former is easier to use and exploit its capabilities than the latter. The participants were in general satisfied with the proposed method and its supporting infrastructure, and expressed interest in using again the functionalities of both components. However, future improvements were suggested, concerning the graphical interface and especially the timeline visualization.

6 Conclusions

In the previous sections of this paper an ICT-based method for 'passive expert-sourcing' was presented, which allows the collection of high quality policy relevant information, knowledge and ideas from knowledgeable experts, aiming at supporting policy making in the European Union (EU) by leveraging its large policy community. Its theoretical foundation is previous theoretical work on the relationships and the required balance between democracy and technocracy, and also on policy networks. The proposed method is based on EU policy experts' profiling and reputation management, relevant documents' opinion mining and relevance rating, and finally advanced visualized presentation of them. At the political level, its objective is to enable a better interconnection of the two important bases of modern public policy making, the democratic processes and the technocratic expertise (which is of critical importance, as discussed in more detail in Sect. 2.2), by supporting the transfer of knowledge from the latter to the former. In particular, it aims to support the efficient and effective retrieval by various actors of the democratic processes (e.g. representatives of stakeholder groups, journalists, government employees, active citizens, etc.) of diverse expert information, knowledge and ideas on a specific topic/policy, which is included in postings and texts authored by knowledgeable experts and published in various web-sites and social media. Furthermore, the proposed method of passive expert-sourcing aims to increase the density of interactions among the actors participating in public policy networks, which is highly important for their stability, the development of shared values and beliefs, and finally the effectiveness and the outcomes of such networks (as discussed in more detail in Sect. 2.3), by supporting the exchange of expertise and knowledge between network participants.

Also, a first evaluation of the proposed method has been presented, which gave encouraging results, with respect to its ease of use and usefulness. However, further evaluation of this method is required, based on realistic pilot applications of it, in order to assess better its value and potential with respect to its abovementioned ambitious objectives: to what extent it enables and supports the transfer of information, knowledge and proposals from experts to the participants in the democratic processes of modern policy making, and under what conditions? to what extent it can enable and support the exchange of information, knowledge and proposals among the participants in public policy networks, and under what conditions? to what extent can this method can assist the EU institutions to collect high quality information, knowledge, opinions and proposals from their policy networks? Research in this directions is already in progress as part of the abovementioned EU-Community project. Also, further research is required concerning the use of ICT for the transfer of knowledge in the opposite direction, from the democratic processes towards experts/technocracy (e.g. concerning diverse needs, values and concerns of different stakeholder groups on the particular social problem/public policy the experts analyze, and also existing diverse perspectives, approaches and ideologies). This is quite important for the construction of better and more multi-dimensional comprehensive and inclusive expert analyses and plans, which do not miss or neglect important aspects of the social problems or public policies they are dealing with and might be quite important for large social groups, and also do not underestimate existing diverse perspectives, approaches and ideologies.

References

1. Androutsopoulou, A., Charalabidis, Y., Loukis, E.: Using social media monitoring for public policy making – an evaluation. In: Proceedings of 9th Mediterranean Conference on Information Systems (MCIS 2015), October 2015, Samos, Greece (2015)
2. Atkinson, M., Coleman, W.: Strong states and weak states: sectoral policy networks in advanced capitalist economies. Br. J. Polit. Sci. **19**, 47–67 (1989)

3. Bekkers, V., Edwards, A., de Kool, D.: Social media monitoring: responsive governance in the shadow of surveillance? Gov. Inf. Q. **30**(4), 335–342 (2013)

4. Brabham, D.C.: Crowdsourcing as a model for problem solving: an introduction and cases. Converg.: Int. J. Res. New Media Technol. **14**(1), 75–90 (2008)

5. Brabham, D.C.: Crowdsourcing: a model for leveraging online communities. In: Delwiche, A., Henderson, J. (eds.) The Routledge Handbook of Participative Cultures. Routledge, Abingdon (2012)

6. Brabham, D.C.: Crowdsourcing. MIT Press, Cambridge (2013)

7. Brown, M.B.: Science in Democracy: Expertise, Institutions, and Representation. MIT Press, Cambridge (2009)

8. Charalabidis, Y., Loukis, E.: Participative public policy making through multiple social media platforms utilization. Int. J. Electron. Gov. Res. **8**(3), 78–97 (2012)

9. Charalabidis, Y., Loukis, E., Androutsopoulou, A., Karkaletsis, V., Triantafillou, A.: Passive crowdsourcing in government using social media. Transform. Gov.: People Process Policy **2**(8), 283–308 (2014)

10. Charalabidis, Y., Maragoudakis, M., Loukis, E.: Opinion mining and sentiment analysis in policy formulation initiatives: the EU-community approach. In: Tambouris, E., Panagiotopoulos, P., Sæbø, Ø., Tarabanis, K., Wimmer, M.A., Milano, M., Pardo, T. (eds.) ePart 2015. LNCS, vol. 9249, pp. 147–160. Springer, Heidelberg (2015)

11. Davis, F.D.: Perceived usefulness, perceived ease of use, and user acceptance of information technology. MIS Q. **13**(3), 319–339 (1989)

12. Ferro, E., Loukis, E., Charalabidis, Y., Osella, M.: Policy making 2.0: from theory to practice. Gov. Inf. Q. **30**(4), 359–368 (2013)

13. Fischer, F.: Technocracy and the Politics of Expertise. Sage, London (1990)

14. Harcourt, A., Radaelli, C.: Limits to EU technocratic regulation? Eur. J. Polit. Res. **35**, 107–122 (1999)

15. Hetmank, L.: Components and functions of crowdsourcing systems – a systematic literature review. In: Proceedings of 2013 International Conference on Wirtschaftsinformatik (2013)

16. Hilgers, D., Ihl, C.: Citizensourcing: applying the concept of open innovation to the public sector. Int. J. Public Particip. **4**(1), 67–88 (2010)

17. Howe, J.: The rise of crowdsourcing. Wired **14**(6) (2006). http://www.wired.com/wired/archive/14.06/crowds.html

18. Howe, J.: Crowdsourcing, Why the Power of the Crowd is Driving the Future of Business. Crown Business, New York (2008)

19. Howlett, M.: Do networks matter? Linking policy network structure to policy outcome: evidence from four canadian policy sectors 1990–2000. Can. J. Polit Sci. **35**(2), 235–267 (2002)

20. Hsiao, C.H., Yang, C.: The intellectual development of the technology acceptance model: a co-citation analysis. Int. J. Inf. Manage. **31**(2), 128–136 (2011)

21. Kurki, M.: Democracy through technocracy? Reflections on technocratic assumptions in EU democracy promotion discourse. J. Interv. Statebuilding **5**(2), 211–234 (2011)

22. Linders, D.: From e-government to we-government: defining a typology for citizen coproduction in the age of social media. Gov. Inf. Q. **29**, 446–454 (2012)

23. Loukis, E., Charalabidis, Y., Androutsopoulou, A.: An analysis of multiple social media consultations in the european parliament from a public policy perspective. In: European Conference on Information Systems (ECIS) 2014, Tel Aviv, Israel (2014)

24. Lukensmeyer, C.J., Torres, L.H.: Citizensourcing: citizen participation in a networked nation. In: Yang, K., Bergrud, E. (eds.) Civic Engagement in a Network Society, pp. 207–233. Information Age Publishing, Charlotte (2008)

25. Marsh, D., Smith, M.: Understanding policy networks: towards a dialectical approach. Polit. Stud. **48**, 4–21 (2000)
26. Maylor, H., Blackmon, K.: Researching Business and Management. Palgrave-Macmillan, New York (2005)
27. Mergel, I., Desouza, K.C.: Implementing open innovation in the public sector: the case of challenge.gov. Public Adm. Rev. **73**(6), 882–890 (2013)
28. Nam, T.: Suggesting frameworks of citizen-sourcing via government 2.0. Gov. Inf. Q. **29**, 12–20 (2012)
29. Pedersen, J., Kocsis, D., Tripathi, A., Tarrell, A., Weerakoon, A., Tahmasbi, N., Xiong, J., Deng, W., Oh, O., Vreede, G.J.: Conceptual foundations of crowdsourcing: a review of IS research. In: Proceedings of the 46th Annual Hawaii International Conference on System Sciences, Maui, HI, USA (2013)
30. Radaelli, C.M.: The role of knowledge in the policy process. J. Eur. Public Policy **2**(2), 159–183 (1995)
31. Radaelli, C.M.: The public policy of the european union: whither politics of expertise? J. Eur. Public Policy **6**(5), 757–774 (1999)
32. Ragin, C., Amoroso, L.: Constructing Social Research: The Unity and Diversity of Method, 2nd edn. Pine Forge Press – Sage Publications, California (2011)
33. Rhodes, R.A.W.: Policy network analysis. In: Moran, M., Rein, M., Goodin, R.E. (eds.) The Oxford Handbook of Public Policy, pp. 423–445. Oxford University Press, Oxford (2006)
34. Rhodes, R.A.W.: Understanding governance: ten years on. Organ. Stud. **28**(8), 1243–1264 (2007)
35. Rechenberger, T., Jung, V., Schmidt, N., Rosenkranz, C.: Utilizing the crowd – a literature review on factors influencing crowdsourcing initiative success. In: Pacific Conference on Information Systems (PACIS) 2015 Proceedings, Paper 250 (2015)
36. Rouse, A.C.: A preliminary taxonomy of crowdsourcing In: Proceedings of the Austalasian Conference on Information Systems (ACIS) 2010, Paper 76 (2010)
37. Prpić, J., Taeihagh, A., Melton, J.: The fundamentals of policy crowdsourcing. Policy Internet **7**(3), 340–361 (2015)
38. Schepers, J., Wetzels, M.: A meta-analysis of the technology acceptance model: investigating subjective norm and moderation effects. Inf. Manag. **44**, 90–103 (2007)
39. Seltzer, E., Mahmoudi, D.: Citizen participation, open innovation, and crowdsourcing: challenges and opportunities for planning. J. Plan. Lit. **28**(1), 3–18 (2012)
40. Skogstad, G.: Policy networks and policy communities: conceptual evolution and governing realities. In: Workshop on "Canada's Contribution to Comparative Theorizing" Annual Meeting of the Canadian Political Science Association, University of Western Ontario, London, Ontario (2005)
41. Tarrell, A., Tahmasbi, N., Kocsis, D., Tripathi, A., Pedersen, J., Xiong, J., Oh, O., Vreede, G.J.D.: Crowdsourcing: a snapshot of published research. In: Proceedings of the Nineteenth Americas Conference on Information Systems (AMCIS) 2013, Chicago, Illinois, USA (2013)
42. United Nations Research Institute for Social Development. Technocratic Policy Making and Democratic Accountability, UNRISD Research and Policy Brief no. 3, United Nations Research Institute for Social Development (UNRISD), Switzerland (2004)
43. Van Waarden, F.: Dimensions and types of policy networks. Eur. J. Polit. Res. **21**, 29–52 (1992)
44. Wandhöfer, T., Taylor, S., Alani, H., Joshi, S., Sizov, S., Walland, P., Thamm, M., Bleier, A., Mutschke, P.: Engaging politicians with citizens on social networking sites: the WeGov Toolbox. Int. J. Electron. Gov. Res. **8**(3), 22–43 (2012)

Multi-stakeholder Preference Analysis in Ex-ante Evaluation of Policy Options - Use Case: Ultra Low Emission Vehicles in UK

Anton Talantsev[1], Osama Ibrahim[1(✉)], and Aron Larsson[1,2]

[1] Department of Computer and Systems Sciences,
Stockholm University, Stockholm, Sweden
{antontal, osama, aron}@dsv.su.se
[2] Department of Information and Communications Systems,
Mid Sweden University, Sundsvall, Sweden

Abstract. While the simulation-based impact assessment of public policy proposals allows policy makers to identify the feasible policy options and verify their economic, social and environmental impacts, it does not provide the explicit evaluation of policy options. Multi-criteria decision analysis (MCDA) techniques can support an in-depth performance evaluation of policy options taking into account the preferences of decision makers and stakeholders. These preferences reflect acceptable trade-offs of performance among objectives. This study reviews multi-attribute decision-making (MADM) technique and presents a common policy appraisal format using main evaluation criteria linked to a set of measurable, context dependent attributes. We argue for a rank-based approach for eliciting preferences, select a novel method for attribute weight elicitation, and show how it can be integrated within a public policy multi-criteria evaluation framework. A use case for policymaking, 'Ultra-Low Emission Vehicles (ULEV) Uptake in UK', is used for demonstration of the proposed approach for policy decision analysis. This approach seeks to couple systems modelling and simulation of policy scenarios with MCDA, stakeholder analysis and preference elicitation. The outputs can further provide analytical insights in controversy/acceptability of policy options, and consequently guide further policy formulation and the design of better options.

Keywords: Public policy analysis · Multi-criteria decision analysis · Stakeholders · Preference elicitation · Decision support tools · Ultra low emission vehicles

1   Introduction

Public policy decision processes are often characterized by the presence of multiple and conflicting objectives and multiple stakeholders or decision makers who may have differing point-of-views. Using decision analysis practices to provide informed public policy decisions is not a novel approach per se. What might differ public policy decision analysis from a traditional decision analysis endeavor is that the former does

© IFIP International Federation for Information Processing 2016
Published by Springer International Publishing Switzerland 2016. All Rights Reserved
E. Tambouris et al. (Eds.): ePart 2016, LNCS 9821, pp. 176–188, 2016.
DOI: 10.1007/978-3-319-45074-2_14

not explicitly aim to reveal a clear recommendation of choice, but also to explore the problem and reveal conflicts, cf. (Quade 1982).

Prescriptive approaches for the study of such decision processes have been suggested within the field of systems thinking and in the field of multi-criteria decision analysis (MCDA). In (Larsson and Ibrahim 2015), we presented a work process with associated operational research (OR) modeling and analysis tools that supports a prescriptive analysis for policy that includes: the problem definition, ex-ante impact assessment and evaluation activities carried out at the policy formulation stage of the policymaking process. The proposed approach exploited the use of causal maps for problem structuring and scenario-based simulation for the design of policy options, together with decision analysis for evaluating generated scenarios. Having a set of feasible policy options identified, there are two main tasks remaining in structuring MCDA evaluation models; (i) representation of objectives in a structure, commonly a value tree, and (ii) the definition of attributes to measure the achievement of objectives (Franco and Montibeller 2010).

Multi-criteria evaluation can be organised with an objective to produce a single synthetic conclusion or to produce conclusions adapted to the preferences and priorities of several actors. Thus, applying MCDA should provide the relative global performance of each alternative taking preferences of decision makers and stakeholders into account. This is particularly useful when selecting one out of a finite set of feasible alternatives.

Since the rise of the graphical user interface, a flora of computer based decision analysis tools have emerged, aiming to exploit the strengths of graphic interaction with users and thereby enabling for users with less know-how of decision analysis to conduct decision modelling and evaluation, see, e.g., (Riabacke et al. 2014). A prerequisite to increase the practical aspects of decision analysis is to offer accessible tools, and of greatest importance for practical applicability of decision analysis methods seems to be how "easy" they are to use (Stewart 1992, Hülle et al. 2011).

This work is carried out within the contexts of the research project Sense4us[1], which is developing a web portal that integrates public policy decision support tools to linked open data search tools and social media analytics, in order to enable easy access to information sources and knowledge creation. The aim of this paper is the design of a preference elicitation method based on a multi-criteria evaluation model for policy decision analysis. The method should: (i) not require substantial formal decision analysis knowledge; (ii) not be too cognitively demanding by forcing people to express unrealistic precision or to state more than they are able to; (iii) not require too much time; (iv) make use of the information the decision-maker is actually able to supply, and (v) be supported through a graphical user interface (GUI) accessible from different client operating systems.

This paper is structured as follows. Section 1, introduces the research problem, context, challenges and tasks. Section 2 provides a review of the state-of-the-art research related to concept and application of decision analysis and preference elicitation for policy analysis. Section 3 presents the proposed criteria model for ex-ante

---

[1] EU FP7 research project 'Data insights for policymakers and citizens', http://sense4us.eu/.

evaluation of policy options. Section 4 presents the proposed rank-based preference elicitation method. Section 5, describes the public policy use case, as real example for demonstration of the use of the proposed policy decision analysis process. Finally, Sect. 6, provides the conclusions and possibilities for future work.

2   Related Work

Elicitation of preferences in policy making requires that there exists a basis for decision, typically in the form of more or less objective so-called "impact assessment reports" describing the impact of different alternatives on objectives but strive to be neutral with respect to decision maker preferences. The impact assessment approaches can be more or less formalized, and examples used together with decision analysis approaches within the context of policy making published in the literature include, e.g., life-cycle assessment (Miettinen and Hämäläinen 1997), quality adjusted life-years (Drake et al. 2009, Kivunike et al. 2014), life micro-level simulation and system dynamics (Hansson et al. 2008, Gou et al. 2001), scenario planning (Montibeller et al. 2006), and problem structuring using causal maps (Comes et al. 2011). One important feature of problem structuring approaches is to facilitate the context-setting activity and defining the environment of a decision problem to be modelled and subsequently evaluated, (see, e.g. Belton and Stewart (2002) for an introduction to how problem structuring relates to the decision analysis process).

Further, the use of decision analytic support in participatory/group decision processes involving several decision makers and/or stakeholders has received increasing attention during the last few decades. The decision makers can actually disagree on what the best alternative is but they need to select a common alternative having sufficient support from the group. Within such a context, a number of proposed decision analytic approaches and cases of its use have been published in the literature. For instance, Danielson et al. (2007) propose the analytical decision layer process, incorporating the stakeholders and decision maker views in an interaction layer and aggregating these preferences in a decision layer exploiting methods from interval decision analysis to accommodate for differing preferences such that all decision maker values are captured by each interval. Hansson et al. (2008) presents an MCDA approach for evaluating flood management strategies, putting weights on the stakeholders when aggregating their preferences. Schroeder and Lambert (2011) outlines a decision analysis process for comparison of transportation policies in the case of an emergency exploiting scenario planning in order to set the context.

Multi-Attribute Decision Making (MADM) techniques can be applied when the decision consists of selecting one out of a finite set of feasible alternatives, (Belton and Stewart 2002). The process of MADM is an analytical process that brings together three components; the decision objectives as measured by their associated attributes, the decision options or alternatives and the decision maker's preferences toward the importance of the attributes as reflected by the attribute weights.

The determination of attribute weights is an important and time consuming process. Attribute weight elicitation methods, given the decision problem's structural elements, include: the Balance Beam (BB), Lottery Technique (LT), Paired Comparison (PC), Point

Allocation (PA), Pricing Out (PO), Ratio Weighting (RW) and Trade-off Weighting (TW), (for a comparative review see (Crain 2003)). These methods can be distinguished by the specific technique employed to compute the attribute weight and whether the technique is designed to determine an attribute importance weight or an attribute swing weight. Importance weights reflect the relative preference without regard to the decision problem at hand, whereas swing weights are sensitive to the values that the attributes possess for the particular decision problem. Crain (2003) emphasized the greater utility and correctness of eliciting swing weights in a MADM problem versus importance weights because of the sensitivity of the swing weight to the range of values taken on by the associated attribute.

A common practicability issue of applying decision analysis methods is that often too hard requirements are put on the users. It can be argued that much of the applicability issues in employing formal decision analysis in practical settings roots in the need to elicit beliefs and preferences from decision makers and stakeholders. One recurrent practicability issue reported in the literature is the need to obtain the decision-maker's preferences in such a way that they can be formally represented. That leads to cognitively demanding methods less encouraging for decision makers to use. See, for instance (Riabacke et al. 2012, Riabacke et al. 2014). One increasingly popular way of relaxing the cognitive burden on decision makers is to rank criteria and/or alternatives and using cardinal rankings surrogate values can be generated. Recent studies of rank based approaches include (Sarabando and Dias 2010, Wang and Zionts 2015, Danielson and Ekenberg 2015a), showing that by allowing for the user to provide preference strength information, the equitability of the generated surrogate numbers will improve, (i.e. preferences of the decision maker are more properly reflected).

3 A Common Policy Appraisal Format

In MADM techniques, the decision process starts by structuring the problem as an attribute tree hierarchically ordering the decision makers' aims at different abstraction levels. It is generally assumes that each criterion can be operationalised by a set of measurable attributes allowing for assessing the consequences arising from the implementation of any particular alternative. In the next step preferential information is elicited. The relative importance of criteria is captured in weights w_{jl} for each criterion j at each abstraction level l. At the lowest level of the value tree these objectives are translated into attributes, with each one of them evaluating a given characteristic of the decision options (for example, an objective 'efficiency' may be measured by the attribute 'operating cost'). The performance of each decision option against each attribute is determined and weights are elicited from the decision-makers (Comes et al. 2011).

Figure 1, illustrates a multi-attribute value tree, with measurable attributes in gradient boxes, criteria and overall goal in white boxes. Dependence of attributes on the alternatives (represented as diamonds) is shown by dashed lines.

Given a set of decision options, $A = \{a_1, \ldots, a_N\}$ and M evaluation criteria, we can represent a decision option a_k with a vector of performance levels $(x_{k1}, x_{k2}, \ldots, x_{kM})$.

Conforming to multi-attribute value theory (MAVT), the global value of a decision option a_k is given according to the additive value function:

$$V(a_k) = \sum_{i=1}^{M} w_i v_i(x_{ki}) \qquad (1)$$

where $v_i(x_{ki})$ is a value function representing the value of alternative a_k under criterion i, w_i is the weight of criterion i, $0 \leq w_i \leq 1$ and $\Sigma w_i = 1$.

This additive model cannot capture the dependencies between criteria, (i.e., being substitutes or complements of each other). We refrain from eliciting such dependencies from decision makers, to achieve the use of use of the elicitation method.

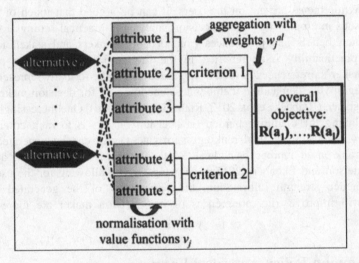

Fig. 1. Multi-attribute value tree. (Comes et al. 2011)

We propose a criteria model for ex-ante evaluation of EU policy interventions, based on a set of main evaluation criteria[2] *Effectiveness, Efficiency, Coherence, Relevance* and *Added value* and the underlying measurable attributes. For each of the policy options, the observed changes on the targeted policy impact variables and the policy financial impacts are provided by the impact assessment results. Figure 2, illustrates the structure of the proposed common policy appraisal format as a multi-attribute value tree. The figure shows k policy options to be evaluated.

Each of the attributes underlying the "*effectiveness*" evaluation criterion reflects how successful a policy option is in achieving the policy goals by comparing the observed change (OC) to the targeted change (TC) for each impact variable. The attributes underlying the "*efficiency*" criterion are concerned with the financial impacts of a policy option, whether financial costs or benefits (cost savings). The evaluation of

---

[2] The European commission's better regulation guidelines for evaluations and fitness checks of EU policy interventions. http://ec.europa.eu/smart-regulation/guidelines/index_en.htm.

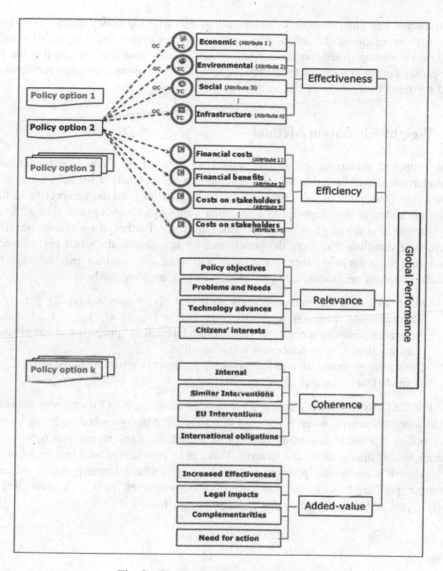

Fig. 2. Common policy appraisal format

the impact of the action is expressed as the costs involved on governmental departments given the achieved changes. In addition costs on businesses (including small businesses), or different stakeholder groups are expressed in terms of different attributes. The efficiency evaluations can be made in a quantitative or a qualitative way. The attributes underlying the "*relevance*" criterion are using qualitative descriptors (or value scales) to assess the relevance of a policy option to the policy objectives, to the problems/needs, to the technological advances and to the citizens. The attributes underlying the "*coherence*" criterion are using qualitative descriptors or value scales to assess the coherence of a policy option: (i) internally if it includes multiple policy instruments, (ii) with other similar interventions, (iii) with EU policy interventions and (iv) with international obligations. Finally the attributes underlying the "*added-value*" criterion are using qualitative descriptors or value scales to assess the added value of the policy option in terms of legal impacts, increased effectiveness, complementarities and the need for continuing this intervention.

4 Weight Elicitation Method

The proposed preference elicitation method to be used is a rank-based approach complemented with intuitive ways of generating a value function for policy decision evaluation. The value of each option under each criterion from the perspective of the decision maker is then captured in a so-called value function $v(x)$ such that $v : X \to [0, 1]$ where X is the range of the performance indicator. Further, if we assume positive preference direction (the more the better) and let x_{min} denote the worst performance level and x_{max} the best, then $v(x_{min}) = 0$ and $v(x_{max}) = 1$. Two simple ways of obtaining values on intermediate performance levels are suggested.

(1) Either to assign them proportionally such that $v(x) = (x - x_{min})/(x_{max} - x_{min})$ if the preference direction is positive, or $v(x) = (x_{max} - x)/(x_{max} - x_{min})$ if the preference direction is negative. This is often labelled as "proportional scores" and is an intuitive way to generate a value function.
(2) Use surrogate values derived from ranking statements according to the novel CAR method (Danielson and Ekenberg, 2015b).

For the CAR method, we use $>_{s(i)}$ to denote the strength of the rankings between criteria or alternatives, where $=_0$ means that they are equally ranked, $a_i >_1 a_j$ means that option i is better important than option j, and, $a_j >_2 a_k$ means that option j is "much better" than option k and so forth. This can be represented such that each option is assigned a preference position $p(i) \in \{1, \dots, Q\}$ where lower position indicate stronger preference such that for two options whenever, $a_i >_{s(i)} a_k$ then $s(i) = |p(i) - p(k)|$ and the surrogate value is simply given from

$$v_i = \frac{(Q - p(i) + 1)}{Q} \tag{2}$$

Given a slider with in total Q number of importance scale positions. Each criterion i has the position $p(i) \in \{1, \dots, Q\}$ on this importance scale where lower position indicate more importance, such that whenever $c_i >_{s(i)} c_j$, $s(i) = |p(i) - p(j)|$, then the surrogate weight is given by:

$$w_i = \frac{\frac{1}{p(i)} + \frac{(Q - p(i) + 1)}{Q}}{\sum_{j=1}^{N} \left(\frac{1}{p(j)} + \frac{(Q - p(j) + 1)}{Q} \right)} \tag{3}$$

For example, Fig. 3 shows four criteria and a scale with eight steps where scale position 1 is at the right end of the slider and scale 8 at the left end of the slider.

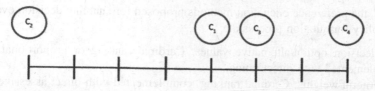

Fig. 3. Ranking of criteria

The ranking visualized is $c_4 >_2 c_3, c_3 >_1 c_1$ and $c_1 >_4 c_2$, yielding surrogate weights $w_1 = 0.21, w_2 = 0.06, w_3 = 0.26$, and $w_4 = 0.47$.

Further, following proportional scores value assignments for all three criteria but the Social criterion, for which we have the following ranking for options 1, 2, and 3, $a_1 >_3 a_3, a_3 >_2 a_2$ yielding values $v_3(x_{13}) = 1$, $v_3(x_{33}) = 0.4$, and $v_3(x_{23}) = 0$.

This can be illustrated using a multi-criteria evaluation matrix, constructed with as many columns as there are criteria and as many rows as there are decision options to be compared. Table 1 shows exemplary impact assessment results, each cell represents the performance x_{ij} of option i under criterion j in the performance indicator used for that particular criterion. Note that: MCDA requires an evaluation of all the decision options for all the criteria, but does not require that all the evaluations take the same form. The technique can support a mix of quantitative criteria expressed by indicators, qualitative criteria expressed by descriptors, and intermediate criteria expressed by scores (e.g., a scale 0–10).

Table 1. Impact assessment matrix

	Criterion 1	Criterion 2	Criterion 3	Criterion 4
Decision option 1	$x_{11} = 20\ \%$	$x_{12} = 510.5$	$x_{13} = $ High	$x_{14} = 4$
Decision option 2	$x_{21} = 35\ \%$	$x_{22} = 312$	$x_{23} = $ Low	$x_{24} = 2$
Decision option 3	$x_{31} = 10\ \%$	$x_{32} = 615$	$x_{33} = $ Neutral	$x_{34} = 6$

In Table 2 below, we denote positive preference direction with '$\nearrow$' and negative direction with '$\searrow$' together with S or R representing "proportional scores" or "ranking" respectively for the value function model. Unequal weights are assigned to criteria (note that the sum of the weights $w_1, \ldots, w_n$ equals 1).

Table 2. Multi-criteria evaluation matrix

Criteria	$C_1 \nearrow S$	$C_2 \nearrow S$	$C_3 \nearrow R$	$C_4 \searrow S$
Weights	$w_1 = 21\ \%$	$w_2 = 6\ \%$	$w_3 = 26\ \%$	$w_4 = 47\ \%$
Decision option 1	$v_1(x_{11}) = 0.4$	$v_2(x_{12}) = 0.66$	$v_2(x_{13}) = 1$	$v_2(x_{14}) = 0.5$
Decision option 2	$v_1(x_{21}) = 1$	$v_2(x_{22}) = 0$	$v_2(x_{23}) = 0$	$v_2(x_{24}) = 0$
Decision option 3	$v_1(x_{31}) = 0$	$v_2(x_{32}) = 1$	$v_2(x_{33}) = 0.4$	$v_2(x_{34}) = 1$

Thus, the preference elicitation methods proposed for enabling decision evaluation in the policy formulation process are:

- For decision option/alternative values: Cardinal ranking or proportional scores, complemented with direct rating.
- For criteria weights: Cardinal ranking, complemented with direct assessment.

The reason for complementing the ranking approach with direct rating is that the latter provides flexibility for exploiting other preference elicitation schemes for advanced users.

5   Use Case: Ultra Low Emission Vehicles (ULEVs) in UK[3]

The British Government wants to increase take up of Ultra Low Emission Vehicles (ULEVs) throughout the UK, as part of its wider plans for reducing greenhouse gas emissions. Electric cars are deemed to reduce CO2 emissions, improve urban air quality, create new jobs, and provide other benefits to society. Amongst a set of initiatives to improve the uptake of electric cars, Plug-in Car Grant, Plugged-in Places, London congestion charge, while many others are being proposed, such as creating exclusive city "green-zones", free parking for electric cars, investing in public recharging infrastructure, arranging hands-on trials for electric cars for citizens, and others. While all these policy interventions can be argued for with means-end rationality, they inevitably impact different stakeholders. Finally, when considering several policy options it's not clear how to compare their acceptability.

Analysis of the national UK stakeholders for the use case is needed to provide answers to the following questions:

1. What are the key stakeholder groups and how are they related to the policy instruments?
2. How would a policy option affect the variety of stakeholders?
3. In what extent might the stakeholders be favouring or be against the transition or a specific policy option?
4. How to accommodate this information to prescriptive decision and policy analysis?

The identified stakeholders have been grouped in order to better articulate potential opponents, reflect the national (UK) level, and reduce the number of stakeholder groups to a manageable number. The list of selected stakeholder groups includes: government, citizens likely to switch to plug-in cars, citizens unlikely to switch to plug-in cars, electricity suppliers, plug-in car manufacturers, conventional cars manufacturers, renewable energy producer s, fossil fuel energy producers, power grid operators, petrol producers. "Citizens likely to buy plug-in cars" fully or partially encapsulate other stakeholder groups (citizens) with particular characteristics, such as early adopters, urban citizens, can drive, sufficient income to buy an EV, etc. Similarly,

---

[3] Department for Transport, UK, (2015),' Uptake of Ultra Low Emission Vehicles in the UK'. A Rapid Evidence Assessment, available on: https://www.gov.uk/government/uploads/system/uploads/attachment_data/file/464763/uptake-of-ulev-uk.pdf (Accessed 1/4/2016).

"Citizens unlikely to buy plug-in cars" can be characterised as risk-averse to new technologies, citizens with insufficient income to buy an EV, etc.

Preference elicitation implies (1) defining the direction of preference and (2) intensity of preference for each concept/stakeholder pair. The direction of preference refers to whether the higher value of a concept corresponds to a higher preference value (unidirectional, denoted by +1) or lower (oppositely directed, denoted by −1). The preference intensity is a weight showing relative importance of a concept. Each stakeholder group has been profiled in terms of their needs, goals and means for their achievement. Then, for each stakeholder assessing how increase or decrease in each concept would impact (positively, negatively, or no impact) stakeholders' needs, goals and means. In this way, it was relatively straightforward to define preference directions or neutrality (no interest) with respect to the policy evaluation criteria. The selection of the concepts as evaluation criteria and/or attributes for each stakeholder group, has been based on the following principles: (1) the criteria set should represent balance and diversity of aspects for a given stakeholder group, (2) the criteria in the set should be relevant and representative, and (3) preferentially independent for a focal stakeholder group.

For instance, as a representative of the "Government" stakeholder group the Office for Low Emission Vehicles (OLEV) of the British government has been selected.

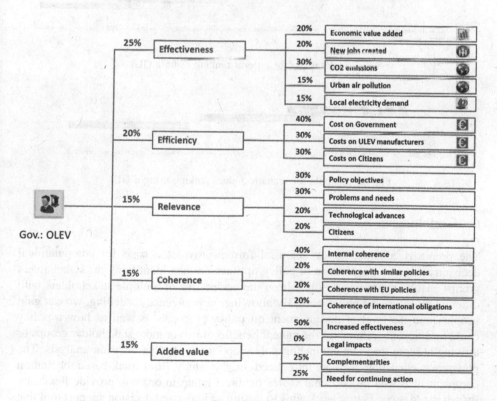

Fig. 4. Visual hierarchy of the evaluation criteria for the use case

The following attributes were considered for evaluation of the effectiveness of policy options by the government stakeholder group: ULEV industry economic value added, new jobs created, green-house gas (GHG)/CO2 emissions, urban air pollution and local electricity demand.

The proposed policy decision analysis process supports a visual hierarchy of criteria. Figure 4, shows an example for the resulting criteria hierarchy tree with exemplary criteria and attributes weights.

A relative global performance of the policy options for stakeholders can be calculated through a step-wise decision evaluation process to define: (i) Stakeholder groups and/or individual stakeholders; (ii) Evaluation criteria and/or the underlying attributes, each stakeholder stipulates its own set of criteria and attributes; (iii) Scenarios/ Alternative policy options are common for all stakeholders; (iv) Scenario values: using cardinal ranking statements or surrogate value statements (a point, an interval or both) by each stakeholder; (v) Criteria weights: using cardinal ranking statements.

Figures 5 and 6 provide examples for ranking of criteria or scenario values utilizing a friendly GUI.

Fig. 5. Example for criteria ranking using a GUI

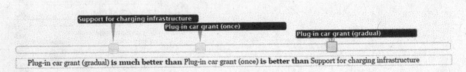

Fig. 6. Example for scenario values ranking using a GUI

6   Conclusions

The proposed common policy appraisal format provides a basis for computational decision analysis for evaluation of policy options. Further, identifying the stakeholders groups enables appraising a policy from the perspective of multiple stakeholders with different priorities and preferences. By allowing for preference modelling, we can gain insights into the level of disagreement on policy proposals as well as how a policy could be efficiently refined for the mutual benefits of two or more stakeholder groups or arriving at more than one competing policy options for further decision analysis. The preference elicitation method introduced in this study, uses rank-based elicitation complemented with proportional scores or direct rating in order to provide flexibility for advanced users. Future work aims to design an integrated decision support tool that couples systems modelling and simulation of public policy problems with MCDA techniques and preference elicitation methods. The implementation of the proposed decision analysis process using an online GUI, enables policy makers and stakeholders to provide preferential statements over their respective goals in a simple way.

References

Belton, V., Stewart, T.J.: Multiple Criteria Decision Analysis: An Integrated Approach. Kluwer Academic Publishers, Berlin (2002)

Comes, T., Hiete, M., Wijngaards, N., Schultmann, F.: Decision maps: a frame-work for multi-criteria decision support under severe uncertainty. Decis. Support Syst. **52**, 108–118 (2011)

Crain, W.F.: Multiattribute weight determination: elicitation & approximation. George Mason University (2003). https://books.google.se/books?id=84IkOAAACAAJ

Danielson, M., Ekenberg, L., Idefeldt, J., Larsson, A.: Using a software tool for public decision analysis: the case of Nacka municipality. Decis. Anal. **4**(2), 76–90 (2007)

Danielson, M., Ekenberg, L.: The CAR method for using preference strength in multi-criteria decision making. Group Decis. Negot. **25**(4), 775–797 (2015a)

Danielson, M., Ekenberg, L.: Using surrogate weights for handling preference strength in multi-criteria decisions. In: Kamiński, B., Kersten, G.E., Szapiro, T. (eds.) GDN 2015. LNBIP, vol. 218, pp. 107–118. Springer, Heidelberg (2015b)

Drake, J.M., Kulkarni, A.V., Kestle, J.: Endoscopic third ventriculostomy versus ventriculoperitoneal shunt in pediatric patients: a decision analysis. Child's Nerv. Syst. **25**, 467–472 (2009)

Franco, L.A., Montibeller, G.: Facilitated modelling in operational research. Eur. J. Oper. Res. **205**, 489–500 (2010)

Gou, H.C., Liu, L., Huang, G.H., Fuller, G.A., Zou, R., Yin, Y.Y,: A system dynamics approach for regional environmental planning and management: a study for the Lake Erhai Basin. J. Environ. Manage. **61**, 93–111 (2001)

Hansson, K., Danielson, M., Ekenberg, L.: A framework for evaluation of flood management strategies. J. Environ. Manage. **86**(3), 465–480 (2008)

Hülle, J., Kaspar, R., Möller, K.: Multiple criteria decision-making in management accounting and control – state of the art and research perspectives based on a bibliometric study. J. Multi Criteria Decis. Anal. **18**(5–6), 253–265 (2011)

Kivunike, F.N., Ekenberg, E., Danielson, M., Tusubira, F.F.: Towards an ICT4D evaluation model based on the capability approach. Int. J. Adv. ICT Emerg. Reg. **7**(1), 1–7 (2014)

Larsson, A., Ibrahim, O.: Modeling for policy formulation: causal mapping, scenario generation, and decision evaluation. In: Tambouris, E., Panagiotopoulos, P., Sæbø, Ø., Tarabanis, K., Wimmer, M.A., Milano, M., Pardo, T. (eds.) ePart 2015. LNCS, vol. 9249, pp. 135–146. Springer, Heidelberg (2015)

Miettinen, K., Hämäläinen, R.P.: How to benefit from decision analysis in environmental life cycle assessment (LCA). Eur. J. Oper. Res. **102**, 279–294 (1997)

Montibeller, G., Gummer, H., Tumidei, D.: Combining scenario planning and multi-criteria decision analysis in practice. J. Multi-Criteria Dec. Anal. **14**(1–3), 5–20 (2006)

Quade, E.S.: Analysis for Public Decisions. Elsevier, New York (1982)

Riabacke, A., Larsson, A., Danielson, M.: Conceptualisation of the gap between managerial decision-making and the use of decision analytic tools. Int. J. Inf. Technol. Bus. Manage. **21**(1), 30–46 (2014)

Riabacke, M., Danielson, M., Ekenberg, L.: State-of-the-art prescriptive criteria weight elicitation. Adv. Dec. Sci. **2012**, 24 p. (2012)

Sarabando, P., Dias, L.C.: Simple procedures of choice in multicriteria problems without precise information about the alternatives' values. Comput. Oper. Res. **37**(12), 2239–2247 (2010)

Schroeder, M.J., Lambert, J.H.: Scenario-based multiple criteria analysis for infrastructure policy impacts and planning. J. Risk Res. **14**(2), 191–214 (2011)

Stewart, T.J.: A critical survey on the status of multiple criteria decision making theory and practice. Omega **20**(5–6), 569–586 (1992)

Wang, J., Zionts, S.: Using ordinal data to estimate cardinal values. J. Multi-Criteria Dec. Anal. **22**, 185–196 (2015)

Author Index

Printed in the United States
By Bookmasters